Money and the Mechanism of Exchange

Jevons, William Stanley, Pacific Coast Numismatic Society. C

Copyright © BiblioLife, LLC

This historical reproduction is part of a unique project that provides opportunities for readers, educators and researchers by bringing hard-to-find original publications back into print at reasonable prices. Because this and other works are culturally important, we have made them available as part of our commitment to protecting, preserving and promoting the world's literature. These books are in the "public domain" and were digitized and made available in cooperation with libraries, archives, and open source initiatives around the world dedicated to this important mission.

We believe that when we undertake the difficult task of re-creating these works as attractive, readable and affordable books, we further the goal of sharing these works with a global audience, and preserving a vanishing wealth of human knowledge.

Many historical books were originally published in small fonts, which can make them very difficult to read. Accordingly, in order to improve the reading experience of these books, we have created "enlarged print" versions of our books. Because of font size variation in the original books, some of these may not technically qualify as "large print" books, as that term is generally defined; however, we believe these versions provide an overall improved reading experience for many.

THE INTERNATIONAL SCIENTIFIC SERIES.

MONEY AND

THE MECHANISM OF EXCHANGE.

BY

W. STANLEY JEVONS, M.A., F.R.S.,

PROFESSOR OF LOGIC AND POLITICAL ECONOMY IN THE
OWENS COLLEGE, MANCHESTER.

NEW YORK:
D. APPLETON AND COMPANY,
72 FIFTH AVENUE.
1896.

PREFACE.

In preparing this volume, I have attempted to write a descriptive essay on the past and present monetary systems of the world, the materials employed to make money, the regulations under which the coins are struck and issued, the natural laws which govern their circulation, the several modes in which they may be replaced by the use of paper documents, and finally, the method in which the use of money is immensely economized by the cheque and clearing system now being extended and perfected.

This is not a book upon the currency question, as that question is so often discussed in England. I have only a little to say about the Bank Charter Act, and upon that, and other mysteries of the money market, I refer my readers to the admirable essay of Mr. Bagehot on "Lombard Street," to which this book may perhaps serve as an introduction.

There is much to be learnt about money before entering upon those abstruse questions, which barely admit of decided answers. In studying a language, we begin with the grammar before we try to read or write. In mathematics, we practice ourselves in simple arithmetic before we proceed to the subtleties of algebra and the differential calculus. But it is the grave misfortune of the moral and political sciences, as well shown by Mr. Herbert Spencer, in his "Study of Sociology," that they are continually discussed by those who have never laboured at the elementary grammar or the simple arithmetic of the subject. Hence the extraordinary schemes and fallacies every now and then put forth.

Currency is to the science of economy what the squaring of the circle is to geometry, or perpetual motion to mechanics. If there were a writer on Currency possessing some of the humour and learning of the late Professor De Morgan, he could easily produce a Budget of Currency Paradoxes more than rivalling De Morgan's Circle-Squaring Paradoxes. There are men who spend their time and fortunes in endeavouring to convince a dull world that poverty can be abolished by the issue of printed bits of paper. I know one gentleman who holds that exchequer bills are the panacea for the evils of humanity. Other philanthropists wish to make us all rich by coining the national debt, or coining the lands of the country, or coining everything. Another class of persons have long been indignant that, in this age of free trade, the Mint price of gold should still remain arbitrarily fixed by statute. A member of Parliament lately discovered a new grievance, and made his reputation by agitating against the oppressive restrictions on the coinage of silver at the Mint. No wonder so many people are paupers when there is a deficiency of shillings and sixpences, and when the amount merely of the rates and taxes paid in a year exceeds the whole sum of money circulating in the kingdom.

The subject of money as a whole is a very extensive one, and the literature of it would fill a very great library. Many changes are now taking place in the currencies of the world, and important inquiries have been lately instituted concerning the best mode of constituting the circulating medium. The information on the subject stored up in evidence given before Government Commissions, in reports of International Conferences, or in researches and writings of private individuals, is quite appalling in extent. It has been my purpose to extract from this mass of literature just such facts as seem to be generally interesting and useful in enabling the public to come to some conclusion upon many currency questions which press for solution. Shall we count in pounds, or dollars, or francs, or marks? Shall we have gold or silver, or gold *and* silver, as the measure of value? Shall we employ a paper currency or a metallic one? How long shall we in England allow our gold coinage to degenerate in weight? Shall we recoin it at the expense of the State or of the unlucky individuals who happen to hold light sovereigns?

In America the questions are still more important and pressing, involving the return to specie payments, the future regulation of the paper currency, its partial replacement by coin, and the exact size and character of the American dollar, regarded in relation to international currency. Germany is in the midst of a great, and probably a sound and successful, reorganization of the currency, both metallic and paper. In France the great debate upon the double *versus* the single standard is hardly yet terminated, and active measures are being taken to place the paper issues on a convertible basis. Among the other countries of Europe—Italy, Austria, Holland, Belgium, Switzerland, the Scandinavian kingdoms and Russia—there is hardly one which is not at present reforming its currency, or has lately done so, or is discussing the proper method of attempting the task. As regards all such changes, we should remember that in the present we are ever moulding the future, and that a world-wide system of international money, though it may seem impracticable at the moment, is an object at which all those should aim who wish to leave the world better than they found it.

I wish to acknowledge the assistance which I have derived from the works of Mr. Seyd, especially his treatise on "Bullion and the Foreign Exchanges," from Professor Sumner's "History of the American Currency," M. Chevalier's work "La Monnaie," M. Wolowski's various important publications upon money, and many valuable articles in the *Journal des Economistes*. I must express my thanks to many bankers and gentlemen for information and assistance kindly rendered to me, especially to Mr. John Mills, Mr. T. R. Wilkinson, Mr. Roberts, the chemist of the Royal Mint, and Mr. E. Helm.

I should also like to take this opportunity of thanking those gentlemen who have from time to time sent me documents and publications bearing upon the subject of money, which have proved very valuable. I may mention especially a series of reports and documents concerning the American mint and currency received through the kindness of the Director of the Mint, and of Mr. Walker and Mr. E. Dubois.

I am much indebted to Mr. W. H. Brewer, M.A., for carefully reading the whole of the proofs, and to Professor T. E. Cliffe Leslie, Mr. R. H. Inglis Palgrave, and Mr. Frederick Hendriks for examining particular portions.

May 31*st*, 1875.

CONTENTS.

CHAPTER I.

BARTER.

	PAGE
Want of Coincidence in Barter	3
Want of a Measure of Value	5
Want of Means of Subdivision	6

CHAPTER II.

EXCHANGE.

Utility and Value are not Intrinsic	9
Value expresses Ratio of Exchange	10

CHAPTER III.

THE FUNCTIONS OF MONEY.

A Standard of Value	14
A Store of Value	15
Separation of Functions	16

CHAPTER IV.

EARLY HISTORY OF MONEY.

Currency in the Hunting State	19
Currency in the Pastoral State	21
Articles of Ornament as Currency	24
Currency in the Agricultural State	25
Manufactured and Miscellaneous Articles as Currency	27

CHAPTER V.

QUALITIES OF THE MATERIAL OF MONEY.

		PAGE
1. Utility and Value		32
2. Portability		34
3. Indestructibility		36
4. Homogeneity		37
5. Divisibility		38
6. Stability of Value		38
7. Cognizability		40

CHAPTER VI.

THE METALS AS MONEY.

Iron	43
Lead	44
Tin	44
Copper	45
Silver	46
Gold	47
Platinum	48
Nickel	49
Other Metals	51
Alloys of Metals	51

CHAPTER VII.

COINS.

The Invention of Coining	55
What is a Coin?	57
Various Forms of Coins	57
The Best Form for Coins	59
Coins as Works of Art	62
Historical Coins	62
The Royal Attribute of Coining	63

CHAPTER VIII.

THE PRINCIPLES OF CIRCULATION.

	PAGE
The Standard Unit of Value	67
Coin, Money of Account, and Unit of Value	70
Standard and Token Money	74
Metallic and Nominal Values of Coins	75
Legal Tender	76
The Force of Habit in the Circulation of Money	78
Gresham's Law	80
Extension of Gresham's Law	84

CHAPTER IX.

SYSTEMS OF METALLIC MONEY.

Currency by Weight	88
Unrestricted Currency by Tale	92
Single Legal Tender System	96
Multiple Legal Tender System	98
Composite Legal Tender	101

CHAPTER X.

THE ENGLISH SYSTEM OF METALLIC CURRENCY.

English Gold Coin	105
English Silver Coin	108
English Bronze Coin	110
Deficiency of Weight of the English Gold Coin	111
Withdrawal of Light Gold Coin	113
Supply of Gold Coin	115
Supply of Silver Coin	118
The Royal Mint	120

CHAPTER XI.

FRACTIONAL CURRENCY.

	PAGE
Equivalent Weights of the Principal Metals	123
Billon Coin	125
Composite Coin	127
Bronze Coin	128
English Bronze Coin	129
Weight of the Currency	130
Nickel, Manganese, Aluminium, and other Metals and Alloys	132

CHAPTER XII.

THE BATTLE OF THE STANDARDS.

The Double Standard	136
Compensatory Action	139
The Demonetization of Silver	140
Disadvantages of the Double Standard	143
The Monetary Systems of the World	147

CHAPTER XIII.

TECHNICAL MATTERS RELATING TO COINAGE.

The Alloy in Coins	151
The Size of Coins	155
The Wear of Coins	156
Methods of Counting Coins	161
Cost of the Metallic Currency	163

CHAPTER XIV.

INTERNATIONAL MONEY.

Advantages of International Money	167
Disadvantages of International Money	169
Conflict of Monetary Systems	171

CONTENTS.

	PAGE
International Monetary Negotiations	172
Decimalization of English Money	175
The Future American Dollar	178
German Monetary Reform	180
Systems of Fractional Mone	181
Final Selection of the Unit of International Money	184

CHAPTER XV.

THE MECHANISM OF EXCHANGE.

Progressive Development of the Methods of Exchange	190
Representative Money	191
Cheque and Clearing System	192

CHAPTER XVI.

REPRESENTATIVE MONEY.

Early History of Representative Money	196
Reasons for the Use of Representative Money	199
Inconvenience of Metallic Money	200
The Weight of Currency	202
Saving of Interest	203

CHAPTER XVII.

THE NATURE AND VARIETIES OF PROMISSORY NOTES.

Specific Deposit Warrant	207
General Deposit Warrant	208
Difference Between a Special and a General Promise	209
Pecuniary Promissory Notes	212
Principles of the Circulation of Representative Money	214

CHAPTER XVIII.

METHODS OF REGULATING A PAPER CURRENCY.

	PAGE
1. Simple Deposit	221
2. Partial Deposit	222
3. Minimum Reserve	223
4. Proportional Reserve	223
5. Maximum Issue	225
6. Elastic Limit	226
7. Documentary Reserve	227
8. Real Property Reserve	228
9. Regulation by the Foreign Exchanges	229
10. Free Issue System	230
11. The Gold Par Method	231
12. Convertibility by Revenue Payments	232
13. Deferred Convertibility	233
14. Inconvertible Paper Money	234
Over Issue of Paper Money	235
Want of Elasticity of Paper Money	236

CHAPTER XIX.

CREDIT DOCUMENTS.

Measurement of Credit	239
Bank-notes	239
Cheques	240
Bills of Exchange	244
Interest-bearing Documents	245
Definition of Money	248

CHAPTER XX.

BOOK CREDIT AND THE BANKING SYSTEM.

Single Bank System	252
System of Two Banks	254

CONTENTS.

	PAGE
Complex Bank System	255
Branch Bank System	257
Bank Agency System	259
London Agency System	260
Country Clearing System	260

CHAPTER XXI.

THE CLEARING-HOUSE SYSTEM.

Transaction of Business at the London Clearing House	265
Manchester Clearing House	269
New York Clearing House	278
Extension of the Clearing System	279
Advantages of the Cheque and Clearing System	283
Proportion of Cash Payments	285
Cases to which the Clearing System is inapplicable	287

CHAPTER XXII.

THE CHEQUE BANK.

Relation of the Cheque Bank to other Banks	291
The Cheque Bank as a Monetary Agent	293
Payment of Wages by Cheques	295
The Cheque Bank as a Savings Bank	296
Results of the Cheque Bank System	298

CHAPTER XXIII.

FOREIGN BILLS OF EXCHANGE.

Origin and Nature of Bills of Exchange	300
Trade in Foreign Bills	302
The World's Clearing House	303
Centralization of Financial Transactions in London	305
Representation of Foreign Bankers in London	307

CHAPTER XXIV.

THE BANK OF ENGLAND AND THE MONEY MARKET.

	PAGE
Expansion of Trade	310
Competition of Bankers	311
The Bank Charter Act of 1844	312
The Free-banking School	314
Possibility of Over-issue	314
The Right of Coining Bank-notes	317
Scotch and English Banking	319
Cash Reserves of Bankers	320
Remedy for the Sensitiveness of the Money Market	322

CHAPTER XXV.

A TABULAR STANDARD OF VALUE.

Corn Rents	326
A Multiple Legal Tender	327
Lowe's Proposed Table of Reference	328
Poulett Scrope's Tabular Standard of Value	329
Difficulties of the Scheme	331

CHAPTER XXVI.

THE QUANTITY OF MONEY NEEDED BY A NATION.

Quantity of Work to be done by Money	335
Efficiency of the Currency	336
Effects of the Cheque and Clearing System	337
Conclusion	340
INDEX	343

MONEY

AND THE MECHANISM OF EXCHANGE.

CHAPTER I.

BARTER.

Some years since, Mademoiselle Zélie, a singer of the Théâtre Lyrique at Paris, made a professional tour round the world, and gave a concert in the Society Islands. In exchange for an air from *Norma* and a few other songs, she was to receive a third part of the receipts. When counted, her share was found to consist of three pigs, twenty-three turkeys, forty-four chickens, five thousand cocoa-nuts, besides considerable quantities of bananas, lemons, and oranges. At the Halle in Paris, as the prima donna remarks in her lively letter, printed by M. Wolowski, this amount of live stock and vegetables might have brought four thousand francs, which would have been good remuneration for five songs. In the Society Islands, however, pieces of money were very scarce; and as Mademoiselle could not consume any considerable portion of the receipts herself, it became necessary in the mean time to feed the pigs and poultry with the fruit.

When Mr. Wallace was travelling in the Malay Archipelago, he seems to have suffered rather from the scarcity than the superabundance of provisions. In his most interesting account of his travels, he tells us that in some of the islands, where there was no proper currency, he could not procure supplies for dinner without a special bargain and much chaffering upon each occasion. If the vendor of fish or other coveted eatables did not meet with the sort of exchange desired, he would pass on, and Mr. Wallace and his party had to go without their dinner. It therefore became very desirable to keep on hand a supply of articles, such as knives, pieces of cloth, arrack, or sago cakes, to multiply the chance that one or other article would suit the itinerant merchant.

In modern civilized society the inconveniences of the primitive method of exchange are wholly unknown, and might almost seem to be imaginary. Accustomed from our earliest years to the use of money, we are unconscious of the inestimable benefits which it confers upon us; and only when we recur to altogether different states of society can we realize the difficulties which arise in its absence. It is even surprising to be reminded that barter is actually the sole method of commerce among many uncivilized races. There is something absurdly incongruous in the fact that a joint-stock company, called "The African Barter Company, Limited," exists in London, which carries on its transactions upon the

West Coast of Africa entirely by bartering European manufactures for palm oil, gold dust, ivory, cotton, coffee, gum, and other raw produce.

The earliest form of exchange must have consisted in giving what was not wanted directly for that which was wanted. This simple traffic we call *barter* or *truck*, the French *troc*, and distinguish it from sale and purchase in which one of the articles exchanged is intended to be held only for a short time, until it is parted with in a second act of exchange. The object which thus temporarily intervenes in sale and purchase is money. At first sight it might seem that the use of money only doubles the trouble, by making two exchanges necessary where one was sufficient; but a slight analysis of the difficulties inherent in simple barter shows that the balance of trouble lies quite in the opposite direction. Only by such an analysis can we become aware that money performs not merely one service to us, but several different services, each indispensable. Modern society could not exist in its present complex form without the means which money constitutes of valuing, distributing, and contracting for commodities of various kinds.

Want of Coincidence in Barter.

The first difficulty in barter is to find two persons whose disposable possessions mutually suit each other's wants. There may be many people wanting, and many possessing those things wanted; but to allow of an act of barter, there must be a double coincidence, which will rarely happen. A hunter having returned from a successful chase has plenty of game, and may want arms and ammunition to renew the chase. But those who have arms may happen to be well supplied with game, so that no direct exchange is possible. In civilized society the owner of a house may find it unsuitable, and may have his eye upon another house exactly fitted to his needs. But even if the owner of this second house wishes to part with it at all, it is exceedingly unlikely that he will exactly reciprocate the feelings of the first owner, and wish to barter houses. Sellers and purchasers can only be made to fit by the use of some commodity, some *marchandise banale*, as the French call it, which all are willing to receive for a time, so that what is obtained by sale in one case, may be used in purchase in another. This common commodity is called a *medium of exchange*, because it forms a third or intermediate term in all acts of commerce.

Within the last few years a curious attempt has been made to revive the practice of barter by the circulation of advertisements. *The Exchange and Mart* is a newspaper which devotes itself to making known all the odd property which its advertisers are willing to give for some coveted article. One person has some old coins and a bicycle, and wants to barter them for a good concertina. A young lady desires to possess "Middlemarch," and offers a variety of old songs, of which she has become tired. Judging from the size and circulation of the paper, and the way in which its scheme has been imitated by some other weekly papers, we must assume that the offers are sometimes accepted, and that the printing press can bring about, in some degree, the double coincidence necessary to an act of barter.

Want of a Measure of Value.

A second difficulty arises in barter. At what rate is any exchange to be made? If a certain quantity of beef be given for a certain quantity of corn, and in like manner corn be exchanged for cheese, and cheese for eggs, and eggs for flax, and so on, still the question will arise—How much beef for how much flax, or how much of any one commodity for a given quantity of another? In a state of barter the price-current list would be a most complicated document, for each commodity would have to be quoted in terms of every other commodity, or else complicated rule-of-three sums would become necessary. Between one hundred articles there must exist no less than 4950 possible ratios of exchange, and all these ratios must be carefully adjusted so as to be consistent with each other, else the acute trader will be able to profit by buying from some and selling to others.

All such trouble is avoided if any one commodity be chosen, and its ratio of exchange with each other commodity be quoted. Knowing how much corn is to be bought for a pound of silver, and also how much flax for the same quantity of silver, we learn without further trouble how much corn exchanges for so much flax. The chosen commodity becomes *a common denominator* or *common measure of value*, in terms of which we estimate the values of all other goods, so that their values become capable of the most easy comparison.

Want of Means of Subdivision.

A third but it may be a minor inconvenience of barter arises from the impossibility of dividing many kinds of goods. A store of corn, a bag of gold dust, a carcase of meat, may be portioned out, and more or less may be given in exchange for what is wanted. But the tailor, as we are reminded in several treatises on political economy, may have a coat ready to exchange, but it much exceeds in value the bread which he wishes to get from the baker, or the meat from the butcher. He cannot cut the coat up without destroying the value of his handiwork. It is obvious that he needs some medium of exchange, into which he can temporarily convert the coat, so that he may give a part of its value for bread, and other parts for meat, fuel, and daily necessaries, retaining perhaps a portion for future use. Further illustration is needless; for it is obvious that we need a means of dividing and distributing value according to our varying requirements.

In the present day barter still goes on in some cases, even in the most advanced commercial countries, but only when its inconveniences are not experienced. Domestic servants receive part of their wages in board and lodging: the farm labourer may partially receive payment in cider, or barley, or the use of a piece of land. It has always been usual for the miller to be paid by a portion of the corn which he grinds. The *truck* or barter system, by which workmen took their wages in kind, has hardly yet been extinguished in some parts of England. Pieces of land are occasionally exchanged by adjoining landowners; but all these are comparatively trifling cases. In almost all acts of exchange money now intervenes in one way or other, and even when it does not pass from hand to hand, it serves as the measure by which the amounts given and received are estimated. Commerce begins with barter, and in a certain sense it returns to barter; but the last form of barter, as we shall see, is very different from the first form. By far the greater part of commercial payments are made at the present day in England apparently without the aid of metallic money; but they are readily adjusted, because money acts as the common denominator, and what is bought in one direction is balanced off against what is sold in another direction.

CHAPTER II.

EXCHANGE.

MONEY is the measure and standard of value and the medium of exchange, yet it is not necessary that I should enter upon more than a very brief discussion concerning the nature of value, and the advantage of exchange. Every one must allow that the exchange of commodities depends upon the obvious principle that each of our wants taken separately requires a limited quantity of some article to produce satisfaction. Hence as each want becomes fully satiated, our desire, as Senior so well remarked, is for variety, that is, for the satisfaction of some other want. The man who is supplied daily with three pounds of bread, will not desire more bread; but he will have a strong inclination for beef, and tea, and alcohol. If he happen to meet with a person who has plenty of beef but no bread, each will give that which is less desired for that which is more desired. Exchange has been called *the barter of the superfluous for the necessary*, and this definition will be correct if we state it as *the barter of the comparatively superfluous for the comparatively necessary.*

It is impossible, indeed, to decide exactly how much bread, or beef, or tea, or how many coats and hats a person needs. There is no precise limit to our desires, and we can only say, that as we have a larger supply of a substance, the urgency of our need for more is in some proportion weakened. A cup of water in the desert, or upon the field of battle, may save life, and become infinitely useful. Two or three pints per day for each person are needful for drinking and cooking purposes. A gallon or two per day are highly requisite for cleanliness; but we soon reach a point at which further supplies of water are of very minor importance. A modern town population is found to be satisfied with about twenty-five gallons per head per day for all purposes, and a further supply would possess little utility. Water, indeed, may be the reverse of useful, as in the case of a flood, or a damp house, or a wet mine.

Utility and Value are not intrinsic.

It is only, then, when supplied in moderate quantities, and at the right time, that a thing can be said to be useful. Utility is not a quality *intrinsic* in a substance, for, if it were, additional quantities of the same substance would always be desired, however much we previously possessed. We must not confuse the usefulness of a thing with the physical qualities upon which the usefulness depends. Utility and value are only accidents of a thing arising from the fact that some one wants it, and the degree of the utility and the amount of resulting value will depend upon the extent to which the desire for it has been previously gratified.

Regarding utility, then, as constantly varying in degree, and as variable even for each different portion of commodity, it is not difficult to see that we exchange those parts of our stock which have a low degree of utility to us, for articles which, being of low utility to others, are much desired by us. This exchange is continued up to the point at which the next portion given would be equally useful to us with that received, so that there is no gain of utility: there would be a loss in carrying the exchange further. Upon these considerations it is easy to construct a theory of the nature of exchange and value, which has been explained in my book* called "The Theory of Political Economy." It is there shown that the well-known laws of supply and demand follow from this view of utility, and thus yield a verification of the theory. Since the publication of the work named, M. Léon Walras, the ingenious professor of political economy at Lausanne, has independently arrived at the same theory of exchange,† a remarkable confirmation of its truth.

Value expresses Ratio of Exchange.

We must now fix our attention upon the fact that, in every act of exchange, a definite quantity of one sub-

* "The Theory of Political Economy." 8vo. 1871 (Macmillan).
† Walras, Éléments d'Économie politique pure. Lausanne, Paris (Guillaumin), 1874.

stance is exchanged for a definite quantity of another. The things bartered may be most various in character, and may be variously measured. We may give a weight of silver for a length of rope, or a superficial extent of carpet, or a number of gallons of wine, or a certain horse-power of force, or conveyance over a certain distance. The quantities to be measured may be expressed in terms of space, time, mass, force, energy, heat, or any other physical units. Yet each exchange will consist in giving so many units of one thing for so many units of another, each measured in its appropriate way.

Every act of exchange thus presents itself to us in the form of *a ratio between two numbers*. The word *value* is commonly used, and if, at current rates, one ton of copper exchanges for ten tons of bar iron, it is usual to say that the value of copper is ten times that of the iron, weight for weight. For our purpose, at least, this use of the word value is only an indirect mode of expressing a ratio. When we say that gold is more valuable than silver, we mean that, as commonly exchanged, the weight of silver exceeds that of the gold given for it. If the value of gold rises compared with that of silver, then still more silver is given for the same quantity of gold. But value like utility is no intrinsic quality of a thing; it is an extrinsic accident or relation. We should never speak of the value of a thing at all without having in our minds the other thing in regard to which it is valued. The very same substance may rise and fall in value at the same time. If, in exchange for a given weight of gold, I can get more silver, but less copper, than I used to do, the value of gold has risen with respect to silver, but fallen with respect to copper. It is evident that an intrinsic property of a thing cannot both increase and decrease at the same time; therefore value must be a mere relation or accident of a thing as regards other things and the persons needing them.

CHAPTER III.

THE FUNCTIONS OF MONEY.

We have seen that three inconveniences attach to the practice of simple barter, namely, the improbability of coincidence between persons wanting and persons possessing; the complexity of exchanges, which are not made in terms of one single substance; and the need of some means of dividing and distributing valuable articles. Money remedies these inconveniences, and thereby performs two distinct functions of high importance, acting as—

(1) A medium of exchange.
(2) A common measure of value.

In its first form money is simply any commodity esteemed by all persons, any article of food, clothing, or ornament which any person will readily receive, and which, therefore, every person desires to have by him in greater or less quantity, in order that he may have the means of procuring necessaries of life at any time. Although many commodities may be capable of performing this function of a medium more or less perfectly, some one article will usually be selected, as money *par excellence*, by custom or the force of circumstances. This article will then begin to be used as a measure of value. Being accustomed to exchange things frequently for sums of money, people learn the value of other articles in terms of money, so that all exchanges will most readily be calculated and adjusted by comparison of the money values of the things exchanged.

A Standard of Value.

A third function of money soon develops itself. Commerce cannot advance far before people begin to borrow and lend, and debts of various origin are contracted. It is in some cases usual, indeed, to restore the very same article which was borrowed, and in almost every case it would be possible to pay back in the same kind of commodity. If corn be borrowed, corn might be paid back, with interest in corn; but the lender will often not wish to have things returned to him at an uncertain time, when he does not much need them, or when their value is unusually low. A borrower, too, may need several different kinds of articles, which he is not likely to obtain from one person; hence arises the convenience of borrowing and lending in one generally recognized commodity, of which the value varies little. Every person making a contract by which he will receive something at a future day, will prefer to secure the receipt of a commodity likely to be as valuable then as now. This commodity will usually be the current money, and it will thus come to perform the function of a *standard of value*. We must not suppose that the substance serving as a standard of value is really invariable in value, but merely that it is chosen as that measure by which the value of future payments is to be regulated. Bearing in mind that value is only the ratio of quantities exchanged, it is certain that no substance permanently bears exactly the same value relatively to another commodity; but it will, of course, be desirable to select as the standard of value that which appears likely to continue to exchange for many other commodities in nearly unchanged ratios.

A Store of Value.

It is worthy of inquiry whether money does not also serve a fourth distinct purpose—that of embodying value in a convenient form for conveyance to distant places. Money, when acting as a medium of exchange, circulates backwards and forwards near the same spot, and may sometimes return to the same hands again and again. It subdivides and distributes property, and *lubricates* the action of exchange. But at times a person needs to condense his property into the smallest compass, so that he may hoard it away for a time, or carry it with him on a long journey, or transmit it to a friend in a distant country. Something which is very valuable, although of little bulk and weight, and which will be recognised as very valuable in every part of the world, is necessary for this purpose. The current money of a country is perhaps more likely to fulfil these conditions than anything else, although diamonds and other precious stones, and articles of exceptional beauty and rarity, might occasionally be employed.

The use of esteemed articles as a store or medium for conveying value may in some cases precede their employment as currency. Mr. Gladstone states that in the Homeric poems gold is mentioned as being hoarded and treasured up, and as being occasionally used in the payment of services, before it became the common measure of value, oxen being then used for the latter purpose. Historically speaking, such a generally esteemed substance as gold seems to have served, firstly, as a commodity valuable for ornamental purposes; secondly, as stored wealth; thirdly, as a medium of exchange; and, lastly, as a measure of value.

Separation of Functions.

It is in the highest degree important that the reader should discriminate carefully and constantly between the four functions which money fulfils, at least in modern societies. We are so accustomed to use the one same substance in all the four different ways, that they tend to become confused together in thought. We come to regard as almost necessary that union of functions which is, at the most, a matter of convenience, and may not always be desirable. We might certainly employ one substance as a medium of exchange, a second as a measure of value, a third as a standard of value, and a fourth as a store of value. In buying and selling we might transfer portions of gold; in expressing and calculating prices we might speak in terms of silver; when we wanted to make long leases we might define the rent in terms of wheat, and when we wished to carry our riches away we might condense it into the form of precious stones. This use of different commodities for each of the functions of money has in fact been partially carried out. In Queen Elizabeth's reign silver was the common measure of value; gold was employed in large payments in quantities depending upon its current value in silver, while corn was required by the Act 18th Elizabeth, c. VI. (1576), to be the standard of value in drawing the leases of certain college lands.

There is evident convenience in selecting, if possible, one single substance which can serve all the functions of money. It will save trouble if we can pay in the same money in which the prices of things are calculated. As few people have the time or patience to investigate closely the history of prices, they will probably assume that the money in which they make all minor and temporary bargains, is also the best standard in which to register debts and contracts extending over many years. A great mass of payments too are invariably fixed by law, such as tolls, fees, and tariffs of charges: many other payments are fixed by custom. Accordingly, even if the medium of exchange varied considerably in value, people would go on making their payments in terms of it, as if there had been no variation, some gaining at the expense of others.

One of our chief tasks in this book will be to consider the various materials which have been employed as money, or have been, or may be, suggested for the purpose. It must be our endeavour, if possible, to discover some substance which will in the highest degree combine the characters requisite for all the different functions of money, but we must bear in mind that a partition of these functions amongst different substances is practicable. We will first proceed to a brief review of the very various ways in which the need of currency has been supplied from the earliest ages, and we will afterwards analyse the physical qualities and circumstances which render the substances employed more or less suited to the purpose to which they were applied. We may thus arrive at some decision as to the exact nature of the commodity which is best adapted to meet our needs in the present day.

CHAPTER IV.

EARLY HISTORY OF MONEY.

LIVING in civilized communities, and accustomed to the use of coined metallic money, we learn to identify money with gold and silver; hence spring hurtful and insidious fallacies. It is always useful, therefore, to be reminded of the truth, so well stated by Turgot, that every kind of merchandise has the two properties of measuring value and transferring value. It is entirely a question of degree what commodities will in any given state of society form the most convenient currency, and this truth will be best impressed upon us by a brief consideration of the very numerous things which have at one time or other been employed as money. Though there are many numismatists and many political economists, the natural history of money is almost a virgin subject, upon which I should like to dilate; but the narrow limits of my space forbid me from attempting more than a brief sketch of the many interesting facts which may be collected.

Currency in the Hunting State.

Perhaps the most rudimentary state of industry is that in which subsistence is gained by hunting wild animals. The proceeds of the chase would, in such a state, be the property of most generally recognised value. The meat of the animals captured would, indeed, be too perishable in nature to be hoarded or often exchanged; but it is otherwise with the skins, which, being preserved and valued for clothing, became one of the earliest materials of currency. Accordingly, there is abundant evidence that furs or skins were employed as money in many ancient nations. They serve this purpose to the present day in some parts of the world.

In the book of Job (ii. 4) we read, "Skin for skin, yea, all that a man hath will he give for his life;" a statement clearly implying that skins were taken as the representative of value among the ancient Oriental nations. Etymological research shows that the same may be said of the northern nations from the earliest times. In the Esthonian language the word *rāha* generally signifies money, but its equivalent in the kindred Lappish tongue has not yet altogether lost the original meaning of skin or fur. Leather money is said to have circulated in Russia as late as the reign of Peter the Great, and it is worthy of notice, that classical writers have recorded traditions to the effect that the earliest currency used at Rome, Lacedæmon, and Carthage, was formed of leather.

We need not go back, however, to such early times to study the use of rude currencies. In the traffic of the Hudson's Bay Company with the North American Indians, furs, in spite of their differences of quality and size, long formed the medium of exchange. It is very instructive, and corroborative of the previous evidence to find that, even after the use of coin had become common among the Indians the skin was still commonly used as the money of account. Thus Whymper says,* "a gun, nominally worth about forty shillings, brought twenty 'skins.' This term is the old one employed by the company. One skin (beaver) is supposed to be worth two shillings, and it represents two marten, and so on. You heard a great deal about 'skins' at Fort Yukon, as the workmen were also charged for clothing, etc., in this way."

Currency in the Pastoral State.

In the next higher stage of civilization, the pastoral state, sheep and cattle naturally form the most valuable and negotiable kind of property. They are easily transferable, convey themselves about, and can be kept for many years, so that they readily perform some of the functions of money.

We have abundance of evidence, traditional, written, and etymological, to show this. In the Homeric poems oxen are distinctly and repeatedly mentioned as the commodity in terms of which other objects are valued. The arms of Diomed are stated to be worth nine oxen, and are compared with those of Glaucos, worth one hundred. The tripod, the first prize for wrestlers in the 23rd Iliad, was valued at twelve oxen, and a woman captive, skilled in industry, at four.† It is peculiarly

---

* "Travels in Alaska, etc.," by F. Whymper, p. 225.
† Gladstone, "Juventus Mundi," p. 53 l.

interesting to find oxen thus used as the common measure of value, because from other passages it is probable, as already mentioned, that the precious metals, though as yet uncoined, were used as a store of value, and occasionally as a medium of exchange. The several functions of money were thus clearly performed by different commodities at this early period.

In several languages the name for money is identical with that of some kind of cattle or domesticated animal. It is generally allowed that *pecunia*, the Latin word for money, is derived from *pecus*, cattle. From the Agamemnon of Æschylus we learn that the figure of an ox was the sign first impressed upon coins, and the same is said to have been the case with the earliest issues of the Roman *As*. Numismatic researches fail to bear out these traditions, which were probably invented to explain the connection between the name of the coin and the animal. A corresponding connection between these notions may be detected in much more modern languages. Our common expression for the payment of a sum of money is *fee*, which is nothing but the Anglo-Saxon *feoh*, meaning alike money and cattle, a word cognate with the German *vieh*, which still bears only the original meaning of cattle. As I am informed by my friend, Professor Theodores, the same connection of ideas is manifested in the Greek word for property, κτῆμα, which means alike possession, flock, or cattle, and is referred by Grimm to an original verb κέτω or κετάω, to feed cattle. It is even supposed by Grimm that the same root reappears in the Teutonic and Scandinavian languages, in the

Gothic, *skatts*, the modern High German, *schatz*, the Anglo-Saxon, *scät*, or *sceat*, the ancient Norsk *skat*, all meaning wealth, property, treasure, tax, or tribute, especially in the shape of cattle. This theory is confirmed by the fact that the Frisian equivalent, *sket*, has retained the original meaning of cattle to the present day. In the Norsk, Anglo-Saxon, and English, *scat* or *scot* has been specialized to denote tax or tribute.

In the ancient German codes of law, fines and penalties are actually defined in terms of live-stock. In the Zend Avesta, as Professor Theodores further informs me, the scale of rewards to be paid to physicians is carefully stated, and in every case the fee consists in some sort of cattle. The fifth and sixth lectures in Sir H. S. Maine's most interesting work on "The Early History of Institutions," which has just been published, are full of curious information showing the importance of live-stock in a primitive state of society. Being counted *by the head*, the kine was called *capitale*, whence the economical term *capital*, the law term *chattel*, and our common name *cattle*.

In countries where slaves form one of the most common and valuable possessions, it is quite natural that they should serve as the medium of exchange like cattle. Pausanias mentions their use in this way, and in Central Africa and some other places where slavery still flourishes, they are the medium of exchange along with cattle and ivory tusks. According to Earl's account of New Guinea, there is in that island a large traffic in slaves, and a slave forms the unit of value. Even in England slaves are believed to have been exchanged at one time in the manner of money.

Articles of Ornament as Currency.

A passion for personal adornment is one of the most primitive and powerful instincts of the human race, and as articles used for such purposes would be durable, universally esteemed, and easily transferable, it is natural that they should be circulated as money. The wampumpeag of the North American Indians is a case in point, as it certainly served as jewellery. It consisted of beads made of the ends of black and white shells, rubbed down and polished, and then strung into belts or necklaces, which were valued according to their length, and also according to their colour and lustre, a foot of black peag being worth two feet of white peag. It was so well established as currency among the natives that the Court of Massachusetts ordered, in 1649, that it should be received in the payment of debts among settlers to the amount of forty shillings. It is curious to learn, too, that just as European misers hoard up gold and silver coins, the richer Indian chiefs secrete piles of wampum beads, having no better means of investing their superfluous wealth.

Exactly analogous to this North American currency, is that of the cowry shells, which, under one name or another—chamgos, zimbis, bouges, porcelanes, etc.—have long been used in the East Indies as small money. In British India, Siam, the West Coast of Africa, and elsewhere on the tropical coasts, they are still used as small change, being collected on the shores of the Maldive and Laccadive Islands, and exported for the purpose. Their value varies somewhat, according to the abundance of the yield, but in India the current rate used to be about 5000 shells for one rupee, at which rate each shell is worth about the two-hundredth part of a penny. Among our interesting fellow-subjects, the Fijians, whale's teeth served in the place of cowries, and white teeth were exchanged for red teeth somewhat in the ratio of shillings to sovereigns.

Among other articles of ornament or of special value used as currency, may be mentioned yellow amber, engraved stones, such as the Egyptian scarabæi, and tusks of ivory.

Currency in the Agricultural State.

Many vegetable productions are at least as well suited for circulation as some of the articles which have been mentioned. It is not surprising to find, then, that among a people supporting themselves by agriculture, the more durable products were thus used. Corn has been the medium of exchange in remote parts of Europe from the time of the ancient Greeks to the present day. In Norway corn is even deposited in banks, and lent and borrowed. What wheat, barley, and oats are to Europe, such is maize in parts of Central America, especially Mexico, where it formerly circulated. In many of the countries surrounding the Mediterranean, olive oil is one of the commonest articles of produce and consumption; being, moreover, pretty uniform in quality, durable, and easily divisible, it has long served as currency in the Ionian Islands, Mytilene, some towns of Asia Minor, and elsewhere in the Levant.

Just as cowries circulate in the East Indies, so cacao nuts, in Central America and Yucatan, form a perfectly recognised and probably an ancient fractional money. Travellers have published many distinct statements as to their value, but it is impossible to reconcile these statements without supposing great changes of value either in the nuts or in the coins with which they are compared. In 1521, at Caracas, about thirty cacao nuts were worth one penny English, whereas recently ten beans would go to a penny, according to Squier's statements. In the European countries, where almonds are commonly grown, they have circulated to some extent like the cacao nuts, but are variable in value, according to the success of the harvest.

It is not only, however, as a minor currency that vegetable products have been used in modern times. In the American settlements and the West India Islands, in former days, specie used to become inconveniently scarce, and the legislators fell back upon the device of obliging creditors to receive payment in produce at stated rates. In 1618, the Governor of the Plantations of Virginia ordered that tobacco should be received at the rate of three shillings for the pound weight, under the penalty of three years' hard labour. We are told that, when the Virginia Company imported young

EARLY HISTORY OF MONEY. 27

women as wives for the settlers, the price per head was one hundred pounds of tobacco, subsequently raised to one hundred and fifty. As late as 1732, the legislature of Maryland made tobacco and Indian corn legal tenders; and in 1641 there were similar laws concerning corn in Massachusetts. The governments of some of the West India Islands seem to have made attempts to imitate these peculiar currency laws, and it was provided that the successful plaintiff in a lawsuit should be obliged to accept various kinds of raw produce, such as sugar, rum, molasses, ginger, indigo, or tobacco.* Such endeavours to establish a kind of multiple currency will be found to possess considerable interest for us in a later chapter.

The perishable nature of most kinds of animal food prevents them from being much used as money; but eggs are said to have circulated in the Alpine villages of Switzerland, and dried codfish have certainly acted as currency in the colony of Newfoundland.

Manufactured and Miscellaneous Articles as Currency.

The enumeration of articles which have served as money may already seem long enough for the purposes in view. I will, therefore, only add briefly that a great number of manufactured commodities have been used as a medium of exchange in various times and places.

---

* See a scarce tract, entitled "Two Letters to Mr. Wood on the Coin and Currency in the Leeward Islands," p. 34. London, 1740.

Such are the pieces of cotton cloth, called *Guinea pieces*, used for traffic upon the banks of the Senegal, or the somewhat similar pieces circulated in Abyssinia, the Soulou Archipelago, Sumatra, Mexico, Peru, Siberia, and among the Veddahs. It is less easy to understand the origin of the curious straw money which circulated until 1694 in the Portuguese possessions in Angola, and which consisted of small mats, called libongos, woven out of rice straw, and worth about $1\frac{1}{2}d.$ each. These mats must have had, at least originally, some purpose apart from their use as currency, and were perhaps analogous to the fine woven mats so much valued by the Samoans, and also treated by them as a medium of exchange.

Salt has been circulated not only in Abyssinia, but in Sumatra, Mexico, and elsewhere. Cubes of benzoin gum or beeswax in Sumatra, red feathers in the Islands of the Pacific Ocean, cubes of tea in Tartary, iron shovels or hoes among the Malagasy, are other peculiar forms of currency. The remarks of Adam Smith concerning the use of hand-made nails as money in some Scotch villages will be remembered by many readers, and need not be repeated. M. Chevalier has adduced an exactly corresponding case from one of the French coalfields.

Were space available it would be interesting to discuss the not improbable suggestion of Boucher de Perthes, that, perhaps, after all, the finely worked stone implements now so frequently discovered were among the earliest mediums of exchange. Some of them are certainly made of jade, nephrite, or other hard stones, only found in distant countries, so that an active traffic in such implements must have existed in times of which we have no records whatever.

There are some obscure allusions in classical authors to a wooden money circulating among the Byzantines, and to a wooden talent used at Antioch and Alexandria, but in the absence of fuller information as to their nature, it is impossible to do more than mention them.

CHAPTER V.

QUALITIES OF THE MATERIAL OF MONEY.

Many recent writers, such as Huskisson, MacCulloch, James Mill, Garnier, Chevalier, and Walras, have satisfactorily described the qualities which should be possessed by the material of money. Earlier writers seem, however, to have understood the subject almost as well. Harris explained these qualities with remarkable clearness in his "Essay upon Money and Coins," published in 1757, a work which appeared before the "Wealth of Nations," yet gave an exposition of the principles of money which can hardly be improved at the present day. Eighty years before, however, Rice Vaughan, in his excellent little "Treatise of Money," had written a brief but satisfactory statement of the qualities requisite in money. We even find that William Stafford, the author of that remarkable dialogue of the Elizabethan age (1581), called "A Brief Conceipte of English Policy," showed perfect insight into the subject. Of all writers, M. Chevalier, however, probably gives the most accurate and full account of the properties which money should possess, and I shall in many points follow his views.

QUALITIES OF THE MATERIAL OF MONEY. 31

The prevailing defect in the treatment of the subject is the failure to observe that money requires different properties as regards different functions. To decide upon the best material for money is thus a problem of great complexity, because we must take into account at once the relative importance of the several functions of money, the degree in which money is employed for each function, and the importance of each of the physical qualities of the substance with respect to each function. In a simple state of industry money is chiefly required to pass about between buyers and sellers. It should, then, be conveniently portable, divisible into pieces of various size, so that any sum may readily be made up, and easily distinguishable by its appearance, or by the design impressed upon it. When money, however, comes to serve, as it will at some future time, almost exclusively as a measure and standard of value, the system of exchange, being one of perfected barter, such properties become a matter of comparative indifference, and stability of value, joined perhaps to portability, is the most important quality. Before venturing, however, to discuss such complex questions, we must proceed to a preliminary discussion of the properties in question, which may thus perhaps be enumerated in the order of their importance:—

1. Utility and value.
2. Portability.
3. Indestructibility.
4. Homogeneity.
5. Divisibility.
6. Stability of value.
7. Cognizability.

1. *Utility and Value.*

Since money has to be exchanged for valuable goods, it should itself possess value, and it must therefore have utility as the basis of value. Money, when once in full currency, is only received in order to be passed on, so that if all people could be induced to take worthless bits of material at a fixed rate of valuation, it might seem that money does not really require to have substantial value. Something like this does frequently happen in the history of currencies, and apparently valueless shells, bits of leather, or scraps of paper, are actually received in exchange for costly commodities. This strange phenomenon is, however, in most cases capable of easy explanation, and if we were acquainted with the history of every kind of money the like explanation would no doubt be possible in other cases. The essential point is that people should be induced to receive money, and pass it on freely at steady ratios of exchange for other objects; but there must always be some sufficient reason first inducing people to accept the money. The force of habit, convention, or legal enactment may do much to maintain money in circulation when once it is afloat, but it is doubtful whether the most powerful government could oblige its subjects to accept and circulate as money a worthless substance which they had no other motive for receiving.

Certainly, in the early stages of society, the use of money was not based on legal regulations, so that the utility of the substance for other purposes must have been the prior condition of its employment as money. Thus the singular *peag* currency, or *wampumpeag*, which was found in circulation among the North American Indians by the early explorers, was esteemed for the purpose of adornment, as already mentioned, (p. 24). The cowry shells, so widely used as a small currency in the East, are valued for ornamental purposes on the West Coast of Africa, and were in all probability employed as ornaments before they were employed as money. All the other articles mentioned in Chapter IV., such as oxen, corn, skins, tobacco, salt, cacao nuts, etc., which have performed the functions of money in one place or other, possessed independent utility and value. If there are any apparent exceptions at all to this rule, they would doubtless admit of explanation by fuller knowledge. We may, therefore, agree with Storch when he says:—"It is impossible that a substance which has no direct value should be introduced as money, however suitable it may be in other respects for this use."

When once a substance is widely employed as money, it is conceivable that its utility will come to depend mainly upon the services which it thus confers upon the community. Gold, for instance, is far more important as the material of money than in the production of plate, jewellery, watches, gold-leaf, etc. A substance originally used for many purposes may eventually serve only as money, and yet, by the demand for currency and the force of habit, may maintain its value. The cowry circulation of the Indian coasts is probably a case in point. The importance of habit, personal or hereditary, is at least as great in monetary science as it is, according to Mr. Herbert Spencer, in morals and sociological phenomena generally.

There is, however, no reason to suppose that the value of gold and silver is at present due solely to their conventional use as money. These metals are endowed with such singularly useful properties that, if we could only get them in sufficient abundance, they would supplant all the other metals in the manufacture of household utensils, ornaments, fittings of all kinds, and an infinite multitude of small articles, which are now made of brass, copper, bronze, pewter, German silver, or other inferior metals and alloys.

In order that money may perform some of its functions efficiently, especially those of a medium of exchange and a store of value, to be carried about, it is important that it should be made of a substance valued highly in all parts of the world, and, if possible, almost equally esteemed by all peoples. There is reason to think that gold and silver have been admired and valued by all tribes which have been lucky enough to procure them. The beautiful lustre of these metals must have drawn attention and excited admiration as much in the earliest as in the present times.

2. *Portability.*

The material of money must not only be valuable, but the value must be so related to the weight and bulk of the material, that the money shall not be inconveniently heavy on the one hand, nor inconveniently minute on the other. There was a tradition in Greece that Lycurgus obliged the Lacedæmonians to use iron money, in order that its weight might deter them from overmuch trading. However this may be, it is certain that iron money could not be used in cash payments at the present day, since a penny would weigh about a pound, and instead of a five-pound note, we should have to deliver a ton of iron. During the last century copper was actually used as the chief medium of exchange in Sweden; and merchants had to take a wheelbarrow with them when they went to receive payments in copper dalers. Many of the substances used as currency in former times must have been sadly wanting in portability. Oxen and sheep, indeed, would transport themselves on their own legs; but corn, skins, oil, nuts, almonds, etc., though in several respects forming fair currency, would be intolerably bulky, and troublesome to transfer.

The portability of money is an important quality not merely because it enables the owner to carry small sums in the pocket without trouble, but because large sums can be transferred from place to place, or from continent to continent, at little cost. The result is to secure an approximate uniformity in the value of money in all parts of the world. A substance which is very heavy and bulky in proportion to value, like corn or coal, may be very scarce in one place and over abundant in another; yet the supply and demand cannot be equalized without great expense in carriage. The cost of conveying gold or silver from London to Paris, including insurance, is only about four-tenths of one per cent.; and between the most distant parts of the world it does not exceed from two to three per cent.

Substances may be too valuable as well as too cheap, so that for ordinary transactions it would be necessary to call in the aid of the microscope and the chemical balance. Diamonds, apart from other objections, would be far too valuable for small transactions. The value of such stones is said to vary as the square of the weight, so that we cannot institute any exact comparison with metals of which the value is simply proportional to the weight. But taking a one-carat diamond (four grains) as worth £15, we find it is, weight for weight, 460 times as valuable as gold. There are several rare metals, such as iridium and osmium, which would likewise be far too valuable to circulate. Even gold and silver are too costly for small currency. A silver penny now weighs $7\frac{1}{4}$ grains, and a gold penny would weigh only half a grain. The pretty octagonal quarter-dollar tokens circulated in California are the smallest gold coins I have seen, weighing less than four grains each, and are so thin that they can almost be blown away.

3. *Indestructibility.*

If it is to be passed about in trade, and kept in reserve, money must not be subject to easy deterioration or loss. It must not evaporate like alcohol, nor putrefy like animal substances, nor decay like wood, nor rust like iron. Destructible articles, such as eggs dried codfish, cattle, or oil, have certainly been used as currency; but what is treated as money one day must soon afterwards be eaten up. Thus a large stock of such perishable commodities cannot be kept on hand, and their value must be very variable. The several kinds of corn are less subject to this objection, since, when well dried at first, they suffer no appreciable deterioration for several years

4. *Homogeneity.*

All portions or specimens of the substance used as money should be *homogeneous*, that is, of the same quality, so that equal weights will have exactly the same value. In order that we may correctly count in terms of any unit, the units must be equal and similar, so that twice two will always make four. If we were to count in precious stones, it would seldom happen that four stones would be just twice as valuable as two stones. Even the precious metals, as found in the native state, are not perfectly homogeneous, being mixed together in almost all proportions; but this produces little inconvenience, because the assayer readily determines the quantity of each pure metal present in any ingot. In the processes of refining and coining, the metals are afterwards reduced to almost exactly uniform degrees of fineness, so that equal weights are then of exactly equal value.

5. *Divisibility.*

Closely connected with the last property is that of divisibility. Every material is, indeed, mechanically divisible, almost without limit. The hardest gems can be broken, and steel can be cut by harder steel. But the material of money should be not merely capable of division, but the aggregate value of the mass after division should be almost exactly the same as before division. If we cut up a skin or fur the pieces will, as a general rule, be far less valuable than the whole skin or fur, except for a special intended purpose; and the same is the case with timber, stone, and most other materials in which reunion is impossible. But portions of metal can be melted together again whenever it is desirable, and the cost of doing this, including the metal lost, is in the case of precious metals very inconsiderable, varying from $\frac{1}{4}d.$ to $\frac{1}{2}d.$ per ounce. Thus, approximately speaking, the value of any piece of gold or silver is simply proportional to the weight of fine metal which it contains.

6. *Stability of Value.*

It is evidently desirable that the currency should not be subject to fluctuations of value. The ratios in which money exchanges for other commodities should be maintained as nearly as possible invariable on the average. This would be a matter of comparatively minor importance were money used only as a measure of values at any one moment, and as a medium of exchange. If all prices were altered in like proportion as soon as money varied in value, no one would lose or gain, except as regards the coin which he happened to have in his pocket, safe, or bank balance. But, practically speaking, as we have seen, people do employ money as a standard of value for long contracts, and they often maintain payments at the same invariable rate, by custom or law, even when the real value of the payment is much altered. Hence every change in the value of money does some injury to society.

It might be plausibly said, indeed, that the debtor gains as much as the creditor loses, or *vice versâ*, so that on the whole the community is as rich as before; but this is not really true. A mathematical analysis of the subject shows that to take any sum of money from one and give it to another will, on the average of cases, injure the loser more than it benefits the receiver. A person with an income of one hundred pounds a year would suffer more by losing ten pounds than he would gain by an addition of ten pounds, because the degree of utility of money to him is considerably higher at ninety pounds than it is at one hundred and ten. On the same principle, all gaming, betting, pure speculation, or other accidental modes of transferring property involve, on the average, a dead loss of utility. The whole incitement to industry and commerce and the accumulation of capital depends upon the expectation of enjoyment thence arising, and every variation of the currency tends in some degree to frustrate such expectation and to lessen the motives for exertion.

7. *Cognizability.*

By this name we may denote the capability of a substance for being easily recognized and distinguished from all other substances. As a medium of exchange, money has to be continually handed about, and it will occasion great trouble if every person receiving currency has to scrutinize, weigh, and test it. If it requires any skill to discriminate good money from bad, poor ignorant people are sure to be imposed upon. Hence the medium of exchange should have certain distinct marks which nobody can mistake. Precious stones, even if in other respects good as money, could not be so used, because only a skilled lapidary can surely distinguish between true and imitation gems.

Under cognizability we may properly include what has been aptly called *impressibility*, namely, the capability of a substance to receive such an impression, seal, or design, as shall establish its character as current money of certain value. We might more simply say, that the material of money should be *coinable*, so that a portion, being once issued according to proper regulations with the impress of the state, may be known to all as good and legal currency, equal in weight, size, and value to all similarly marked currency. We shall afterwards consider more minutely what is involved in the manufacture of a good coin.

CHAPTER VI.

THE METALS AS MONEY.

It need not be pointed out in detail that, though the numerous commodities mentioned in Chapter IV. possess, in a greater or less degree, the qualities essential to the material of money, they cannot for a moment compare in this respect with many of the metals. Some of the metals seem to be marked out by nature as most fit of all substances for employment as money, at least when acting as a medium of exchange and a store of value. Accordingly, we find that gold, silver, copper, tin, lead, and iron have been more or less extensively in circulation in all historical ages. So closely have silver and copper become associated in people's minds with their use as money, that we find their names adopted as the names of money. In Greek, ἄργυρος means equally silver, silver coin, and money generally; in Latin, *aes* is copper, bronze, or brass, and also money and wages; in French, *argent* is both silver and money. The same association of meanings could be pointed out in many other languages, including our own. Though our pence are now made of bronze, we still speak of them as *coppers*.

With the exception of iron, the principal metals are peculiarly indestructible, and undergo little or no deterioration when hoarded up or handed about. Each kind of metal is approximately homogeneous, piece differing from piece in nothing but weight, the differences of fineness being ascertained and allowed for in the case of gold and silver. The metals are also perfectly divisible, either by the chisel or the crucible, and yet a second melting will always reunite the pieces again with little cost or loss of material. Most of them possess the properties of cognizability and impressibility in the highest degree. Each metal has its characteristic colour, density, and hardness, so that it is easy for a person with very slight experience to distinguish one metal from another. Their malleability enables us to roll, cut, and hammer them into any required form, and to impress a permanent design by means of dies. With the exception of porcelain coins, which have been used in Siam, I am not aware that coins have ever been made of any substance except metal.

In respect to steadiness of value the metals are probably less satisfactory, regarded as a standard of value, than many other commodities, such as corn. From the earliest ages metals must have been most highly valued, as we may learn from the way in which they are esteemed by savages in the present day. But their value has suffered and is suffering an almost continuous decline, owing to the progress of industry, and the discovery of new mechanical and chemical means for their extraction. Even the order of their values becomes changed. According to Mr. Gladstone, iron was, in the Homeric age, much more valued than *chalkos*, or copper, which latter was then the most common and useful metal. Lead was little known or valued, but gold, silver, and tin held the same places at the head of the list which they hold at the present day.

Iron.

Proceeding to consider briefly each of the more important metals, the statements of Aristotle, Pollux, and other writers prove that iron was extensively employed as money in early times. Not a single specimen of such money is now known to exist, but this is easily accounted for by the rapidity with which the metal rusts. In the absence of specimens, we do not know the form and size of the money, but it is probable that it consisted of small bars, ingots, or spikes, somewhat similar to the small bars of iron which are still used in trading with the natives of Central Africa. Iron money is still, or was not long since, used in Japan for small values; but its issue from the mint has been discontinued.

The use of pure iron coins in civilized countries at the present day is out of the question, both because of the cheapness of the metal, and because the coins would soon lose the sharpness of their impressions by rusting, and become dirty and easily counterfeited. But it is quite possible that iron or steel might still be alloyed with other metals for the coining of pence.

Lead.

Lead has often been used as currency, and is occasionally so mentioned by the ancient Greek and Latin poets. In 1635 leaden bullets were used for change at the rate of a farthing a piece in Massachusetts. At the present day it is still current in Burmah, being passed by weight for small payments. The extreme softness of the metal obviously renders it quite unfit for coining in the pure state. It is one of the components of pewter, which has frequently been coined.

Tin.

Tin has also been employed as money at various times. Dionysius of Syracuse issued the earliest tin coinage of which anything is certainly known; but as tin was in early times procured from Cornwall, it can hardly be doubted that the first British currency was composed of tin. In innumerable cabinets may be found series of tin coins issued by the Roman emperors; the kings of England also often coined tin. In 1680 tin farthings were struck by Charles II., a stud of copper being inserted in the middle of the coin to render counterfeiting more difficult. Tin halfpence and farthings were also issued in considerable quantities in the reign of William and Mary (1690 to 1691). Tin coins were formerly employed among the Javanese, Mexicans, and many other peoples, and the metal is said to be still current by weight in the Straits of Malacca.

Tin would be in many respects admirably suited for making pence, possessing a fine white colour, perfect freedom from corrosion, and a much higher value than copper. Unfortunately, its softness and tendency to bend and break when pure are insuperable obstacles to its employment as money.

Copper.

This metal is in many respects well suited for coining. It does not suffer from exposure to dry air, possesses a fine distinct red colour, and takes a good impression from the dies, which impression it retains better than the majority of other metals. Accordingly, we find that it has been continually employed as currency, either alone or in subordination to gold and silver. The earliest Hebrew coins were composed chiefly of copper, and the metallic currency of Rome consisted of the impure copper, called *aes*, until B.C. 269, when silver was first coined. In later times copper has not only been generally used for coins of minor value, but, in Russia and in Sweden, a hundred years ago, it formed the principal mass of the currency. Its low value now stands in the way of its use. A penny, if made so as to contain metal equivalent to its nominal value, would weigh 870 grains, or more than an ounce and three-quarters troy. Its value is also subject to considerable fluctuations. Moreover, it is unlikely that copper in a pure state will be coined for the future, since bronze is now known to be so much more suitable for coinage.

Silver.

I need hardly say that silver is distinguished by its exquisite white lustre, which is not rivalled by that of any other pure metal. Certain alloys, indeed, such as speculum metal, or Britannia metal, have been made of almost equal lustre, but they are either brittle, or so soft as not to give the metallic ring of silver. When much exposed to the air silver tarnishes by the formation of a black film of silver sulphide; but this forms no obstacle to its use as currency, since the film is always very thin, and its peculiar black colour even assists in distinguishing the pure metal from counterfeit. When suitably alloyed, silver is sufficiently hard to stand much wear, and next after gold it is the most malleable and impressible of all the metals.

A coin or other object made of silver may be known by the following marks:—(1) a fine pure white lustre, where newly rubbed or scraped; (2) a blackish tint where the surface has long been exposed to the air; (3) a moderate specific gravity; (4) a good metallic ring when thrown down; (5) considerable hardness; (6) strong nitric acid dissolves silver, and the solution turns black if exposed to light.

Silver has been coined, it need hardly be said, in all ages since the first invention of the art, and its value relatively to gold and copper suits it for taking the middle place in a monetary system. Its value too remains very stable for periods of fifty or a hundred years, because a vast stock of the metal is kept in the form of plate, watches, jewellery, and ornaments of various kinds, in addition to money, so that a variation in the supply for a few years cannot make any appreciable change in the total stock. Productive silver mines exist in almost all parts of the world, and wherever lead is produced, a small but steady yield of silver is obtained from it by the Pattinson method of extraction.

Gold.

Silver is beautiful, yet gold is even more beautiful, and presents indeed a combination of useful and striking properties quite without parallel among known substances. To a rich and brilliant yellow colour, which can only be adequately described as golden, it joins astonishing malleability and a very high specific gravity, exceeded only by that of platinum and a few of the rarest or almost unknown metals. We can usually ascertain whether a coin consists of gold or not, by looking for three characteristic marks: (1) the brilliant yellow colour; (2) the high specific gravity; (3) the metallic ring of the coin when thrown down, which will prove the absence of lead or platinum in the interior of the coin.

If there remain any doubt about a metal being gold, we have only to appeal to its solubility. Gold is remarkable for its freedom from corrosion or solution, being quite unaffected and untarnished after exposure of any length of time to dry, or moist, or impure air, and being also insoluble in all the simple acids. Strong nitric acid will rapidly attack any coloured counterfeit metal, but will not touch standard gold, or will, at the most, feebly dissolve the copper and silver alloyed with it.

In almost all respects gold is perfectly suited for coining. When quite pure, indeed, it is almost as soft as tin, but when alloyed with one-tenth or one-twelfth part of copper, becomes sufficiently hard to resist wear and tear, and to give a good metallic ring; yet it remains perfectly malleable and takes a fine impression. Its melting point is moderately high, and yet there is no perceptible oxidization or volatilization of the metal at the highest temperature which can be produced in a furnace. Thus old coin and fragments of the metal can be melted into bullion at a very slight loss, and at a cost of not more than one halfpenny per ounce troy, or little more than one-twentieth of one per cent.

Platinum.

This is one of those comparatively rare metals which have been known only in recent times. Its extremely high melting-point, and low affinity for oxygen, render it one of the most indestructible of all substances, whilst its white colour, joined to its excessively high specific gravity, are marks which cannot be mistaken. As it seemed in these respects well suited for currency, the Russian government, which owns the principal platinum mines in the Ural mountains, commenced to coin it, in 1828, into pieces intended to have the values of twelve, six, and three roubles. Several objections to this use of the metal soon presented themselves. The appearance of platinum

being inferior to that of silver or gold, it is seldom
or never employed for purposes of ornament, and its only
extensive use is in the construction of chemical apparatus.
Hence there is no large stock of the metal kept on hand,
and the localities where it is found being few, the supply
is incapable of being much increased, so that any variation of demand is sure to cause a great change in its
value. Moreover, the cost of making the coins was very
great, owing to the extreme difficulty of melting platinum, and the worn coins could not be withdrawn and
recoined without much additional cost. Platinum being
thus found to be quite unfitted for currency, the scheme
was abandoned in 1845, and the existing coins withdrawn
from circulation.

Great improvements having been lately made in the
modes of working platinum, it was proposed by M. de
Jacobi, the representative of Russia at the International
Monetary Conference held at Paris, in 1867, that
platinum should be employed for the coinage of five-
franc pieces. It is not likely that such a suggestion
will be adopted.

Nickel.

This metal was formerly regarded as the bane of the
metallurgist, but has recently assumed an important
place in manufacturing industry, and even in monetary
science. It is used only in alloy with other metals, and
for the purposes of coinage it is usual to melt up one
part of nickel with three of copper. Some of the coins
of Belgium, and the one-cent pieces of the United States

have been made of this material and seem to be very convenient. In 1869 and 1870-1, pence and halfpence, to the value of £3000, were executed in the same alloy, at the English mint, for the colony of Jamaica. These are some of the most beautiful coins which have ever been issued from Tower Hill, and are in most respects admirably suited for circulation. But they were unfortunately made much too large and heavy; not only were they thus rendered less convenient, but when in 1873, the Deputy Master of the Mint was requested to supply a further quantity of the same coins, he found that the price of nickel had risen very much, so that the materials for the coinage alone would cost more than the nominal value of the coins to be produced. This rise in price was due partly to the small number of nickel mines yet worked, and partly to the great demand for the metal occasioned by the German government, which has chosen the same alloy for the ten and five-pfennig pieces of its new monetary system. These coins, which are now being issued, are of a convenient size, rather less than a shilling and sixpence respectively, and appear to be in every way admirably suited to their purpose. The German empire will soon possess the best instead of the worst fractional currency in the world. The variableness in the price of nickel, which is at present a cause of embarrassment, may after a time become less serious, when the stock in use and the annual produce become larger.

Other Metals.

The metals yet mentioned are but a small number of those now known by chemists to exist, and it would be unwise to assume as certain that money must always be made in the future of the same materials as in the past. It is just conceivable, on the one hand, that in the course of time, some metal still more valuable than gold may be introduced. Roughly speaking, the order in which the metals have hitherto acted, as the principal medium of exchange, is (1) copper, (2) silver, (3) gold; as a general decline in the values of the metals took place, the more valuable replaced the less valuable, and the more portable gold is now rapidly taking the place of silver. Some still more valuable metal, such as the scarce and intractable iridium or osmium, or the remarkable metal palladium, might possibly take the place of gold. This, however, is barely more than a matter of scientific fancy.

On the other hand, many metals exist which might be produced more cheaply than silver, such as aluminium or manganese. It may be well worthy of inquiry whether in such metals may not be found the best solution of the fractional currency difficulty, to be afterwards more fully discussed (p. 132).

Alloys of Metals.

At one time or another an immense number of different alloys or mixtures of metals have been coined. It would be strictly correct to say, indeed, that metals have seldom been issued except in the state of alloy. Even gold and silver, as usually coined, are either alloyed with each other or with copper. The latter metal, too, has generally been employed in union with other metals. The Roman *as* consisted, not of pure copper, but of the mixed metal *aes*, an alloy of copper and tin, partially resembling the bronze which has quite recently been introduced for small money in France, England, and other countries. Brass was largely coined by some of the Roman emperors. In many cases, no doubt, the early metallurgists in smelting an ore obtained a natural alloy of all the metals contained therein, and being unable to separate them were obliged to use the mixture. Thus we may explain the curious metal containing from sixty to seventy parts of copper, twenty to twenty-five of zinc, five to eleven of silver, with small quantities of gold, lead, and tin, which was employed to make the *stycas*, or small money, of the early kings of Northumbria.

Monarchs or states in difficulty have often coined the metal which they could most easily obtain. The Irish money issued by James II. was said to have been coined from a mixture of old guns, broken bells, waste copper, brass, and pewter, old kitchen furniture, and in fact any refuse metal which his officers could lay their hands upon. He attempted to make pewter crowns circulate for the value of silver ones.

CHAPTER VII.

COINS.

It is clear that the metals far surpass all other substances in suitability for the purpose of circulation, and it is almost equally clear that certain metals surpass all the other metals in this respect. Of gold and silver especially we may say, with Turgot, that, by the nature of things, they are constituted the universal money independently of all convention and law. Even if the art of coining had never been invented, gold and silver would probably have formed the currency of the world; but we have now to consider how, by shaping weighed pieces of these metals into coins, we can make use of their valuable properties to the greatest advantage.

The primitive mode of circulating the metals, indeed, was simply that of buying and selling them against other commodities, the weights or portions being rudely estimated. Some of the earliest specimens of money consist of the *aes rude,* or rough, shapeless lumps of native copper employed as money by the ancient Etruscans. In the Museum of the Archiginnasio at Bologna may be seen the skeleton of an Etruscan, half embedded in earth, with the piece of rough copper yet within the grasp of the bony hand, placed there to meet the demands of Charon. Pliny, moreover, tells us that, before the time of Servius Tullius, copper was circulated in the rude state. Afterwards copper, brass, or iron were, it is probable, employed in the form of small bars or spikes, and the name of the Greek unit of value, *drachma*, is supposed to have been derived from the fact that six of these metal spikes could be grasped in the hand, each piece being called an *obolus*. Such is supposed to have been the first system of money which was passed purely by *tale*, or number of pieces.

Gold is most readily obtained from alluvial deposits, and then has the form of grains or dust. Hence this is the primitive form of gold money. The ancient Peruvians enclosed the gold dust for the sake of security in quills, and thus passed it about more conveniently. At the gold diggings of California, Australia, or New Zealand, gold dust is to the present day sold directly against other goods by the aid of scales. The art of melting gold and silver, and fashioning them by the hammer into various shapes was early invented. Even in the present day the poor Hindoo, who has saved up a few rupees, employs a silversmith to melt them up and beat them into a simple bracelet, which he wears in the double character of an ornament and a hoard of wealth.

Similarly, the ancient Goths and Celts were accustomed to fashion gold into thick wires, which they rolled up into spiral rings and probably wore upon their fingers

COINS. 55

until the metal was wanted for trading purposes. There can be little doubt that this ring money, of which abundant specimens have been found in various parts of Europe and Asia, formed the first approximation to a coinage. In some cases the rings may have been intentionally made of equal weight; for Cæsar speaks of the Britons as having iron rings, adjusted to a certain weight, to serve as money. In other cases the rings, or amulets, were bought and sold by aid of the balance; and in certain Egyptian paintings men are represented as in the act of weighing rings. It is probable that the necessity for frequent weighings was avoided by making up sealed bags containing a certain weight of rings, and such perhaps are the bags of silver given by Naaman to Gehazi in the Second Book of Kings (v. 23). Ring money is said to be still current in Nubia.

Gold and silver have been fashioned into various other forms to serve as money. Thus the Siamese money consists of very small ingots or bars bent double in a peculiar manner In Pondicherry and elsewhere gold is circulated in the form of small grains or buttons.

The Invention of Coining.

The date of the invention of coining can be assigned with some degree of probability. Coined money was clearly unknown in the Homeric times, and it was known in the time of Lycurgus. We might therefore assume, with various authorities, that it was invented in the mean time. or about 900 B.C. There is a tradition, moreover, that Pheidon, King of Argos, first struck silver money in the island of Ægina about 895 B.C., and the tradition is supported by the existence of small stamped ingots of silver, which have been found in Ægina. Later inquiries, however, lead to the conclusion that Pheidon lived in the middle of the eighth century B.C., and Grote has shown good reasons for believing that what he did accomplish was done in Argos, and not in Ægina.

The mode in which the invention happened is sufficiently evident. Seals were familiarly employed in very early times, as we learn from the Egyptian paintings or the stamped bricks of Nineveh. Being employed to signify possession, or to ratify contracts, they came to indicate authority. When a ruler first undertook to certify the weights of pieces of metal, he naturally employed his seal to make the fact known, just as, at Goldsmiths' Hall, a small punch is used to certify the fineness of plate. In the earliest forms of coinage there were no attempts at so fashioning the metal that its weight could not be altered without destroying the stamp or design. The earliest coins struck, both in Lydia and in the Peloponnesus, were stamped on one side only. The Persian money, called the *larin*, consists of a round silver wire, about six centimetres long, bent in two, and stamped on one part which is flattened for the purpose. It is probably a relic of ring money. The present circulation of China is composed to a considerable extent of the so-called Sycee silver, which consists of small shoe-shaped ingots, assayed and stamped, according to some accounts, by the government.

What is a Coin?

Although, in rings, grains, or stamped ingots, we have an approximation to what we call coin, it is plain that we must do something more to make convenient money. The stamp must be so impressed as to certify, not only the fineness and the original weight, but also the absence of any subsequent alteration. To coin metal, as we now understand the art, is to form it into flat pieces of a circular, oval, square, hexagonal, octagonal, or other regular outline, and then to impress designs from engraved dies upon both sides, and sometimes upon the edges. Not only is it very costly and difficult to counterfeit coins well executed in this manner, but the integrity of the design assures us that no owner of the coin has tampered with it. Even the amount of ordinary wear and tear, which the coin has suffered, may be rudely inferred from the sharpness or partial effacement of the designs, and the roundness of the edges. "Pieces of money," says M. Chevalier, "are ingots of which the weight and the fineness are certified." There is nothing in this definition to distinguish coins from Sycee silver, or from the ordinary stamped bars and ingots of bullion. I should prefer, therefore, to say, *coins are ingots of which the weight and fineness are certified by the integrity of designs impressed upon the surfaces of the metal.*

Various Forms of Coins.

From time to time coins have been manufactured in very many forms, although circular coins vastly predominate in number. Among the innumerable issues of the German states may be found octagonal and hexagonal coins. A singular square coin, with a circular impress in the centre, was issued from Salzburg by Rudbert in 1513. Siege-pieces have been issued in England and elsewhere in the form of squares, lozenges, etc. Some of the most extraordinary specimens of money ever used are the large plates of pure copper which circulated in Sweden in the eighteenth century. These were about three-eighths of an inch in thickness, and varied in size, the half-daler being $3\frac{1}{2}$ inches square, and the two-daler piece as much as $7\frac{1}{2}$ inches square, and $3\frac{1}{2}$ pounds in weight. As the whole surface could not be covered with a design, a circular impress was struck near to each corner, and one in the centre, so as to render alteration as difficult as possible.

Among Oriental nations the shapes of coins are still more curious. In Japan, the principal part of the circulation consists of silver *itzibus,* which are oblong, flat pieces of silver, covered on both sides with designs and legends, the characters being partly in relief and partly incised. The smaller silver coins have a similar form. Among the minor Japanese coins are found large, oval, moulded pieces of copper or mixed metal, each with a square hole in the centre. The Chinese *cash* are well known to be round discs of a kind of brass, with a square hole in the centre to allow of their being strung together. The coins of Formosa are similar, except that they are much larger and thicker. All the copper and base metal coins of China, Japan, and Formosa are distinguished by a broad flat rim, and they have characters in relief upon a sunk ground, somewhat in the manner of Boulton and Watt's copper pence. They are manufactured by moulding the metal, and then filing the protuberant parts smooth. Such coins stand wear, and preserve their design better than European coins, but they are easily counterfeited.

The most singular of all coins are the scimitar-shaped pieces formerly circulated in Persia.

The best Form for Coins.

It is a matter of considerable importance to devise the best possible form for coins, and the best mode of striking them. The use of money creates, as it were, an artificial crime of false coining, and so great is the temptation to engage in this illicit art that no penalty is sufficient to repress it, as the experience of two thousand years sufficiently proves. Thousands of persons have suffered death, and all the penalties of treason have been enforced without effect. Ruding is then unquestionably right in saying, that our efforts should be directed not so much to the punishment of the crime, as to its prevention by improvements in the art of coining. We must strike our coins so perfectly that successful imitation or alteration shall be out of the question.

There are four principal objects at which we should aim in deciding upon the exact design for a coin.

1. To prevent counterfeiting.
2. To prevent the fraudulent removal of metal from the coin.

3. To reduce the loss of metal by legitimate wear and tear.

4. To make the coin an artistic and historical monument of the state issuing it, and the people using it.

For the prevention of counterfeiting, our principal resource is to render the mechanical execution of the piece as perfect as possible, and to strike it in a way which can only be accomplished with the aid of elaborate machinery. When all coins were made by casting, the false coiner could work almost as skilfully as the moneyer. Hence, in the Roman empire, it was difficult to distinguish between true and false coin. Hammered money was a great improvement on moulded money, and milled money on hammered money. The introduction of the steam coining press by Boulton and Watt was the next great improvement; and the knee-joint press of Ulhorn and Thonnelier, now used in nearly all mints, except that on Tower Hill, forms the last advance in the mechanism for striking coin.

The utmost attention ought to be paid to the perfect execution of the milling, legend, or other design, impressed upon the edge of modern coins. This serves at once to prevent clipping or tampering with the coin, and to baffle the skill of the counterfeiter. The coins of ancient nations were issued with rough, unstamped edges, and the first coin marked with a legend on the edge was a silver coin of Charles IX. of France, issued in the year 1573. The English coinage was first grained or marked on the edge in 1658 or 1662, when the use of the mill and screw was finally established in the mint. All the larger coins now issued from the English, and, indeed, from most other mints, bear a milled or serrated edge, produced by ridges on the internal surface of the collar which holds the coin when being struck between the two dies. These collars are difficult to make, and useless when made except in the coining-press, and the counterfeiter cannot imitate the milling by hand work, it being almost impossible to use a file with sufficient regularity.

The French five-franc pieces bear a legend on the edge in raised letters, the words being "Dieu protége la France." Such raised letters are quite beyond the art of the counterfeiter. The English crown has a legend, "Decus et Tutamen," and the year of the reign in incised letters, which could obviously be imitated by the use of punches. The new German gold coins are issued with smooth edges, the ten-mark piece having only a few slight incised marks, and the twenty-mark piece bearing the legend, "Gott mit uns," in faint letters; this is surely a far less satisfactory protection than the milled edge adopted in most other mints. It may be worthy of inquiry, whether the milled edge might not be combined with a legend or other design in relief, so as to render imitation still more difficult. One or two centuries ago, silver coins used to have a kind of ornamental beading on the edge. Elaborate patterns, produced by machinery with perfect regularity, and altogether incapable of imitation by hand, might now be substituted.

Coins as Works of Art.

I have in the previous section considered the best form of a coin as regards the prevention of counterfeiting. The falsification of coins, the loss which they undergo by abrasion, and the best means of avoiding these evils will be treated in Chapter XIII. Of the use of coins as artistic medals it would not be appropriate to speak at any length. I must however remark that many of the coins still issued from the English mint are monuments of bad taste. It is difficult to imagine poorer designs than those upon the shilling and sixpence, descending from a time when art in many branches was at its apogee in England. As our architecture and art manufactures of many kinds are regenerated by the efforts of private persons, is it too much to hope that a government department will follow? The florin is indeed an immense advance upon the shilling, being in some respects a reversion to the style of old English money. A very beautiful pattern crown piece was produced in 1847, in a somewhat similar style, but never issued. Mr. Lowe, when Master of the Mint, gave us back the old George and Dragon sovereign, which is much superior to the shield and wreaths. I think, however, that the time has come for a general improvement in our coins.

Historical Coins.

Some states have utilized their coins as monuments of important events, such as conquests, jubilees, the accession of monarchs, etc. The German states, especially Prussia, have struck a long series of beautiful coins down to the Krönung's Thaler of 1861, and the Sieges Thaler of 1871. Some of these coins are at once treasured up in cabinets in the manner of medals. If it is possible to conceive literature destroyed, and modern cities and their monuments in ruins and decay, such medallic coins would become the most durable memorials, and the history of the kings of Prussia would be traced out by future numismatists as that of the great dynasties of Bactria has lately been recovered.

In 1842 M. Anténor Joly brought before the French legislative chambers a scheme for a system of historical money, and he renewed his proposal in 1852. M. Ernest Dumas has also suggested the issue of twenty-centime bronze pieces, which should serve either as money or as historical medals. Such schemes have not been carried out in France, and in England no coins of the sort have been struck. Except the mere expense of a new set of dies, I see no objection to the issue of historical money.

The Royal Attribute of Coining.

Every civilized community requires a supply of well-executed coins, and there arises the question, How shall this money be provided? The coins of each denomination must contain exactly equal weights of fine metal, and must bear an impress proving that they do so. Can we trust to the ordinary competition of manufacturers and traders to keep up a sufficient supply of such coins, just as they supply buttons or pins and needles? Or must we establish a government department, under strict legislative control, to secure good coinage?

As almost every opinion finds some advocate, there are not wanting a few who believe that coinage should be left to the free action of competition. Mr. Herbert Spencer especially, in his "Social Statics," advanced the doctrine that, as we trust the grocer to furnish us with pounds of tea, and the baker to send us loaves of bread, so we might trust Heaton and Sons, or some of the other enterprising firms of Birmingham, to supply us with sovereigns and shillings at their own risk and profit. He held that just as people go by preference to the grocer who sells good tea, and to the baker whose loaves are sound and of full weight, so the honest and successful coiner would gain possession of the market, and his money would drive out inferior productions.

Though I must always deeply respect the opinions of so profound a thinker as Mr. Spencer, I hold that in this instance he has pushed a general principle into an exceptional case, where it quite fails. He has overlooked the important law of Gresham (to be explained in the next chapter), that better money cannot drive out worse. In matters of currency self-interest acts in the opposite direction to what it does in other affairs, as will be explained, and if coining were left free, those who sold light coins at reduced prices would drive the best trade.

This conclusion is amply confirmed by experience; for at many times and places coins have been issued by private manufacturers, and always with the result of debasing the currency. For a long time the copper currency of England consisted mainly of tradesmen's tokens, which were issued very light in weight and excessive in number. In Mr. Smiles' "Lives of Boulton and Watt" (p. 391), there is printed an interesting letter, in which Boulton complains that in his journeys he received on an average at the toll-gates two counterfeit pennies for one true one. The lower class of manufacturers, he says, purchased copper coin to the nominal value of thirty-six shillings for twenty shillings in silver, and distributed it to their work-people in wages, so as to make a considerable profit. The multitude of these depreciated pieces in circulation was so great, that the magistrates and inhabitants of Stockport held a public meeting, and resolved to take no halfpence in future but those of the Anglesey Company, which were of full weight. This shows, if proof were needed, that the separate action of self-interest was inoperative in keeping bad coin out of circulation, and it is not to be supposed that the public meeting could have had any sufficient effect. In China the current small money called *cash* or *le*, is commonly manufactured by private coiners, and the consequence is that the size, quality, and value of the coins have fallen very much.

In my opinion there is nothing less fit to be left to the action of competition than money. In constitutional law the right of coining has always been held to be one of the peculiar prerogatives of the Crown, and it is a maxim of the civil law, that *monetandi jus principum ossibus inhæret*. To the executive government and its scientific advisers, who have minutely inquired into the intricacies of the subject of currency and coinage, the matter had better be left. It should as far as possible be removed from the sphere of party struggles or public opinion, and confided to the decision of experts. No doubt, in times past, kings have been the most notorious false coiners and depreciators of the currency, but there is no danger of the like being done in modern times. The danger lies quite in the opposite direction, that popular governments will not venture upon the most obvious and necessary improvement of the monetary system without obtaining a concurrence of popular opinion in its favour, while the people, influenced by habit, and with little knowledge of the subject, will never be able to agree upon the best scheme.

CHAPTER VIII.

THE PRINCIPLES OF CIRCULATION.

BEFORE proceeding to consider the actual monetary systems adopted by modern or ancient nations, it is desirable to dwell for a short time upon the different meanings which may be attributed to the word *money*, and upon the natural principles which govern the use and circulation of coins. We must, in the first place, distinguish three things which, in the practical working of a currency system, are often separate, namely, the actual coins employed, the numbers by which they are expressed, and the relation of those numbers to the assumed unit of value. We must further distinguish coins according as their values depend upon the metal they contain, the metal for which they can be exchanged, or the other coins for which they are the legal equivalent.

The Standard Unit of Value.

It is essential, in the first place, to decide clearly what we mean by a *standard unit of value*. This must consist of a fixed quantity of some concrete substance, defined by reference to the units of weight or space. Value may seem to some people to be a purely mental phenomenon, and a pound would then have to be defined, as Lord Castlereagh asserted, by a *sense of value*. But we might as well define a yard by a sense of length, or a grain by a sense of weight. Just as every quantity in physical science is defined by reference to some concrete standard specimen, so, if we are to measure and express value at all, we must fix upon definite quantities of one or more definite and unchangeable commodities for the purpose.

The expression, *standard unit of value*, will indeed be almost inevitably misunderstood as implying the existence of something of fixed value. As we have seen, however (p. 11), value merely expresses the essentially variable ratio in which two commodities exchange, so that there is no reason to suppose that any substance does for two days together retain the same value. All that a standard of value means is, that some uniform unchangeable substance is chosen, in terms of which all ratios of exchange may be expressed and calculated, without any regard whatever to the feelings or mental phenomena which the commodities produce in men. For reasons already stated, one or other of the metals, gold, silver, or copper, has usually been considered most suitable for constituting the standard substance.

The absolute weight or magnitude of the unit of money is a matter of little or no importance, provided that all people agree upon the same unit, and that it be permanently and exactly defined, and afterwards adhered to. Before the English yard was fixed, it would not have mattered whether it was a few inches longer or shorter; it does not matter, indeed, whether the inch, the foot, the furlong, or the mile is the unit, provided that one of them is definitely fixed, and the others referred to it by known ratios. So, it is really indifferent whether we regard the pound troy of standard gold, or the ounce, or the fixed number of grains in the sovereign, as our standard. It is only requisite that every contract expressed in money shall enable us to ascertain exactly how much standard gold is due from one person to another.

M. Chevalier and some other continental economists have argued elaborately in favour of a universal standard unit of value, coinciding with the metric system of weights. They wish the unit of value to be ten grams of gold exactly, and seem to think that there is some magical efficacy in the correspondence of money and weights. This correspondence might perhaps be a slight convenience to those bullion dealers who have to calculate the metallic value of coins before melting or exporting them, or to those mint officials who have to adjust and test the weights of coins; to all other persons it would be a matter of complete indifference. Those who use coins in ordinary business need never inquire how much metal they contain. Probably not one person in ten thousand in this kingdom knows, or need know, that a sovereign should contain 123·27447 grains of standard gold. Besides, if we agree to accept a precise metrical quantity of one metal as our standard, the weights of the coins composed of other metals will be complicated fractional amounts, to be determined with reference to the accidental market values of the metals.

All we can say, then, is that the standard unit of value is some entirely arbitrary weight of the standard metal, the exact amount of which, being a matter of indifference on general grounds, should be fixed as seems most convenient in reference to the habits of nations or other accidental circumstances.

Coin, Money of Account, and Unit of Value.

It is desirable to distinguish clearly between three things which, although definitely related to each other, need not be identical. The unit of value, or standard weight of the selected metal, is not necessarily made into a coin. It may be a quantity too great or too small for coining. All that is requisite is that the current coins shall be multiples or submultiples of the unit, or easily expressible in terms of the unit. Nor is it even requisite that the numbers in which we express value should be numbers of coins, or numbers of units of value. The *money of account,* as it is called, may differ both from the current money and the standard money. This is well illustrated in the Anglo-Saxon system of currency. The unit of value was the Saxon pound of standard silver, which was far too large to be coined. The only coins issued in any considerable quantity by the Anglo-Saxon kings, were silver pennies and a few halfpennies; yet the usual money of account was the shilling, which, after varying from four to five pence, was fixed by William I. at twelve pence, as it has ever since continued. No coin called a shilling was issued before the reign of Henry VII. Though the shilling has survived, other moneys of account have been forgotten, as, for instance, the *mancus*, which was equal to thirty pennies, or six shillings of five pence each. The *mark*, the *ora*, and the *thrimsa* were other moneys of account used by the Anglo-Saxons.

In our present English system the three moneys happen to coincide, which is doubtless a matter of some convenience. The sovereign is at once the principal coin, the unit of value, and the money of account in all the larger transactions, although in the expression of smaller sums the shilling is yet preferred. In France at the present time the money of account and the unit of value is the franc in gold; but as this weighs only 0·3226 gram, or about five grains, it is coined only in five, ten, and twenty-franc gold pieces, with subsidiary silver coins. In Russia, before the time of Peter the Great, the rouble was an imaginary money of account, consisting of one hundred copper copecks.

When Montesquieu affirmed that the negroes on the West Coast of Africa had a purely ideal sign of value called a *macute*, he misunderstood the nature of money of account. The macute served with the negroes as the name for a definite, though probably a variable, number of cowry shells, the number being at one time 2000. The macute has also been coined in silver pieces of eight, six, and four macutes, struck by the Portuguese for use in their colonies, the macute being worth about $2\frac{3}{4}d$.

When the currency of a country undergoes a change, the units of coinage, account and value are likely to become separated. Sometimes a new system of accounts is applied to an old coinage, as in Norway at the present time. The Stockholm government is endeavouring to introduce the Swedish decimal system of currency, and some merchants are said already to keep their accounts in kroner and öre, although the money in circulation consists almost wholly of the old skillings and the paper specie-dalers. On the other hand, the coinage is sometimes changed, and yet the old method of accounts retained, especially as regards foreign transactions. Thus the rates of foreign exchange between the United States and England were, until last year, quoted in terms of a dollar valued at $4s.\ 6d.$, in accordance with a law of 1789. This rate seems to have been the traditional par of exchange of the Mexican dollar, and it was still retained even when the American dollar had been coined so as to be worth only $49\cdot 316$ English pence.

There are two causes which have often led to a difference between coinage and money of account. The coins may, by legitimate abrasion, or by fraudulent clipping and sweating, become much reduced below their proper weights, yet an *agio*, or allowance, being made for the average depreciation, the old standard of value and money of account may be retained, as was the case in Amsterdam, Hamburg, and other towns. When a depreciated currency is issued in a country, the money of account may either change with it or remain as before; and it is an exceedingly difficult, if not insoluble problem, to decide whether, in particular periods of English history, prices were expressed in the new depreciated or the old good money. Professor J. E. T. Rogers has pointed out, in his admirable "History of Agriculture and Prices in England," printed by the Clarendon Press (vol. i. p. 175), that, in the fourteenth century, the coinage, though apparently passed by tale, was often weighed. In the ancient college accounts which he has investigated, he finds charges entered both for the cost of scales to make the weighings, and for the deficiency of weight of the coins.

In many countries, even at the present day, the circulating medium consists not of any one simple and well-connected series of coins, but of a miscellaneous collection of coins of various sizes and values, imported from foreign states. In such cases the money of account must necessarily differ from the mass of the coins, of which the value is usually estimated by a tariff expressed in terms of the money of account. In the German states, a few years ago, French and English gold was freely accepted in this manner. In Canada there was in former years an intricate confusion of monetary systems. Many species of foreign coins, chiefly varieties of the dollar, were in circulation. There were also two separate moneys of account, namely, the Halifax Currency Pound divided into twenty shillings of twenty pence each, and defined by the fact that sixty such pence were equal to one dollar; and, secondly, the Halifax Sterling Currency. The latter is still employed to express the foreign exchanges. The present monetary unit of Canada is the dollar, and the currency consists of bank-notes, with silver coins of 50, 25, 20, 10, and 5 cents; but English sovereigns and half sovereigns are also in circulation.

Standard and Token Money.

We must distinguish between coins according as they serve for *standard money* or for *token money*. A standard coin is one of which the value in exchange depends solely upon the value of the material contained in it. The stamp serves as a mere indication and guarantee of the quantity of fine metal. We may treat such coins as bullion, and melt them up or export them to countries where they are not legally current; yet the value of the metal being independent of legislation will everywhere be recognised.

Token coins, on the contrary, are defined in value by the fact that they can, by force of law or custom, be exchanged in a certain fixed ratio for standard coins. The metal contained in a token coin has of course a certain value; but it may be less than the legal value in almost any degree. In our English silver coinage the difference is from 9 to 12 per cent., according to the market price of silver; in our bronze coinage the difference is 75 per cent. The metal contained in the French bronze coins is in like manner equal in value to little more than one quarter of the current value. In many cases the difference has been far greater, as for instance in some of the old kreutzer pieces lately current in the German states. Woods's halfpence, which at one time created so much discontent in Ireland, or the small money previously issued by James II. in Ireland, are extreme instances of depreciated token money.

Metallic and Nominal Values of Coins.

It has been usual to call the value of the metal contained in a coin the *intrinsic value* of the coin; but this use of the word *intrinsic* is likely to give rise to fallacious notions concerning the nature of value, which is never an intrinsic property, or existence, but merely a circumstance, or external relation (see p. 9). To avoid any chance of ambiguity, I shall substitute the expression, *metallic value*, and I shall distinguish this from the *nominal, customary,* or *legal value*, at which a coin actually does, or is by law required, to exchange for other coins.

There are two ways in which the metallic value of a coin may be reduced below its nominal value, namely, by reducing either the weight or the fineness of the metal. English silver coin is still maintained at the "ancient right standard" of 11 oz. 2 dwts. in the troy pound, which has existed from time immemorial. By the Act of 1816 the silver coins which had previously been, in theory at least, standard money, were reduced in weight by 6 per cent., and thus rendered token money, which they still continue to be. In France and other countries belonging to the Monetary Convention, the smaller silver coins of two francs, one franc, and fifty centimes, have been converted into tokens by reducing the fineness of the silver from 900 to 835 parts in 1000. It does not seem to be a matter of any importance which mode is adopted; but the English mode, so long as it does not render the coins inconveniently small, is perhaps slightly the better, because some persons can satisfy themselves as to the weight of a coin, but none are able to test its fineness, unless they are professional assayers.

It need hard'y be stated that coins which circulate by law in one country as tokens may be accepted in other countries at their metallic value.

Legal Tender.

Money must further be distinguished, according as it is or is not *legal tender*, or has or has not what the French call *cours forcé*. By legal tender is denoted such money as a creditor is obliged to receive in requital of a debt expressed in terms of money of the realm. One great object of legislation is to prevent uncertainty in the interpretation of contracts, and accordingly the Coinage Act defines precisely what will constitute a legal offer of payment on the part of a debtor, as regards a money debt. If a debtor tender to his creditor the amount of a debt due in legal tender money, and it be refused, the creditor may indeed apply for it, or sue for it afterwards, but the costs of the action will be thrown upon him.

But there seems to be no legal necessity that exchanges or contracts shall be made in money of the realm. At common law, contracts for the direct barter of two commodities, or for purchase and sale in terms of any kind of money, will be valid, provided it is clear what the terms of the contract mean. Accordingly, the sixth section of the Coinage Act (33 Vict. c. 10), while enacting that every contract, sale, payment, bill, note, transaction, or matter relating to money, shall be made or done according to the coins which are current and legal tender in pursuance of this Act, yet adds, " unless the same be made, executed, entered into, done or had, according to the currency of some British possession or some foreign state."

If I understand the matter aright, then, every person is at liberty to buy, sell, or exchange in terms of any money or commodity whatsoever which he prefers; and the fact that certain coins, up to certain limits, are legal tender, only means that the state provides a definite medium of exchange and defines precisely what that is. The Act requires that *English money* shall be the money issued by the mint, in accordance with the terms of the Act. Of course it remains quite open to a creditor to receive payment in coins which are not legal tender, if he like to do so, and I presume there would be nothing to prevent him entering into a contract to that effect. If a man contracted to sell goods to the extent of £100, and to receive payment in bronze pence and halfpence, it would no doubt be a valid contract, although no single quantity of pence exceeding twelve pence is a legal tender.

The exact meaning of the term, legal tender, may of course vary from country to country, and the above remarks apply only to countries under the English law.

The Force of Habit in the Circulation of Money.

No one can possibly understand many social phenomena unless he constantly bears in mind the force of habit and social convention. This is strikingly true in our subject of money. Over and over again in the course of history, powerful rulers have endeavoured to put new coins into circulation or to withdraw old ones; but the instincts of self-interest or habit in the people have been too strong for laws and penalties. Though in particular instances it may be difficult to explain occurrences which happen in the circulation of coins, yet a close analysis of the character of those who handle money, and their motives for holding or paying it away, will throw much light upon the subject.

We must notice, in the first place, that the great mass of the population who hold coins have no theories, or general information whatever, upon the subject of money. They are guided entirely by popular report and tradition. The sole question with them on receiving a coin is whether similar coins have been readily accepted by other people. Thus in the remote parts of Norway at the present time, the old paper daler notes are preferred to the beautiful new twenty-kroner gold pieces. By far the greater number of the people possess no means of learning the metallic, or even the legal, value of an unfamiliar coin. Few people have scales and weights suitable for weighing a coin, and no one but an assayer or analytical chemist can decide upon its fineness. Many a traveller who has carried good new coin into a country where it happened to be strange, has had to suffer a loss in paying it away. When our bronze pence were quite a novelty, I happened to take some with me into a remote part of North Wales, and they were rejected.

People in general accept coin simply on the ground of its familiar appearance. So entirely is this the case among very ignorant populations, that it has often been found desirable to maintain unchanged the impress on successive issues of coins. In many cases coins have been struck for this purpose with the date of a long past year, or even the effigy of a dead sovereign. The Maria Theresa dollar is still coined by the Austrian mint, with exactly the same design and date as when first issued in 1780, because it is the favourite coin in some of the states of North Africa, and various parts of the Levant. The British Government, when undertaking the Abyssinian expedition, procured a large stock of these coins for paying the natives. In the same way Mexican dollars are usually worth rather more than silver bullion, because of their easy currency in the East.

To the supremacy of habit, and the absence of means of estimating the real value of coin, is obviously due the depreciation which currencies have undergone. False coiners and kings alike find that, if they can only make new coins look and feel exactly like old coins, the people will accept depreciated money without question.

The annals of coinage, in this and all other countries, are little more than a monotonous repetition of depreciated issues both public and private, varied by occasional meritorious, but often unsuccessful, efforts to restore the standard of the currency. A curious instance of successive attempts to beguile a people are found in certain Roman denarii of the Consular times. False coiners having issued plated denarii among the subject Germans, the people appeared to have notched them with files to test their genuineness. The Germans having thus become accustomed to see genuine *notched* coins, the Roman government found it desirable to issue new coins notched in a similar manner. But the forgers were not to be beaten. They issued plated denarii with the notches all complete, apparently displaying good metal within; and notched false coins of this kind exist to the present day in numismatic cabinets.

Gresham's Law.

Though the public generally do not discriminate between coins and coins, provided there is an apparent similarity, a small class of money-changers, bullion-dealers, bankers, or goldsmiths make it their business to be acquainted with such differences, and know how to derive a profit from them. These are the people who frequently *uncoin* money, either by melting it, or by exporting it to countries where it is sooner or later melted. Some coins are sunk in the sea or lost, and some are carried abroad by emigrants and travellers who do not look closely to the metallic value of the money. But by far the greatest part of the standard coinage is removed from circulation by people who know that they shall gain by choosing for this purpose the new heavy coins most recently issued from the mint. Hence arises the practice, extensively carried on in the present day in England, of *picking and culling*, or, as another technical expression is, *garbling* the coinage, devoting the good new coins to the melting-pot, and passing the old worn coins into circulation again on every suitable opportunity.

From these considerations we readily learn the truth and importance of a general law or principle concerning the circulation of money, which Mr. Macleod has very appropriately named the Law or Theorem of Gresham, after Sir Thomas Gresham, who clearly perceived its truth three centuries ago. This law, briefly expressed, is that *bad money drives out good money*, but that *good money cannot drive out bad money*. At first sight there may seem to be something paradoxical in the fact, that when beautiful new coins of full weight are issued from the mint, the people still continue to circulate, in preference, the old depreciated ones. Many well-intentioned efforts to reform a currency have thus been frustrated, to the great cost of states, and the perplexity of statesmen who had not studied the principles of monetary science.

In all other matters everybody is led by self-interest to choose the better and reject the worse; but in the case of money, it would seem as if they paradoxically retain the worse and get rid of the better. The explanation is very simple. The people, as a general rule, do not reject the better, but pass from hand to hand indifferently the heavy and the light coins, because their only use for the coin is as a medium of exchange. It is those who are going to melt, export, hoard, or dissolve the coins of the realm, or convert them into jewellery and gold leaf, who carefully select for their purposes the new heavy coins.

Gresham's law alone furnishes a sufficient refutation of Mr. Herbert Spencer's doctrine, already noticed (p. 64) that money ought to be provided by private manufacturers. People who want furniture, or books, or clothes, may be trusted to select the best which they can afford, because they are going to keep and use these articles; but with money it is just the opposite. Money is made to go. They want coin, not to keep it in their own pockets, but to pass it off into their neighbours' pockets; and the worse the money which they can get their neighbours to accept, the greater the profit to themselves. Thus there is a natural tendency to the depreciation of the metallic currency, which can only be prevented by the constant supervision of the state.

From Gresham's law we may infer the necessity of two precautions in the regulation of the currency. In the first place, the standard coins, as issued from the mint, should be as nearly as possible of the standard weight, otherwise the difference will form a profit for the bullion-broker and exporter. In the second place, adequate measures must be taken for withdrawing from circulation all coins which are worn below the least legal weight, otherwise they will continue to circulate as token coins for an indefinite length of time. All commerce consists in the exchange of commodities of equal value, and the principal money should consist of pieces of metal so nearly equal in metallic contents, that all persons, including bullion dealers, bankers, and other professed dealers in money, will indifferently substitute one coin for another. But it is obvious that these remarks do not apply to coins intended to serve as tokens, since the current value of tokens exceeds their metallic value, and every one who uses them otherwise than in ordinary circulation will lose the difference. Hence the weight of a token coin is comparatively a matter of indifference, so long as people will receive them, and the deficiency of weight is not too great a temptation to the false coiner.

In England at the present day the force of habit, and the absence of means of discrimination, lead to the depreciation of our gold standard coinage by abrasion. Only while a sovereign exceeds 122·5 grains in weight is it legally a sovereign; but people go on paying and receiving indifferently, in ordinary trade, sovereigns of which the metallic values differ 2d. or 4d., and sometimes even 6d. or 8d. Every standard coin thus tends to degenerate into a token coin, and such a coin can only be withdrawn from circulation by the state.

Extension of Gresham's Law.

Gresham's remarks concerning the inability of good money to drive out bad money, only referred to moneys of one kind of metal, but the same principle applies to the relations of all kinds of money, in the same circulation. Gold compared with silver, or silver with copper, or paper compared with gold, are subject to the same law that the relatively cheaper medium of exchange will be retained in circulation and the relatively dearer will disappear. The most extreme instance which has ever occurred was in the case of the Japanese currency. At the time of the treaty of 1858, between Great Britain, the United States, and Japan, which partially opened up the last country to European traders, a very curious system of currency existed in Japan. The most valuable Japanese coin was the kobang, consisting of a thin oval disc of gold about 2 inches long, and $1\frac{1}{4}$ inch wide, weighing 200 grains, and ornamented in a very primitive manner. It was passing current in the towns of Japan for four silver itzebus, but was worth in English money about 18s. 5d., whereas the silver itzebu was equal only to about 1s. 4d. Thus the Japanese were estimating their gold money at only about one-third of its value, as estimated according to the relative values of the metals in other parts of the world. The earliest European traders enjoyed a rare opportunity for making profit. By buying up the kobangs at the native rating they trebled their money, until the natives, perceiving what was being done, withdrew from circulation the remainder of the gold. A complete reform of the Japanese currency is now being carried out, the English mint at Hong Kong having been purchased by the Japanese government.

What happened in an extreme degree in Japan has often happened in England and other European countries, in a less degree. If the ratio of gold and silver in the coinage, as legally current, differs only one or two per cent. from the commercial ratio, it may become profitable to export the one metal rather than the other, and in this way, as we shall see, the main part of the currency of France was changed from silver into gold between 1849 and 1869. In fact the character of the coinage of most nations has been determined in a similar manner, and England and the United States were thus led to adopt a principal gold currency. There is every reason to believe that in ancient Rome, both in the time of the Republic and of the Empire, great difficulties were encountered in regulating the currency of silver alongside of copper, and the perplexity became worse when gold coin was introduced.

CHAPTER IX.

SYSTEMS OF METALLIC MONEY.

WE are now in a position to analyse the construction of the various systems of metallic money which have existed, or do exist, or which might be conceived to exist. The systems actually brought into operation are more numerous than is commonly supposed, and I have nowhere met with an adequate classification of them. M. Courcelle-Seneuil, indeed, has satisfactorily described some of the principal systems, and MM. Chevalier, Garnier, and other writers, both continental and English, have given other brief classifications. But we must now take a comprehensive view of the possible ways in which two, three, or more metals may be employed in the construction of a more or less useful monetary system.

There seem to be five distinct modes in which a government may deal with metallic money.

1. It may confine itself to providing a system of weights and measures, and may then allow the precious metals to be passed about from hand to hand, like other commodities, in terms of the national weights and measures, and in the form which individuals find to be most

convenient. This we may call the system of *currency by weight*.

2. To save the trouble of frequent weighing, and the uncertainty of fineness of the metal, it may coin one or more metals into pieces of certain specified weights and fineness, and may afterwards allow the public to make their contracts and sales in one or other kind of coin, as they deem expedient. This may be described as the system of *unrestricted currency by tale*.

3. To prevent misunderstandings, the government, while emitting various coins in various metals, may ordain that all contracts expressed in money of the realm shall, in the absence of express provision to the contrary, be taken to mean money of one kind of metal, specially named, while other coin shall be left to circulate at varying market rates compared with this principal kind of coinage. This is *the single legal tender system*.

4. The government may emit coins of two or more kinds of metal, and enact that money contracts may be discharged in one or other kind, at certain rates fixed by law. This is the *multiple legal tender system*.

5. While maintaining one kind of coin as the principal legal tender, in which all large money contracts must be fulfilled, coins of other kinds of metal may be ordered to be received in limited quantities, as equivalent to the principal coin. For this the name *composite legal tender system* may be proposed.

Currency by Weight.

The order in which I have enumerated the principal systems of metallic money, is not only the logical order, but it is the historical order in which the systems have, for the most part, been introduced. There is overwhelming evidence to prove that simple currency by weight is the primitive system. Before the invention of the balance, lumps and grains were no doubt exchanged according to a rude estimation of their bulk or weight; but afterwards the balance became a necessary instrument in all important transactions. In the Old Testament we find several statements clearly implying that the ancient Hebrews used to pass money by weight. In Genesis (xxiii. 16) Abraham is represented as weighing out to Ephron "four hundred shekels of silver, current money with the merchant," but the silver in question is believed to have consisted of rough lumps or rings not to be considered coin. In the Book of Job (xxviii. 15) we are told that "wisdom cannot be gotten for gold, neither shall silver be weighed for the price thereof."

Aristotle, in his Politics (Book I., chap. ix), gives an interesting account of his view of the origin of money, and distinctly tells us that the metals were first passed simply by weight or size, and Pliny makes a similar assertion. That it was so, we may infer from the remarkable fact that, even when no use was made of it, the custom of bringing a pair of scales survived as a legal formality in the sale of slaves at Rome.

There can be little doubt that every system of coinage was originally identical with a system of weights, the unit of value being the unit of weight of some selected metal. The English pound sterling was certainly the Saxon pound of standard silver, which was too large to be made into a single coin, but was divided into two hundred and forty silver pennies, each equal to a *pennyweight*. In the English and Scotch *pounds*, and the French *livre*, we have the vestiges of a uniform international system of money and weights, the establishment of which is attributed to Charlemagne, but which unfortunately became differentiated and destroyed by the various depreciations of the coinage in one country or another. Most of the other principal units of value were originally units of weight, such as the shekel, the talent, the as, the stater, the libra, the mark, the franc, the lira.

In the Old Testament the notion of money is expressed three times by the Hebrew word kesitah, which is translated in certain old versions into words meaning *lamb*. This might seem to be an additional proof of the former use of cattle as a medium of exchange; but I am informed by my learned friend, Professor Theodores, that this translation probably arises from an accidental blunder, and that the original meaning of the word kesitah, was that of "a certain weight," or "an exact quantity." The corresponding word in the Arabic, kist, is said to denote a pair of scales.

Currency by weight still exists among considerable portions of the human race. In the Burman empire, for instance, three kinds of metal are current, namely, lead, silver, and gold, and all payments are made by the balance, the unit of weight for silver being the tical. In the Chinese empire and Cochin China, there is indeed a legal tender currency of *cash* or *sapeks* but gold and silver are usually dealt in by weight, the unit being the tael. A very interesting account of Chinese money, by M. le Comte Rochechouart, will be found in the *Journal des Economistes* for 1869 (vol. xv. p. 103). According to this writer, both gold and silver are treated simply as merchandise, and there is not even a recognized stamp, or government guarantee of the fineness of the metal. The traveller must carry these metals with him, as a sufficient quantity of strings of *cash* would require a waggon for their conveyance. Yet in exchanging silver or gold he is sure to suffer great losses, both from the falsity of balances and weights, and the uncertain fineness of the metal. In buying a tael of gold the traveller may have to give eighteen taels of silver; but in selling it he will often not obtain more than fourteen taels.

Whatever be the inconveniences of the method, currency by weight is yet the natural and necessary system to which people revert whenever the abrasion of coins, the intermixture of currencies, the fall of a state, or other causes destroy the public confidence in a more highly organized system. Though the silver penny among the Anglo-Saxons was supposed to correspond with a *pennyweight*, there was a practice of giving *compensatio ad pensum,* which really amounted to taking the coins by weight, to allow for abrasion and inaccurate or false coinage. The *as* was at first equal in weight to a Roman pound, but it was rapidly lessened, so that at the epoch of the First Punic War, it did not exceed two ounces, and by the time of the Second Punic War it had sunk to one ounce. The Roman people had naturally reverted to weighing the metal, and the *aes grave* was money reckoned by weight instead of by *tale*.

In the present day currency by weight is far more extensively practised then might be supposed, because, in many parts of the world, the currency consists of a miscellaneous assortment of old gold, silver, and even copper coins, which have been brought thither from other countries, and have been variously worn, clipped, or depreciated. In such countries the only means of avoiding loss and fraud is to weigh each coin, and the impress passes for little more than an indication of the fineness of the metals. In all large international transactions, again, currency by weight is the sole method. The regulations of a state concerning its legal tender have no validity beyond its own frontiers; and as all coins are subject to more or less wear and uncertainty of weight, they are received only for the actual weight of metal they are estimated to contain. The coin of well-conducted foreign mints is bought and sold by weight without melting; but the coin of minor states, which have occasionally depreciated their money, is melted up and treated simply as bullion.

Unrestricted Currency by Tale.

The simplest way for a state to manage its money might seem to be to revert to the primitive notion of a coin, and issue pieces of gold, silver, and copper, certified to be equal to units of weight, leaving all persons free to make contracts or sales in terms of any of these metals. These pieces of certified metal would then be so many commodities thrown into the markets and allowed to take their natural relative values.

Such appears to have been the system intended to be established by the French Revolutionary Government in terms of the abortive law of Thermidor, an III. Discs of ten grams each were to be struck in gold, silver, and copper, and then put in circulation, without any attempt to regulate their currency. If I understand his meaning correctly, M. Garnier has recently brought forward a somewhat similar scheme, proposing to make the gram of gold at nine-tenths the unit of value, and to coin pieces of one, two, five, eight, or ten grams concurrently with standard silver pieces, which are in France already multiples of the gram. M. Chevalier's proposed system of international money, partially at least, involves the same notion; for he considers that the principal currency should consist of decagrams of gold. But, as Mr. Bagehot has well remarked, there is no object whatever, as regards the greater mass of the population, in having coins simply related to the system of weights, because most people never need take any account of the weight at all. They need only know how many copper coins are equal to one silver coin, and how many silver to one gold coin. Now, if we carry out M. Chevalier's scheme consistently and fully, and make all the coins multiples of the gram, we shall oblige all people to be constantly working complex arithmetical sums. No one could give exactly correct change without calculating how many silver ten-gram pieces are, at the market price of silver, equal to one gold ten-gram piece. The necessity for calculation occasions needless loss of time and trouble, and a factitious gain is sure to accrue to the expert and unscrupulous at the expense of the poor and ignorant.

Owing to these obvious objections no government has ever, I believe, carried into practice a system of money of the kind described. Nevertheless, currencies approximating to it in nature have come to exist in many parts of the world by the intermixture of coinages of different states. There are many half-civilized nations which have no national coinage, but employ the coins which happen to reach them in the course of trade. On the West Coast of Africa the Spanish dollar is the best known coin, but Danish, French or Dutch coins also circulate. In several of the South American states the currency is in a state of complete confusion, consisting of a mixture of American eagles, gold doubloons, silver dollars, English sovereigns, piastres, etc., together sometimes with several different issues of coinage of the South American states variously depreciated. Even in British possessions we find the same state of things. In the British West Indian Islands, American, Mexican,

Spanish, and other dollars, circulate concurrently with English money; but it should be added that in most cases the Spanish dollar is treated as the standard of value, and other coins are quoted in terms of it.

In Eastern countries there is a similar intermixture of coinage. In Singapore the Indian rupee mingles with Spanish and Mexican dollars. Persia has a rude coinage of its own, so uncertain in weight that it has to be dealt in by the balance, but Russian, Turkish, and Austrian gold coins circulate by tale. Some of the best-regulated nations have allowed, or even promoted, the currency of various foreign coins. In Germany, French and English gold coins used to be accepted, according to a well-recognised tariff. The circulation of English, French, Spanish, Mexican, and other gold coins in the United States was legalized by an Act of June 28th, 1834, repealed by an Act of February 21st, 1857, which however allows certain foreign coins to be received at government offices.

In England we have for many generations enjoyed a very pure currency, so that we are unconscious of the inconveniences arising from a confusion of coins of different values. But in the early part of this century Spanish dollars were put into circulation for a time in England.

In former centuries the mixture of coinages was far more common than at present. No country had a currency free from strange coins. It is impossible to open an old book on commerce without finding long tables of coins which the merchant might expect to meet with; and the business of money-changing was a lucrative and common one.

It will be understood, that only so long as coins are known by the fresh sharp appearance of the impression to be of full weight, and are accepted according to tariff, does the system of currency by tale or number exist. The silver dollar, being a large coin, is subject to comparatively little abrasion, so that people learn to receive dollars of various species at certain well-established rates. Thus the dollar has practically been for several centuries the international money of the tropical countries. But so soon as coins bear evidence of wear or ill-treatment, they must be circulated by weight, and we revert to a more primitive system.

M. Feer-Herzog has described, as the system of *parallel standards*, that in which a state issues coins in two or more metals, and then allows them to circulate by tale at ratios varying according to the market values of the metals. He cites, as recent examples, the rixdaler in silver, employed as the internal money of Sweden in combination with the ducat in gold, serving as international money. The government of India, again, has on several occasions tried to introduce a parallel standard of gold alongside of the single silver legal tender now existing there. Gold mohurs have long been more or less in circulation in India, and are supposed to form at present about one-tenth part of the coinage. They are of exactly the same weight and fineness as the silver rupee, and are usually valued at from 15 to $15\frac{2}{3}$ rupees. It seems probable, however, that what M. Feer-Herzog calls the system of parallel standards will coincide according to circumstances, either with that which I have described as the system of unrestricted currency by tale, or that of a single legal tender, with an additional commercial money of varying value. The Indian currency must certainly be classed under the latter head. There cannot in fact be two different parallel standards used both at the same time; and though it is not uncommon for a state to coin moneys in two metals, and leave its subjects to pay in one or other at will, yet one of the two is generally recognized as the standard of value.

Single Legal Tender System.

The system of currency naturally adopted by the first coiners of money was that of a single legal tender. Coins of one kind of metal, or even a single series of coins of uniform weight, were at first thought sufficient. Iron in small bars was the single legal tender in Lacedæmon, and possibly in some other early states. *Aes* was undoubtedly the legal tender among the Romans for a length of time. In China the sole measure of value and legal tender to the present day consists of brass *cash* or *sapeks*, strung together in lots of a thousand each. In England silver was the only metal coined from the time of Egbert to that of Edward III., with the doubtful exception of a very few small pieces of gold. Silver was the sole legal tender and measure of value, and few coins except silver pennies were issued. In Russia and Sweden, during part of last century, copper was the sole legal tender.

A single metal currency has the great advantages of simplicity and certainty. Every one knows exactly what he is to pay or receive, and when the coins are of one size or of a few sizes, simply related to each other, like the early English coins, no one is subject to loss by errors of calculation. But there is the obvious disadvantage that, according as the metal chosen is cheap or dear, large or small transactions will be troublesome to effect. To pay a few hundred pounds in Swedish copper plates, or Chinese strings of *cash*, a cart would be required for conveyance, and the counting of *cash* is almost impracticable. A silver coinage again does not admit of coins sufficiently small for minor transactions. It is difficult to understand how retail trade was carried on when the silver penny weighed $22\frac{1}{2}$ grains, and the precious metals were far more precious than at present. The penny was, indeed, cut up into halfpence and farthings, *i.e. four-things;* but even the farthing must have been equal in purchasing power to our threepenny or fourpenny piece. The mass of the currency appears to have consisted of silver pennies.

Accordingly it is found that, if a government issue coins only of a single metal, the people will introduce and circulate coins of other metals for their own convenience. In Anglo-Saxon times gold byzants from Byzantium were used in England, and the gold coins of Florence, thence called florins, were much esteemed both here and in other parts of Europe. In later centuries, too, in the absence of a legitimate copper coinage, tradesmen's tokens came into general circulation.

Multiple Legal Tender System.

Out of a single legal tender naturally grew up systems of a double or even a multiple legal tender. The Plantagenet kings of England, for instance, finding that though they coined only silver the people made use of gold, eventually began to issue gold coins, and fixed the rates at which they should be exchanged for silver coins. In the absence of any special regulations to the contrary this constituted a double tender system. As, after a time, the ratio of values of the metals would fail to coincide with that involved in the relative weights of the coins, it became requisite to fix by royal proclamation a new value for one metal in terms of the other. From 1257 to 1664 the gold and silver currency of England was thus regulated, no coins of copper or any inferior metal being then issued. From 1664 to 1717 no proclamations were made upon the subject, and the value of the guinea was allowed to vary in terms of the shilling. At one time it rose nearly to 30s., owing partly to the decreased value of silver, but chiefly to the clipped and worn state of the silver money. During this interval, then, the country had a single silver standard.

In the early part of the last century a great deal of discussion took place upon the unsatisfactory state of the silver currency, and Sir Isaac Newton, the Master of the Mint, was requested to report upon the best measures to be adopted. In 1717 he made a celebrated report, recommending that the government should revert to the practice of fixing the price of the guinea, and he

SYSTEMS OF METALLIC MONEY. 99

suggested 21s. as the best rate. His advice being accepted, the guinea has ever since been valued at 21s. Then there was again a double standard in England, any one being at liberty to pay in either kind of coin. In practice, however, it is almost impossible that the commercial value of the metals should coincide with the legal ratio. At the rate adopted by Sir Isaac Newton, gold was overvalued by rather more than $1\frac{1}{2}$ per cent.; to that extent it was more valuable as currency than as metal. Therefore, in accordance with the Law of Gresham, and the principles laid down in Chapter VIII., the full weight silver coin was withdrawn or exported, and gold became the practical measure of value, which it has ever since continued to be.

In every other part of the world, where attempts have been made to combine two metals as concurrent standards of value, similar results have followed. In Massachusetts, in 1762, gold was made a legal tender, as well as silver, at the rate of $2\frac{1}{2}d.$ per grain; but, being overvalued as much as 5 per cent, the silver coinage rapidly disappeared from circulation. Various laws were passed to remedy this inconvenient state of things, but without success so long as this valuation of gold was maintained.

In these and many other cases which might be quoted, a government had attempted to combine a circulation of gold with that of silver, without being aware of all the principles involved in the experiment. It was hardly, perhaps, till the time of the French Revolution that the double standard system was consciously selected as the best method. Since the celebrated law, known as "La loi du 7 Germinal, an XI.," was adopted by the Revolutionary Government, the system has become identified with the policy of the French economists. The history of the origin of this law was almost unknown, until M. Wolowski described it in a series of valuable articles published in the *Journal des Economistes* for 1869.

As early as 1790 Mirabeau presented to the National Assembly a celebrated memoir on monetary doctrines, in which, amid a curious mixture of true and false views, he decided in favour of silver as the principal money, on the ground of the greater abundance of silver compared with gold. He proposed to make silver the *constitutional money*, that is, the legal tender, and to employ gold and copper as *additional signs* of value. These ideas were only so far carried out that the franc was defined first as ten grams of silver by the decree of the 1st August, 1793, and was afterwards definitively fixed at five grams by the law of the 28th Thermidor, an III. The old gold pieces of twenty-four and forty-eight livres continued to circulate, while the ten-gram gold pieces ordered by the decree to be struck were not really issued.

In the year IX. Gaudin proposed that the ratio of $15\frac{1}{2}$ to 1 should be adopted in fixing the weight of the gold coins relatively to the silver ones. Thus, while the franc was defined as consisting of five grams of silver nine-tenths fine, the twenty-franc gold piece was to contain 6·451 grams of gold of equal fineness. He seems to have thought that this ratio was sufficiently near to that of the markets to allow the coins to circulate side by side for a long time, and in case of a change, he thought that the gold pieces could be melted and reissued at a different weight. After a great amount of discussion, in which Berenger, Lebreton, Daru, and Bosc took the most prominent parts, the proposals of Gaudin were carried out, but not precisely on the ground indicated by him. It appears to have been thought unwise either to demonetize gold altogether, which would have seriously diminished the circulating medium, or to leave the value of the gold coins uncertain, which would give rise to disputes.

The ratio adopted by the legislators of the Revolution happened to overvalue silver in some degree, and hence the currency of France came to consist principally of the heavy five-francs pieces, or écus. Not until the Californian and Australian discoveries caused gold to be the cheaper money in which to make payments, did this heavy silver money gradually disappear. The action of the double standard system will be further considered in Chapter XII.

Composite Legal Tender.

We have seen that with a single metal currency there is inconvenience in making small or large payments, according as the metal chosen is dear or cheap. If two or more series of full-weight coins be issued in different metals, and allowed to vary in relation to each other, the difficulty of calculation intervenes. If they both be made legal tenders at a fixed ratio, the currency will tend to become composed alternately of one or the other metal, and money-changers will make a profit out of the conversion.

There yet remains another possible system, in which coins of one metal are adopted as the standard of value and principal legal tender, and subordinate token coins of other metals are furnished for the purpose of subdivision, being recognized as legal tender only for small amounts. The values of these token coins now depend upon that of the standard coins for which they are legally exchangeable, and care is taken to make their weights such that the metallic value will always be less than the legal value. No profit can ever be made by melting such coins, or removing them from the country, and their ratio of exchange with the principal coins is always a simple ratio fixed by law.

The composite legal tender rises naturally out of the double standard system; for, as we have seen, if, under the latter system, gold be overvalued at the legal rate, all full-weight silver coins will be withdrawn and exported by degrees, so that there will remain practically a token currency of light silver. Lord Liverpool, having in his thorough investigation of the subject of metallic money observed the superior convenience of the composite legal tender to the double legal tender, advocated its adoption in England in the most conclusive manner. His arguments will be found in his admirable "Treatise on the Coins of the Realm in a Letter to the King" (Oxford, 1805), and his recommendations, as carried into effect in 1816, are the foundation of our present monetary system.

SYSTEMS OF METALLIC MONEY.

A composite system of currency has frequently existed in one country or another without being specially designed or recognized. It comes into existence whenever coins of gold and silver are current at rates fixed by law or custom, but the silver coins are reduced by abrasion or clipping below the corresponding weight. From the year 1717, when the guinea was fixed at 21s., until the present system was instituted in 1816, the English currency was based theoretically upon the double standard system. Practically, however, the silver coins were so scarce and worn that they served but as tokens. The tradesmen's copper tokens, too, being always of light weight, and exchangeable by custom for a certain proportion of silver coins, formed the third term in the series. But Lord Liverpool appears to have been the first to apprehend and explain the principles on which such a composite system worked, and there can be no doubt that the system, as he expounded it, is the best adapted for supplying a convenient and economical currency.

Most of the leading nations have now adopted the composite legal tender in a more or less complete form. France, Belgium, Switzerland, and Italy still adhere to the double standard in theory, but have reduced all coins of less value than five francs to the footing of token money, by reducing the fineness of the silver from 900 parts to 835 parts in 1000, or by $7\frac{1}{4}$ per cent., and by limiting the amount for which they are legal tender. The copper money of France had previously been restricted as a legal tender to sums below five francs in any one payment. In the United States, when metallic currency was generally employed, the double standard system existed in theory, but was reduced to a composite standard by the excessive overvaluing of the gold money. Moreover, by a law of 21st February, 1853, the smaller silver coins were reduced in weight and made legal tender only for sums not exceeding five dollars. The silver three-cent pieces, and the several copper, bronze, or nickel coins, issued from the United States' mints, were also token money with various limits as regards egal tender.

The new German monetary system is perfectly organized as a composite legal tender.

CHAPTER X.

THE ENGLISH SYSTEM OF METALLIC CURRENCY.

I now come to describe in more detail the system of metallic currency which has existed in England for more than half a century, and which seems to be the best of all as regards the principles on which coins of three different metals are combined into a composite legal tender. The legal regulations under which the English coinage is issued and circulated, can be ascertained with ease and certainty, thanks to the Act of Parliament (33 Victoria, ch. 10), which Mr. Lowe caused to be passed to simplify and consolidate the statutes on the subject.

English Gold Coin.

The English sovereign is the principal legal tender and the standard of value. It is defined as consisting of 123·27447 grains (7·98805 grams) of English standard gold, composed of eleven parts of fine gold, and one part of alloy, chiefly copper. The sovereign ought, therefore, in theory, to contain 113·00160 grains, or 7·32238 grams, of pure gold. But as it is evidently impossible to make coins of any precise weight, or to maintain them of that weight when in circulation, the weight stated is only that standard weight to which the mint workmen should aim to attain as closely as possible, both in each individual piece, and in the average.

From the weight of the sovereign we deduce the mint price of gold. For if we divide the number of grains in the sovereign into the number of grains—namely, 480—in the troy ounce, we ascertain exactly how many sovereigns and portions of a sovereign the mint ought to return for each ounce delivered in. This we find to be $3·89375$, which is equivalent to £3 17s. $10\frac{1}{2}d$. It comes to exactly the same thing to say in terms of the old mint indentures, that twenty-pounds' weight troy of gold are to be coined into 934 sovereigns, and one half-sovereign. I have heard of people who protested against the government fixing the price at which gold should be bought and sold by the mint, and who yet allowed that the sovereign must have some fixed weight. But the fixed price is convertible with the fixed weight, and *vice versâ*. Either follows from the other.

In practice the weight of a coin is always a matter of limits, and there must be limits both for the weight as sent out and that at which it can legally remain in circulation. The *remedy* is the technical name for the allowance made to the mint-master for imperfection of workmanship, and is defined by the Act as two-tenths of a grain (0·01296 gram). Thus the mint cannot legally issue a sovereign weighing less than 123·074 grains, or more than 123·474 grains. Since the fineness of the gold, again, can never be adjusted exactly to the standard of eleven parts in twelve, or 916·66 in a 1000, a remedy of two parts in 1000 is allowed in this respect. It is understood that the English mint succeeds in working well within the remedy both of weight and fineness.

Every sovereign issued from the mint in accordance with these regulations, and bearing the impress authorized by the Queen, is legal tender, and must be accepted by a creditor in discharge of a debt to that amount, provided that it has not been reduced by wear or ill-treatment below the weight of 122·50 grains (7·93787 grams). If a sovereign of less than this *least current weight* be tendered to any person, he is presumed by the law to detect the deficiency, and is bound to cut or deface the coin, and return it to the tenderer, who must bear the loss. If the coin so defaced should prove not to be below the limit, then the defacer has to receive it and bear the loss arising from his mistake. Any justice of the peace may decide disputes arising concerning light sovereigns in a summary manner.

The only other gold coin actually issued is the half-sovereign, of which the standard weight and remedy are exactly half those of the sovereign, the remedy in fineness the same as in the sovereign, and the least current weight 61·1250 grains (3·96083 grams). The Coinage Act also legalizes the issue of two- and five-pound gold pieces, the weights and remedies in weight being corresponding multiples of those of the sovereign. Coins of the value of five and two guineas were struck by most of the English monarchs from the time of Charles II. to that of

George III. Patterns of five- and two-pound pieces have been prepared under Queen Victoria; but gold coins of this size have not been issued in the present reign, nor is it desirable, for reasons stated in Chapter XIII., that they should be issued.

English Silver Coin.

The further subdivision of the pound is effected by token coins of silver and bronze, which are made of such weights that there is no danger of their metallic values rising above the metallic value of the gold coins for which they are legally equivalent. Previous to the year 1816, the troy pound of standard silver, containing 925 parts of fine silver and 75 parts of alloy in 1000, was coined into 62 shillings, so that each shilling would contain 92·90 grains of standard metal. Under these regulations gold was rated as 15·21 times as valuable as silver. As silver, however, may sometimes become more valuable relatively to gold, Lord Liverpool very wisely recommended in his letter to the king, that the weight of the shilling should be reduced. By the Act 56 Geo. III. ch. 68, it was ordered that the troy pound of silver should be coined into 66 shillings, a reduction of weight of about 6 per cent. The new Coinage Act maintains the chief provisions of that of 1816, so that the English shilling now has the weight of 87·27272 grains of standard silver (5·65518 grams), and the weights of all the other silver coins are exactly corresponding multiples or submultiples of this. The mint remedy in weight for the shilling is a little more than the third part of a grain, and in simple proportion for the other coins. The remedy in fineness is in all cases four parts in one thousand. The denominations of coins authorized are nine in number, namely, the crown, half-crown, florin, shilling, sixpence, groat, or fourpenny piece, threepence, twopence, and penny. All, except the crown, are coined in greater or less quantity, but the fourpence, twopence, and penny, are now only struck in very small quantities as Maundy money, which, after being distributed by the Queen annually in alms, appears to find its way into numismatic cabinets or to be melted down.

All such coins are legally current, irrespective of their weights, so long as they are not called in by proclamation, or so worn and defaced that the impress of the mint cannot be recognized. The coin in circulation is actually reduced in weight by abrasion to a considerable amount, often one-fourth or one-third of its original weight. Moreover, the fall in the value of silver relatively to gold reduces the metallic worth of the coins, so that no one can export them to foreign countries, or melt them for sale as bullion, without losing from 10 to 30 per cent. of their nominal value.

It would obviously be a cause of grievance if a person could be obliged to receive unlimited amounts of this token money in discharge of a debt. Merchants might often have thousands of pounds worth of such coins thrown upon their hands, the full value of which could only be realized by gradually putting it into circulation again. It was therefore provided by the Acts of 1816 and 1870, that silver coin shall be a legal tender only to the amount of forty shillings in any one payment. This limit was chosen apparently because the two-pound piece was in 1816 regarded as the largest coin then in circulation, or likely to be issued.

English Bronze Coinage.

The final subdivision of the pound is effected by bronze pence, halfpence, and farthings, of which the weights when issued should be respectively 145·833, 87·500 and 43·750 grains. They are composed of an alloy of 95 parts by weight of copper, four parts of tin, and one part of zinc, being exactly the same kind of bronze as was previously employed by the French mints. The remedy in weight is one-fifth of one per cent., and as the coins are token money there is no least current weight. As the reasons against allowing them to be a legal tender for large sums are stronger than in the case of silver coin, it is enacted that bronze coins shall be a legal tender only to an aggregate amount of one shilling.

If a copper penny were now made to contain metal equivalent in value to the 240th part of a sovereign, its weight would be 871 grains, at the present market price of copper (£75 per ton). Thus the fractional coinage has been reduced in weight nearly to one-sixth part of what it would be as standard copper coin. The bronze of which the pence are made is worth, according to Mr. Seyd, 10*d*. per troy pound, so that the metallic values of the coins are almost exactly one-fourth part of their

THE ENGLISH SYSTEM OF METALLIC CURRENCY. 111

nominal values. A considerable profit therefore accrues upon the coinage of bronze, amounting up to the end of 1871 to about £270,000; but the reduction of weight is altogether an advantage, and is probably not carried as far as it might properly be done.

Deficiency of Weight of the English Gold Coin.

It is the theory of the present English monetary law, as we have seen (p. 107) that every person weighs a sovereign tendered to him, and assures himself, before accepting it, that it does not weigh less than 122·5 grains. In former days it was not uncommon for people to carry pocket-scales for weighing guineas, and such scales may still be occasionally seen in old curiosity shops. But we know that the practice is entirely given up, and that even the largest receivers of coin, such as the banks and railway companies, and even tax-offices, post-offices, etc., do not pay the least regard to the law. Only the Bank of England, its branches, and a few government offices, weigh gold coin in England. The result is that a large part of the gold coinage is worn below the least current weight, and all persons of experience avoid paying old sovereigns to the Bank of England. Only ignorant and unlucky persons, or else large banks and companies which cannot otherwise get rid of light coin, suffer loss. The quantity of light gold coin withdrawn by the bank did not for many years exceed half a million a year; during the last few years it has varied from £700,000 to £950,000. As the average amount of gold coined annually is four or five millions, and the coins melted or exported are for the most part new and of full weight, it follows necessarily, that the currency is becoming more and more deficient in weight.

In 1869 I ascertained, by a careful and extensive inquiry, that $31\frac{1}{2}$ per cent. of the sovereigns and nearly one-half of the ten-shilling pieces were then below the legal limit. The reader who has attended to the remarks on Gresham's Law (p. 80), will see that no amount of coinage of new gold will drive out of circulation these depreciated old coins, because those who export, or melt, or otherwise treat the coins as bullion, will take care to operate upon good new ones.

Great injustice arises in some cases from this defective state of the gold currency. I have heard of one case in which an inexperienced person, after receiving several hundred pounds in gold from a bullion dealer in the city of London, took them straight to the Bank of England for deposit. Most of the sovereigns were there found to be light, and a prodigious charge was made upon the unfortunate depositor. The dealer in bullion had evidently paid him the residuum of a mass of coins, from which he had picked the heavy ones. In a still worse case, lately reported to me, a man presented a post-office order at St. Martin's-le-Grand, and carried the sovereigns received to the stamp-office at Somerset House, where the coins were weighed, and some of them found to be deficient. Here a man was, so to say, defrauded between two government offices.

It should be stated that the government made, in

July, 1870, a slight effort to promote the withdrawal of light gold, by engaging to receive it through the Bank of England at the full price of £3 17s. 9d. per ounce by weight, the price previously paid by the bank having been only £3 17s. 6½d., owing to the old sovereigns being a little below the standard in fineness. A certain increase in the amounts withdrawn has no doubt followed this measure; but the loss by deficiency in weight is still thrown upon the public, and as long as this is the case the withdrawal of light gold will continue inadequate to maintain the coinage at its standard weight.

Withdrawal of Light Gold Coin.

Some steps must soon be taken to remedy the increasing deficiency of weight of the gold coinage described above. The withdrawal may no doubt be effected in several ways. One method would be for the Queen to issue a proclamation calling in and prohibiting the circulation of all gold coins more than twenty or twenty-five years old, as it is mostly the older coins which are deficient in weight. Another method would be to oblige all revenue officers, post-masters, and others, under the control of government, to weigh all sovereigns presented to them. If necessary, the bankers of the kingdom generally might be obliged to weigh coin. But it is obvious that great trouble and inconvenience would arise from such measures. The progress of the post-office savings banks would be imperilled if every depositor of a pound were liable to be charged 2 per cent. for lightness. Considerable excitement and trouble followed the issue of the last proclamation of June, 1842, calling in light gold. To make the last holder of a coin pay for the whole cost of its circulation during thirty or forty years past, leads in many cases to gross injustice. The present law tends to throw the loss upon the poor, who have usually only one or two sovereigns at a time to pay, whereas rich people, having many, can avoid paying light gold at offices where it will be weighed.

I hold that the only thorough remedy is for the government to bear the loss occasioned by the wear of the gold, as it already bears that of the silver currency. The Bank of England should be authorized to receive all sovereigns *showing no marks of intentional damage or unfair treatment* at their full nominal value, on behalf of the mint, which should recoin the light ones at the public expense. No one would then have any reason for keeping the light gold away from the bank; the currency would soon be purged of the illegally light coins, and would thenceforth be kept up strictly to the standard weight; all loss of time and trouble would be saved to individuals, a consideration which we should not lose sight of; and, lastly, no injustice would be done, as at present, to the last holder of a light sovereign.

In opposition to such a proposal it is usually urged, that encouragement would be given to the criminal practice of sweating or otherwise diminishing the weight of the currency. I answer that, on the contrary, it is the present state of things which gives the best opportunity for illegal practices, because it renders the population perfectly accustomed to handling old and worn coins. No one now actually refuses any gold money in retail business, so that the sweater, if he exists at all, has all the opportunities he can desire. I have met with sovereigns deficient to the extent of four to five grains, or 8d. to 10d., but they nevertheless circulate. If under a better system the gold currency consisted entirely of full-weight, fresh coins, with sharp, new, perfect impressions, attention would quickly be drawn to any coin which appeared to be worn or ill-treated in any degree. As the currency, too, would be constantly passing through the automaton weighing-machines of the Bank of England, without previously undergoing the operation of garbling by bullion brokers, sweated coins, if they existed at all, would soon be detected; whereas, according to the present system, the bank authorities have no opportunity of examining the whole coinage. It is the present state of things, then, which gives the best opportunity for tampering with the currency, though there is no evidence to show that fraudulent practices are carried on to any appreciable extent. Under the proposed new system such practices would be rendered almost impossible.

Supply of Gold Coin.

It is the theory of the English monetary law that every individual is entitled to take gold to the mint and have it coined gratuitously, all the expenses being borne by the public revenues. It is intended that the coin shall be rendered identical in value with an equal quantity of gold bullion, so that it shall, in short, be so much *certified bullion*, and shall be reconvertible into ingots without loss. Though this theory is simple and sound in some respects, it is not perfectly carried into practice. The mint never engages to deliver coin in immediate exchange for gold sent for coining, so that there is a loss of interest during the uncertain interval of coinage. If, instead of sending gold directly to the mint, the owner pursues the customary mode of selling it to the Bank of England, he receives, according to the Bank Charter Act of 1844, only £3 17s. 9d. per ounce, instead of the full mint price of £3 17s. $10\frac{1}{2}d$. Moreover, it has been pointed out by Mr. E. Seyd, that, as the bank used to conduct their bullion business, there was a series of small charges or profits made for weighing, melting, assaying, the turn of the scale, the difference of the assay reports, etc., which amounted on the whole, including the above charge of $1\frac{1}{2}d$. per ounce for demurrage, to 0·2828 per cent. on the value of the gold. The bank has since made some small improvements in the mode of conducting the business, but it may still be considered that the cost of converting gold bullion into sovereigns is about $\frac{1}{4}$ per cent.

Though every person whatever has the right, under the Coinage Act, of taking gold to the mint and having it coined free of charge and in order of priority without undue preference, no one ever does use the privilege, except the Bank of England. During an inquiry into the Bank Act in 1857, Mr. Twells stated that he had once sent £10,000 to the mint, and was afterwards surprised to find his firm of Spooner and Co., mentioned in a parliamentary paper as the only private firm that had ever done such a thing. The directors of the Bank of England have naturally acquired the monopoly of transactions with the mint, because they have to keep large stocks both of coin and bullion to meet the demands of the Issue Department and of their customers, including, directly or indirectly, the whole of the bankers of the United Kingdom. They can convert portions of their bullion into coin without any loss of interest or cost, whenever they find the stock of coin running down. They feel the monetary pulse of the whole community, and they have all the requisite appliances for the custody, assay, or exact weighing of bullion. Even those persons who need to possess large sums of gold often employ the bank to weigh, pack, and warehouse it, and the bank is always willing to do the work for fixed low charges. Hence it is most natural and convenient that the bank should act as the agent of the mint. Though the bank makes a certain profit out of the business, it is hardly earned at the cost of the public, but rather comes out of the economy with which the work is managed. It could in no way improve the currency of the country if every one who owned a few ounces of gold were to run with it to the mint, throwing upon the country the cost of melting and assaying insignificant ingots, and complicating the accounts and transactions of the mint.

118

Supply of Silver Coin.

On account of the absurd misapprehensions recently existing as to the scarcity of silver money, and the supposed right of private individuals to demand the coinage of silver, it may be well to describe exactly how the supply of silver coin is legally regulated and practically carried out. There is no law, statute, or common, which gives any private person, company, or institution, the right to take silver to the mint, and demand coin in exchange. Thus it is left in the hands of the Treasury and the mint to issue so much and such denominations of silver coins as they may think needful for the public service. This state of the law is perfectly right; because, as the silver coins are tokens, they cannot be got rid of by melting or exportation at their nominal values. If individuals were free to demand as much silver coin as they liked, a surplus might be thrown into circulation in years of brisk trade, which in a subsequent year of depressed trade would lie upon people's hands.

Practically speaking, the mint is guided in the supply of silver coin by the Bank of England, not because this bank has by law any special powers, privileges, or duties in the matter, but because, in acting as the bank of banks, and the bank of government departments, it has the best opportunities of judging when more coin is wanted. Not only do all the London bankers draw silver coin from the Bank of England when they need it, but the same is done directly or indirectly by all the other bankers in the kingdom. A deficiency of silver coin in any county is shown by the stock of the local bankers running down. They replenish their stocks either from the nearest branch of the Bank of England or from their London agents, who again draw from the Bank of England. At other times or places the bankers tend to accumulate a surplus of silver coin. Some banks in a large town may happen to have accounts with many shopkeepers, butchers, brewers, cattle-dealers, or dealers of one kind or another, who deposit silver coin in large quantities. Other banks may be largely drawn upon by manufacturers for the payment of wages, and may suffer from a deficiency of silver coin. It is a common practice, therefore, for bankers in any locality to assist each other by buying or selling superfluous silver coin as the case may require. If a superfluity of coin, however, cannot be got rid of in this way, it may be returned to the Bank of England or one of its branches. This bank indeed is in no way bound to provide or receive large sums in silver, and it therefore usually makes a small charge of about five shillings per hundred pounds to cover the trouble and risk. In consideration of this charge the bank bears the cost of transmission by railway, examines the coin for the detection of base pieces and the withdrawal of worn coin—which latter it sends to the mint for recoinage, and acts in general as the agent of the mint.

Having the business so much in its hands, it is obvious that the department of the bank which manages the receipt and issue of silver coin can judge accurately when a fresh supply of coin is wanted. Before the stock runs too low notice is given to the mint, and money is usually advanced to the Master that he may purchase silver bullion for coinage. Under this system it is almost impossible for a deficiency of currency to arise without becoming known to the mint, and if, two or three years ago, the supply could not be made equal to the sudden demand, it was because the mint was not supplied by government with machinery adequate to the growing wants of the country. The existing system, in short, seems to be as nearly perfect as can be desired, provided that the mint be rebuilt and organized in such a manner as to enable it to meet any demand which the fluctuations of trade may occasion.

The Royal Mint.

While treating of the English system of metallic money, it is impossible to avoid expressing the wish that the House of Commons and the government will no longer delay a complete reconstruction of the Royal Mint. The mint factories, as they now stand, were very creditable to the generation which erected them; but it is needless to say that in the last fifty or seventy years we have immensely advanced, both in the art of constructing machinery and in our ideas of the arrangement and economy of manufactories. What should we think of a Cotton Spinning Company, which should propose to use a mill and machinery originally constructed by Arkwright, or to drive a mill by engines turned out of the Soho works in the time of Boulton and Watt? Yet the nation still depends for its coinage upon the presses actually erected by Boulton and Watt, although much more convenient coining presses have since been invented and employed in foreign and colonial mints.

The present mint workshops are quite inadequate for meeting the demands which may be thrown upon them by the increasing industry and wealth of the United Kingdom, not to speak of the British Empire. A few years ago it was impossible to turn out silver coin as quickly as it was required when trade was brisk, and, while one metal is being coined, there are no means of meeting the demand for other kinds of coin. As to the bronze coinage, it has generally to be obtained from Birmingham presses, and bronze blanks have also to be purchased at times. Even silver blanks have been obtained from Birmingham. The British mint ought to represent the skill and wealth of the British nation, and no petty considerations should be allowed to postpone so necessary a reform.

Nothing short of a complete reconstruction of the mint workshops will meet the requirements of the case. If this is to be done, much convenience and economy will arise from abandoning the large and valuable site upon Tower Hill, and erecting an entirely new mint in a more accessible position. The opinions of Mr. E. Seyd upon this subject are worthy of much attention.

CHAPTER XI.

FRACTIONAL CURRENCY.

ONE monetary question which can hardly be said to be satisfactorily solved as yet, is that of selecting the best possible material for coins of small value, called in English *pence*, in French *monnaie d'appoint*. The fractional coins should be equal in value to about a tenth part of the silver ones, coin for coin, but it unfortunately happens that there is no suitable metal of which the value is now one-tenth part of that of silver. In the time of the Romans, gold was about ten times as valuable as silver, and silver about ten times as valuable as copper, so that there would then have been no difficulty in constructing a perfect decimal system of money.

To throw light upon this subject, I have drawn out the following table, in which are shown the weights of the principal commercial metals which are of equal values at present. The numbers in such a table must of course be subject to perpetual fluctuations, according to the changes in the market prices of the metals. In some cases, too, it is difficult to find any accurate quota tions at all, and the price often depends greatly upon the manufactured state of the metal. Gold and silver are taken as of standard fineness, and gold forms the unit.

Equivalent Weights of the Principal Metals.

Gold	1	Tin		942
Platinum	3½	Copper		1,696
Aluminium	7	Lead		6,360
Silver	16	Bar Iron		15,900
Nickel	71	Pig Iron		50,880

It may be worthy of notice that when we thus draw out what may be called the *commercial equivalents* of the metals, they are found to form a series very rudely approximating to a geometrical series with the common ratio 3. Silver, however, is an exception. There is, too, one term missing between nickel and tin, and as tin is not a coinable metal, there is a wide interval between nickel and copper, and a still wider one between silver and copper. At present silver is almost exactly one hundred times as valuable as copper; hence copper pence must either contain in metallic value but a fraction of the nominal value, or else they must be very heavy and bulky. When a new copper coinage was issued in England from the mint of Boulton and Watt in 1797, the coins were made nearly of standard weight, at the rate of an ounce avoirdupois for each penny. There was a double inconvenience in this. Sixteen pence actually weighed a pound avoirdupois, at which rate the people would now be carrying three times as great a weight in their pockets as with our bronze currency. Moreover, the price of copper having risen, Boulton's pence became more valuable as metal than as coins, and were used as material in spite of their beautiful execution.

The first and most obvious course was to reduce the weight of the penny, making it purely a token coin. The old pennies of Victoria weighed about 290 grains each, instead of about 433 grains, as in the coinage of Boulton and Watt, a reduction of about one-third part. The bronze penny has been still further reduced, and ought to weigh 145·8 grains.

There are two inconveniences which may arise from too great and sudden a reduction in the weight of token currency. There is a risk of the population rejecting the new coins as fraudulently light. This was the case with the new copper five- and ten-centime pieces, struck in France in 1794 by the Revolutionary Government, at the rate of one gram for each centime, which was half the previous rate. The government was obliged to call in the light coin and issue it again at the old weight, and only in the time of Napoleon III. could coins of one gram per centime be put into circulation. The people, then, must be educated to receive very light tokens, and the reduction must be made by moderate steps.

In the second place, if the metal is easily coined or manipulated like copper, if it fails to retain a very good impression, and if there is a considerable margin for profit, the temptation to false coiners might become strong. I am not aware that this has ever happened in regard to the English copper coinage, but counterfeit sous used to be manufactured on a large scale in the Faubourg Saint Antoine, in Paris, almost under the eyes of the government.

At the best, too, pure copper makes indifferent coin, being deficient in hardness, so that it soon becomes disfigured; it has a disagreeable odour which it communicates to the fingers; and when exposed to damp air it becomes covered with verdigris, which is both unsightly and poisonous. I proceed to consider the various ways in which it has been attempted to substitute for copper coin some more convenient currency.

Billon Coin.

Pennies and twopenny pieces, if now made of standard silver, like the Maundy money, would be too small and light for use, weighing respectively, $7\frac{1}{4}$ and $14\frac{1}{2}$ grains. Even the threepenny pieces, now so abundant in England, and weighing 21·8 grains each, are inconveniently small. In England, for a very long time, no silver has been coined of less fineness than the old standard of 925 parts in 1000. In many continental countries the smaller currency has been made of a very low alloy of silver and copper, called *billon*. Such coins were at one time current, to a certain extent, in France, the metal containing only one part of silver in five of alloy, but they have long been recalled. In Nor way the small currency now consists partly of half-skilling and one-skilling pieces in copper, the skilling being nearly equal in value to an English halfpenny, but principally of two, three, and four-skilling pieces, composed of billon, containing, according to an analysis performed for me at the Owens' College chemical laboratory, one part of silver and three of copper. These billon pieces are very convenient in size, and, being for the most part newly issued, are clean and neat. Billon is still being coined in Austria.

It is in the states now forming the German empire that billon coins have been most extensively used, especially in pieces of three, four, and six kreutzers, the so-called *scheidemünze* now being recalled. This consists of silver alloyed with three, four, or more times its weight of copper. Before such base silver is passed through the coining press, it is usual to dissolve the copper from the surface of the blank pieces of metal, so as to produce a film of pure white silver upon the surface. This operation, called *colouring*, gives a fine bright appearance to the coins when new, and they are easily put into circulation. But after a little time the silver film is worn off, and the coins assume a very patchy aspect. Billon coinage seems to have, too, an extraordinary power of accumulating a layer of dirt of a very disagreeable character, with which all travellers in Germany in past years must be well acquainted. Moreover, it offers great facilities to the counterfeiter, and for several sufficient reasons cannot be recommended for adoption.

Composite Coin.

It is said that Saint Louis, the great King of France, finding much want of small money to pay his soldiers, caused little pieces of silver wire, weighing nine and eighteen grains, to be fixed on pieces of stamped leather, and circulated for one- and two-dime pieces. The silver gave the value, and the leather served as a case or handle to preserve the small bit of metal from being lost. In recent times, composite coins, having a centre piece of silver and a rim of copper, were constructed on similar principles. A model penny of this kind has an agreeable appearance and a convenient size, but seems to be subject to several objections. The cost of coinage would be considerable; the coins could hardly be made so perfect that the centre would not come out sometimes; the contact of dissimilar metals would set up electro-chemical action, and the copper would be corroded; and, lastly, it would be difficult to detect counterfeit silver pieces inserted by the forger. Composite coins of a similar character were struck in France under Napoleon I., about the year 1810, but were never circulated. Pennies formed of a copper centre with a brass rim have been employed in England, and tin pence, halfpence, or farthings, with a copper plug inserted near the centre, were long used, and are plentiful in numismatic cabinets

Bronze Coin.

It was known, even in prehistoric times, that a small quantity of tin communicated hardness to copper, and the ancient nations were familiar with the use of bronze thus manufactured. The French Revolutionary Government melted up the bells of the churches seized by them, and the *sous de cloche*, as they were called, made from the bell metal, were superior to coins of pure copper. Yet curiously enough no modern government thought of employing a well-chosen bronze for small money, until the government of the late Emperor of the French undertook the recoinage of the old sous in 1852. This recoinage was carried out with great success.

Between the years 1853 and 1867 coins to the nominal value of about two millions sterling, consisting of 800 millions of pieces, and weighing eleven millions of kilograms (10,826 tons) were struck, in addition to a subsequent issue of about 200 millions of pieces. The experiment was in almost every way successful. The ten and five-centime pieces now circulating in France are models of good minting, with a low but sharp and clear impression. They were readily accepted by the people, although only weighing as much as the sous rejected in the time of the Revolution, namely, one gram per centime, and they are wearing well.

The bronze used consists of 95 parts of copper, four of tin, and one of zinc. It is much harder than copper, yet so tough and impressible that it takes a fine impression from the dies, and retains it for a long time. It cannot be struck except by a press of some power, and thus counterfeiting is rendered almost impossible. It can hardly be said to corrode by exposure to air or damp, and merely acquires a natural *patina*, or thin dark film of copper oxide, which throws the worn parts of the design into relief, and increases the beauty of the coin.

Bronze has since been coined by the governments of England, the United States, Italy, and Sweden, and it seems probable that it will entirely take the place of copper. The German government is now using bronze for the one-pfennig pieces.

English Bronze Coin.

The old copper coinage of the United Kingdom was replaced, from ten to fifteen years ago, by a much more convenient and elegant series of pence, halfpence, and farthings, struck in exactly the same kind of bronze as the French centime pieces. The English coins, though far from being so well executed as the French ones, are clean, and likely to wear well. The only great objection which can be raised to them, is that they are still of considerable size and weight, although less than the old copper coins. As all the latter are now withdrawn, and few of the new ones can yet be lost or destroyed, we know very accurately the amount of the English fractional currency. The whole amount issued in the years 1861 to 1873 is as follows:—

	Weight in tons.	Number of pieces.	Nominal value in pounds sterling.
Pennies	1,585	170,419,000	£710,082
Halfpennies	918	164,505,000	342,719
Farthings	149	53,594,000	55,826
	2652	388,518,000	£1,108,627

Including a small amount issued before 1861, the whole value of the bronze coin put into circulation up to the end of 1873 was £1,143,633. It is remarkable that the quantity of small coins used in England is much less than in France, where at least 1000 millions of pieces, chiefly of ten and five centimes, are in use. Thus while the English, Scotch, and Irish seem to be sufficiently supplied with $8\frac{1}{2}d$. per head, the French employ on the average 1 franc 60 centimes, (15 pence), the Belgians, 2 francs 26 centimes ($21\frac{1}{2}$ pence), and the Italians as much as 3 francs 10 centimes ($29\frac{1}{2}$ pence).

Weight of the Currency.

It is curious that the weights of the several kinds of currency vary inversely as their nominal values; thus, taking the paper circulation of the United Kingdom at 40 millions, the gold roughly at 100 millions, the silver at 15 millions, and the bronze as above, I find the weights to be approximately as follows:—

Paper currency	16 tons
Gold ,,	786 ,,
Silver ,,	1670 ,,
Bronze ,,	2652 ,,
	5124 tons

It is impossible to give a satisfactory reason why the least valuable part of the currency should be so much the most weighty. A tendency thus arises for the pence to accumulate upon the hands of retail traders, especially publicans, omnibus proprietors, and newspaper publishers. At one time the London brewers had such large quantities of bronze coins thrown upon their hands from the public-houses which they own, that the mint had eventually to arrange to buy it from them, instead of coining more. In large towns, arrangements have to be made for getting rid of the accumulating pence with the least trouble and loss; the coin is transferred weekly to mills and factories, where it is used in paying wages. Bankers refuse to have anything to do with bronze coin beyond the amount of a shilling, for which it is legal tender, and it is usual for persons to object to receive more than $2d.$ or $3d.$ of change in pence.

It is worthy of inquiry whether this tendency of the fractional currency to stagnation would not be remedied by the substitution of a much lighter and more elegant currency of nickel, or of some alloy yet to be invented. In France, it is found that the bronze coinage circulates much more freely than the old copper and bell-metal sous, which tended to accumulate in certain localities. Our bronze pence are much better than the old copper pence, but it does not follow that we have in any degree approximated to perfection. Coins of about half the weight of those in circulation would be much more convenient.

Nickel, Manganese, Aluminium, and other Metals and Alloys.

The employment of nickel in the manufacture of small money has already been referred to (p. 49), and if the conditions of supply and demand of this metal were more steady we should perhaps want nothing better. The alloy of nickel and copper generally used is hard and difficult to coin, but it takes a fine impression which it will probably require long wear to efface. Nickel coinage is thus very unlikely to be counterfeited, and its peculiar nondescript colour renders it easily distinguishable from silver or gold money. The progress of metallurgy, however, is making us acquainted with several new metals and many new alloys, and it is quite likely that some new material for fractional money will eventually be found. Dr. Percy, having regard to the rising price of nickel, suggests that manganese should be employed instead, as it gives alloys of similar character, and can be procured in greater quantities.

Dr. Clemens Winkler strongly recommends aluminium as suited for monetary purposes. Trial pieces, marked "$\frac{1}{4}$ real, 1872," have been struck, and one of them may be seen in the Monetary Museum at the Paris mint. This metal has a characteristic bluish white colour, but its great advantage is its low specific gravity. The trial piece in question, of which a specimen was furnished to me by Mr. Roberts, the chemist of the English mint, is two centimetres, or 0·79 inch, in diameter, a little wider than a sixpence and much thicker, and yet weighs only one gram, or 15½ grains. Were our pence and halfpennies as light and convenient as this coin, we could carry many of them in the pocket without discomfort. The chief difficulty in adopting such a new metal would arise from the uncertain price at which it can be produced. It is unknown, too, how it would wear. Even if pure aluminium were found to be unsuitable for coining, some of its remarkable alloys might be employed instead. Mr. Graham, the late Master of the Mint, had a series of trial pieces of one to ten cents struck in the so-called "aluminium bronze."

I may suggest that one of the best possible materials for small money would be steel, provided it could be prevented from rusting. Steel coins would be difficult to strike, but when once struck could be hardened, so as to be almost indestructible. The cheapness of the material would allow of their production on a large scale at small cost, while they could not possibly be imitated by the false coiners with any profit. Hence it would be needless to pay any attention to the metallic value of the coins, which might be struck of the most convenient sizes, probably those of the sixpence and shilling. Now it has been pointed out by Sir John Herschel (Physical Geography, reprinted from the "Encyclopædia Britannica," § 320, p. 289), that steel appears to be protected from rusting by being alloyed with a small quantity of nickel; this at least is the effect in the case of meteoric iron. It is much to be desired that such an alloy should be fairly tried. I am informed by Mr. Roberts, that silver also alloys well with iron or steel, and that such mixtures have been proposed for coining purposes. An alloy of silver, copper, and zinc has already, indeed, been fully tested in Switzerland, where it is used for twenty, ten, and five-centime pieces. These coins are convenient in size, but have a poor yellowish white appearance. They have not been adopted, so far as I know, by any other country; and there seems to be no use in putting silver into them, as it would probably be easy to produce a similarly coloured alloy without silver.

It is a misfortune of what may be called the science of monetary technology, that its study is almost of necessity confined to the few officers employed in government mints. Hence we can hardly expect the same advances to be made in the production of money as in other branches of manufacture, where there is wide and free competition. Moreover, it is very difficult to get an opportunity of testing any new kind of coin; in a large currency, like that of the United Kingdom, it is almost impossible to execute experiments. But it may be suggested that the English mint, in supplying coins for some of the smaller British colonies and possessions, enjoys an admirable opportunity for testing new proposals. This need not involve any cost to such colonies, as the English government, in striking a few hundreds or thousands of pounds' worth of small coin for a colony, might readily engage to withdraw them at its own cost if found unsuitable after a certain number of years.

CHAPTER XII.

THE BATTLE OF THE STANDARDS.

EVER since the great discoveries of gold in California and Australia began to disturb the value of that metal relatively to silver and to other commodities, it has been a continual subject of discussion what standard of value should be ultimately adopted. There have been partizans of the now antiquated silver standard, of the double standard, and of the gold standard. Having in England long possessed a gold standard, we have been only in a secondary degree concerned in such discussions, upon which quite a library of works has been written by distinguished French, Belgian, German, Swiss, Italian, and Dutch economists. The changes actually effected in the currencies of Europe since 1849 are of the most extensive character. Some nations have more than once changed their policy. Holland, anticipating a great fall in the value of gold, adopted silver as the single standard of value in 1850. This change had to be effected at considerable pecuniary loss, and it is understood that Holland is again exposed to the trouble and expense of having to admit a gold standard, either as a sole legal tender, like Germany, or else concurrently with a restricted silver coinage, like Belgium and the other monetary allies of France.

From the time of Locke to that of Lord Liverpool, the comparative advantages of gold and silver, as the principal measure of value, were a frequent subject of discussion among English political writers. Locke and most of the earlier English economists upheld silver. Lord Liverpool definitely decided English policy in favour of gold, and the tendency of opinion is now strongly in the same direction. Several countries have recently changed from silver to gold, and since the single example of Holland no nation has passed from gold to silver. Even Austria, which is still supposed to represent the silver standard, has taken a step towards a change by coining ten- and twenty-franc pieces in gold, the inscriptions 10 Francs and 20 Francs now appearing, as well as 4 Gulden and 8 Gulden, on the new gold coins of the Austro-Hungarian empire.

The Double Standard.

The single silver standard having been practically abandoned as regards the currencies of Europe, the battle has more recently waged between the partizans of the double standard, represented in the currencies of France and the Monetary Convention of Western Europe, and those who uphold a gold standard combined with subsidiary coinages of silver and small money, somewhat in the manner of the English system. The advantages of the double standard have been most ably advocated by MM. Wolowski, Courcelle-Seneuil, Seyd, Léon, Prince-

Smith, and others, while MM. Chevalier, De Parieu, Hendriks, Frère Orban, Levasseur, Feer-Herzog, and Juglar, have been some of the leading upholders of the gold standard. The literature of the subject is very extensive and, to most readers, dreary in the extreme, but I will try to give a tolerably concise statement of the principal arguments.

In the first place, I have no doubt whatever that M. Wolowski is theoretically quite correct in what he says about the compensatory action of the double standard system. English writers seem completely to have misunderstood the question, asserting that the system exposes us to the extreme fluctuations of both metals. No doubt, when gold and silver are both legal tenders to unlimited amounts, there will be a tendency to pay in that metal which is overrated in the legal ratio of $15\frac{1}{2}$ to 1. Only when the price of standard silver is exactly 5s. $0\frac{13}{16}d.$ per ounce is it a matter of indifference in France whether a debt be paid in gold or silver, and this exact price has only been quoted a few times in the London market in the last thirty years. Accordingly, it has been urged that the double standard is not really a double one, but only an *alternative gold and silver standard*. When silver is lower in price than 5s. $0\frac{13}{16}d.$ per ounce, silver becomes the standard; when silver rises above this price, gold takes its place as the real measure of value.

So far the English economists are no doubt correct; but, in the first place, it does not follow that the prices of commodities follow the extreme fluctuations of value

138   MONEY.

of both metals, as many writers have inconsiderately
declared. Prices only depend upon the course of the
metal which happens to have sunk in value below the
legal ratio of 15½ to 1. Now, if in the accompanying
figure we represent by the line A the variation of the
value of gold as estimated in terms of some third commodity, say copper, and by the line B the corresponding
variations of the value of silver; then, superposing these
curves, the line C would be the curve expressing the
extreme fluctuations of both metals. Now the standard
of value always follows the metal which *falls* in value;
hence the curve D really shows the course of variation
of the standard of value. This line undergoes more
frequent undulations than either of the curves of gold
or silver, but the fluctuations do not proceed to so great
an extent, a point of much greater importance.

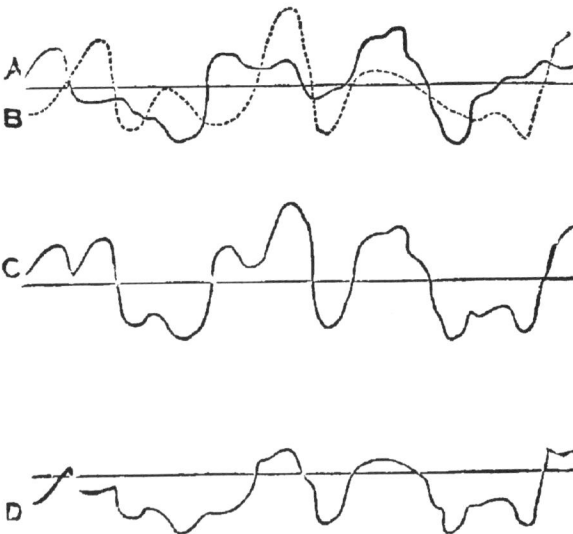

Compensatory Action.

Nor is this the whole error of the English writers. A little reflection must show that MM. Wolowski and Courcelle-Seneuil are quite correct in urging that a *compensatory* or, as I should prefer to call it, *equilibratory action*, goes on under the French currency law, and tends to maintain both gold and silver more steady in value than they would otherwise be. If silver becomes more valuable than in the ratio of 1 to $15\frac{1}{2}$ compared with gold, there arises at once a tendency to import gold into any country possessing the double standard, so that it may be coined there, and exchanged for a legally equivalent weight of silver coin, to be exported again. This is no matter of theory only, the process having gone on in France until the principal currency, which was mainly composed of silver in 1849, was in 1860 almost wholly of gold. France absorbed the cheapened metal in vast quantities and emitted the dearer metal, which must have had the effect of preventing gold from falling and silver from rising so much in value as they would otherwise have done. It is obvious that, if gold rose in value compared with silver, the action would be reversed; gold would be absorbed and silver liberated. At any moment the standard of value is doubtless one metal or the other, and not both; yet the fact that there is an alternation tends to make each vary much less than it would otherwise do. It cannot prevent both metals from falling or rising in value compared with other commodities, but it can throw variations of supply and demand over a larger area, instead of leaving each metal to be affected merely by its own accidents.

Imagine two reservoirs of water, each subject to independent variations of supply and demand. In the absence of any connecting pipe the level of the water in each reservoir will be subject to its own fluctuations only. But if we open a connection, the water in both will assume a certain mean level, and the effects of any excessive supply or demand will be distributed over the whole area of both reservoirs. The mass of the metals, gold and silver, circulating in Western Europe in late years, is exactly represented by the water in these reservoirs, and the connecting pipe is the law of the 7th Germinal, an XI, which enables one metal to take the place of the other as an unlimited legal tender.

The Demonetization of Silver.

M. Wolowski has earnestly warned Europe against the danger of abrogating the law of the double standard, and demonetizing silver. Germany, in adopting a gold standard, is causing a considerable demand for gold, and at the same time throwing many millions of silver coins upon the market. Austria, Denmark, Sweden, and Norway are likely to follow her example. If other countries were to insist upon suddenly having a gold money, it is evident that gold would tend to rise in value compared with silver, which might be largely depreciated. If France, Italy, Belgium, and other countries now possessing theoretically the double standard, were to allow the free action of their monetary laws, the depreciated silver would flow in and replace the appreciated gold, so that the change of values would be moderated. M. Wolowski asserts that if this compensatory action be suspended, and the demonetization of silver be extended, there must ensue a disastrous rise in the value of gold, thus rendered the sole standard of value. All debts private and public will be legally due in this metal, and all burdens will be greatly increased.

Within the last year or two the predictions of M. Wolowski may seem to have been verified in some degree. The price of standard silver, which was at one time $62\frac{1}{2}d.$ per ounce, has already fallen as low as $57\frac{3}{4}d.$ while the demonetization of silver in Germany is only partially accomplished. The whole effect of the great discoveries of gold was only to raise the price from about $59\frac{3}{4}d.$ to a maximum of $62\frac{1}{2}d.$, while the double standard system freely worked; but since its action has been, as we shall see, suspended, the minting operations of a single government can affect the price in a greater degree.

Agreeing that M. Wolowski is entirely correct in an abstract point of view, and is justified to some extent by the course of events, I must adhere to the opinion which I expressed at his request in 1868, and which was partially published in his volume, "L'Or et l'Argent" (p. 62).

The question seems to be entirely one of degree, and in the absence of precise information is quite indeterminate. If all the nations of the globe were suddenly and simultaneously to demonetize silver, and require gold money, a revolution in the value of gold would be inevitable. But M. Wolowski seems to forget that the nations of Europe constitute only a small part of the population of the world. The hundreds of millions who inhabit India and China, and other parts of the eastern and tropical regions, employ a silver currency, and there is not the least fear that they will make any sudden change in their habits. The English government has repeatedly tried to introduce a gold currency into our Indian possessions, but has always failed, and the gold coins now circulating there are supposed not to exceed one tenth part of the metallic currency. Although the pouring out of forty or fifty millions sterling of silver from Germany may for some years depress the price of the metal, it can be gradually absorbed without difficulty by the eastern nations, which have for two or three thousand years received a continual stream of the precious metals from Europe. If other nations should one after another demonetize silver, yet the East may be found quite able to absorb all that is thrust upon it, provided that this be not done too rapidly.

As regards the gold required to replace silver, it does not seem to be evident that there will be any scarcity. The adoption of the gold standard does not necessarily involve the coining of much gold, for some countries may, like Norway, or Italy, or Scotland, have a principal currency almost entirely composed of paper. In other countries, such as France and Germany, the cheque and clearing system, which we shall shortly consider, may be gradually introduced, and may economize to a great extent the use of the metallic currency. The current supply of gold from the mines is still very large, and we cannot be sure that it will not be increased by fresh discoveries in New Guinea, South Africa, North and South America, and elsewhere.

In short, then, the amount of supply and amount of demand of both the precious metals depend upon a a number of accidents, changes, or legislative decisions, which cannot be in any way predicted. The price of silver has fallen in consequence of the German currency reforms, but it is by no means certain that it will fall further than it has already done. That any great rise will really happen in the purchasing power of gold is wholly a matter of speculation. We cannot do more than make random guesses on the subject, and, as a mere guess, I should say that it is not likely to rise. Gold has since 1851 been falling in value, and an increased demand for gold is not likely to do more than slacken, or at the most arrest, the progress of depreciation.

Disadvantages of the Double Standard.

While the need for maintaining the system of the double standard is a matter of speculation, the inconveniences of the system are beyond doubt. So long, indeed, as its operation resulted in substituting a beautiful coinage of napoleons, half-napoleons, and five-franc pieces in gold for the old heavy silver écus, there was no complaint, and the French people admired the action of their compensatory system. But when, a year or two ago, it became evident that the heavy silver currency was coming back again, and that the gold coin was likely to form the circulating medium of other nations, the matter assumed a different aspect. The French, in short, have been educated to the use of gold, and they are not likely to wish for the return of a currency $15\frac{1}{2}$ times as heavy and cumbrous. Moreover, the change involves a loss to the community in general, who receive their debts in a metal of lessened value; and a part of the benefit is reaped by bullion-brokers, money-changers, and bankers, for whom a factitious trade in gold and silver money is created by the law of the 7th Germinal, an XI. The statesmen of the countries still maintaining the double standard must have reflected that other nations showed no tendency whatever to adopt the same system. Thus, if France were to continue to act as a great compensatory currency pendulum, she would bear the cost and inconvenience, while other nations would reap equally with herself the advantage of the increased steadiness of value of the precious metals. The founders of the Monetary Convention and the advocates of International Currency never intended to sacrifice themselves to this extent for the benefit of the world. Accordingly they have in effect abandoned the double standard.

When the renewed tendency to coin silver five-franc pieces in large quantities first became apparent, the French government at once suspended the coinage.

Subsequently an agreement has been made from year to year between France, Switzerland, Belgium, and Italy, that each country shall coin only a fixed quantity of silver écus proportional to its population. An agreement to the same effect had before existed as regards the silver token currency of two-franc and smaller pieces; but the coinage of écus, which were in theory standard coins and legal tender for unlimited amounts, had been left unrestricted. The result of the limitation of coinage now imposed is to destroy the action of the double standard system. Silver being coined only in limited quantities cannot replace and drive out the gold, and the five-franc pieces, although worth more than five single franc pieces, are worth less than the fourth part of a napoleon or twenty-franc piece in gold. Although, so far as I understand, they remain a legal tender for unlimited amounts, they cannot be had in unlimited quantities, and are thus practically reduced to the rank of token coins. By the least possible legislative change, the French and other governments of the Monetary Convention have thus practically abandoned the double standard, and have adopted one which is hardly distinguishable from the composite legal tender of England and Germany. Ever since 1810 copper or bronze money had only been legal tender in France to the amount of 4 francs 99 centimes, and since the fineness of the smaller silver currency was lowered, this money also was restricted as a legal tender to the amount of 50 francs for any one payment between individuals, or to the amount of 100 francs for any payment to the public treasuries. The silver ecu forms the single link by which France holds to the double standard, and this link is half severed.

It is remarkable that the changes thus effected in the money of Western Europe are almost the same as those by which the United States had previously abandoned the double standard. Until the year 1853 the silver dollar of the United States mint was a standard coin of unrestricted legal tender, concurrently with the gold coinage of eagles and their fractions. The legal ratio of silver to gold in weight indeed, was 16 to 1, instead of $15\frac{1}{2}$ to 1 as in France. More silver being thus required to make a legal payment in America than elsewhere, gold was naturally preferred for this purpose, and the silver was sent abroad. To remedy this state of things the government of Washington, in 1853, reduced the half-dollar and smaller silver pieces to the condition of token coins, and though the single silver dollar pieces remained of standard weight, they were coined in very small quantities and were practically suppressed. The predominance of an inconvertible paper currency suspended the question of metallic money for a time. The Coinage Act of the United States Congress came into operation on 1st April, 1873, and constituted the gold one-dollar piece the sole unit of value, whilst it restricted the legal tender of the new silver trade dollar, and of the half-dollar and its subdivisions, to an amount not exceeding five dollars in any one payment. Thus the double standard previously existing in theory was finally abolished, and the United States was added to the list of nations adopting the single gold standard.

The Monetary Systems of the World.

On reviewing the changes which have recently taken place in the currencies of the principal nations, we notice an unmistakable tendency to the adoption of gold as the measure of value, and the sole principal medium of exchange. This system is now adopted throughout Great Britain and Ireland, the Australian colonies, and New Zealand, the African colonies, and many of the minor possessions of the British empire. It has existed for some time in Portugal, Turkey, Egypt, and in several of the South American States, such as Chili and Brazil. It has been established by recent legislation in the German empire, and also in the Scandinavian kingdoms of Denmark, Norway, and Sweden, where a gold currency, and principal legal tender, of twenty-kroner pieces, is now being issued. Even Japan has imitated European nations, and introduced a gold coinage of twenty, ten, five, two, and one-yen pieces, the *yen* being only three per mille less in value than the American gold dollar. The new fractional money of Japan is to consist of fifty, twenty, ten, and five-sen pieces in silver, the *sen* corresponding to a cent, and forming a token money at the fineness of eight parts in ten.

The double standard is still theoretically maintained in France, Italy, Belgium, Switzerland. Spain, Greece, and Roumania have also in recent years reformed their currencies in imitation of the French system, and must, I suppose, be considered as having a double standard.

In the New World, Peru, Ecuador, and New Grenada, profess to have the same system.

A few years ago a very considerable part of Europe might have been classed as retaining the ancient system of a single silver standard, with gold coins circulating, if at all, at varying rates, as commercial money. The whole of Germany, north and south, together with Austria, the Scandinavian kingdoms, and Russia, belonged to this group. Owing to the changes already mentioned, only Austria and Russia now clearly represent the silver standard in Europe, and even Austria has begun, since 1870, to coin gold pieces of eight and four florins, the same in weight and fineness as the French gold twenty- and ten-franc pieces. By an imperial decree, dated Vienna, 12th July, 1873, it is ordered that the French, Belgian, Italian, and Swiss gold pieces of twenty, ten, and five francs shall be internationally accepted in the Austro-Hungarian empire in the ratio of eight gold florins to twenty francs of gold coin of the other nations. Nevertheless the silver standard practically prevails over a large part of the world. The vast populations of India and China, Cochin China, the East Indian Islands, portions of Africa and the West Indies, Central America and Mexico, have a currency mainly consisting of silver coins, either rupees as in India, sycee bars as in China, or silver dollars as in many other places.

The gold standard has thus made great progress, and it will probably continue to progress. When the United States return to specie payments, they will certainly adopt gold, and Canada, whose currency can hardly be classed at all at present, must do the same. The Latin nations, having once abandoned the double standard in practice, are not likely to return to it, and Austria must follow. An extensive monetary change is hardly to be expected in Russia, although it is very remarkable that in the province of Finland, a part of the empire highly distinguished for intelligence and good education, Russia has positively admitted the franc system and its decimal subdivisions, the Finnish marc or quarter-rouble having the precise silver weight and value of the franc, lira, and peseta. A great step towards a future international coinage is thus effected. Like changes are impossible among the poor, ignorant, conservative nations of India, China, and the tropics generally. Hence we arrive, as it seems to me, at a broad, deep distinction. The highly civilized and advancing nations of Western Europe and North America, including also the rising states of Australasia, and some of the better second-rate states, such as Egypt, Brazil, and Japan, will all have the gold standard. The silver standard, on the other hand, will probably long be maintained throughout the Russian empire, and most parts of the vast continent of Asia; also in some parts of Africa, and possibly in Mexico. Excluding, however, these minor and doubtful cases, Asia and Russia seem likely to uphold silver against the rest of the world adopting gold. In such a result there seems to be nothing to regret.

CHAPTER XIII.

TECHNICAL MATTERS RELATING TO COINAGE.

In this chapter I propose to consider several minor points relating to the construction and regulation of metallic currency. Although the first principles of money are simple, it is surprising how many little details have to be considered before we can attain the maximum of convenience. We have already discussed the selection of metals to be employed, the modes in which they may be combined into a system, the regulations as to issue, etc. In this and the following chapters we still have to consider the character of the alloy which is best adapted for coining; the most convenient sizes for coins; the method of counting large numbers of coins; the cost at which the currency is maintained; the advantages and disadvantages of international currency of money; the difficulty of selecting a single standard unit; the best series of multiples and submultiples of the unit. At the most I cannot in this work attempt to give more than a slight sketch of the complicated questions of detail which have to be considered before making any change in the currency.

The Alloy in Coins.

Although we commonly speak of money as consisting of gold or silver, the coins actually used contain alloys either of silver and copper, or of gold and copper, or of gold, silver, and copper. Money struck in nearly pure gold has indeed been issued both in early and recent times, and among such gold coins may be mentioned the ancient bezant, the recent Austrian ducat, containing 986 parts of gold in 1000, the six-ducat piece of Naples, containing 996 parts, or the Tuscan sequin, which is said to be almost pure gold, namely 999 parts in 1000. Pure gold and silver are, however, soft metals, so that even if they were found naturally in the pure state, it would be desirable to add copper, which communicates hardness and reduces very much the abrasion of the coins. The proportion of copper to be adopted has been a matter of frequent discussion, and is determined partly on historical, partly on scientific grounds.

The exact alloy employed in England appears to have been decided by the system of weights used. Silver was weighed by the troy pound of 12 ounces, of which 11 oz. 2 dwts. were to be pure silver, and 18 dwts. copper. This proportion, which, even in 1357, was called the "old right standard of England," has, in spite of temporary depreciations, been maintained to the present day, and corresponds to the proportion of 925 parts in 1000. Gold having been weighed by the ancient and curious system of *carat* weights, said to be derived from the seeds of an Abyssinian plant, the unit weight of gold was 24 carats, of which 22 were to be of pure gold and two of alloy. This ratio, which has existed for many centuries, is decimally expressed by 916·66 parts in 1000.

The degrees of fineness employed in one country or another at different times are infinitely various. Silver has been coined of only 200 or even 150 parts in 1000, and gold of 750 or 700 parts; and coins exist of almost every fineness from these limits up to nearly pure metal. The only standards of fineness which it is needful to discuss in the present day are those of 900 and 835 which are proposed for general adoption in international money. A few years ago, indeed, the Berlin government contemplated the adoption of a standard German crown, consisting of ten grams of pure gold and one gram of alloy, which would give a fineness of $\frac{10}{11}$ or 909·09. This scheme had no apparent advantages, and was fortunately abandoned in favour of the present German coinage, which is, both as regards gold and silver, of the fineness of 900 parts in 1000. This simple decimal proportion was adopted by the French in the time of the Revolution; it has been extended over the countries belonging to the Monetary Convention of 1865, and over Spain, Greece, and other countries which have more or less imitated the French system. It was long ago adopted by the United States, and has been recently introduced into the gold currency of the Scandinavian kingdoms. The German government, having now decided to accept it, the simple decimal fineness is established in all the more advanced countries, excepting England and some of her colonies, and a few nations, such as Russia, Portugal, and Turkey, which have imitated the English currency and coined gold at 916·66.

In a chemical and mechanical point of view the exact degree of fineness is not a matter of importance. The difference between $\frac{11}{12}$ and $\frac{9}{10}$ is only $\frac{1}{60}$, and though the often-quoted experiments of Hatchett were said to show that our standard was slightly better than that of the French, the difference is so slight and questionable as to afford no ground for preference. The late Master of the Mint, Professor Graham, was quite willing to accept the standard of 900, both for gold and silver, and there are really no reasons, except prejudice and traditional usage, why we should not do so as soon as we make any change at all. Uniformity in the practice of nations is desirable in this and many other points, and the French economists lay great stress upon this question of fineness. It appears to me, however, that the exact degree of fineness is altogether a matter of secondary importance. If we were now to make our sovereign nine-tenths fine, we should have to raise its weight from 123·274 grains to 125·557 grains, and the mixture of old and new coins would entirely frustrate the method of counting gold money by the scales adopted in all banks. We must certainly, therefore, postpone a change of fineness in gold until we make a more considerable monetary reform. I see no reason, on the other hand, why the mint should not at once be authorized to coin silver of the decimal fineness of nine-tenths. This would merely involve an imperceptible increase in the thickness of the coins, which would, in the case of the smaller ones, be advantageous.

The fineness of 835 parts in 1000 was adopted by France, as already stated (p. 76), in order to reduce the two-franc and smaller pieces to the rank of tokens, without making any change in their weight and appearance. There is no special objection to this alloy, which is perfectly coinable and of good colour; but it is not likely that it will be adopted by the English government, instead of the present fineness of 925 parts in 1000 of our silver coinage, and does not need further discussion. It may be added that, in former years, the alloy contained in gold coins consisted in part of silver, which is always present in a greater or less quantity in native gold wherever it is found. The yellow appearance of guineas, and also of many Australian sovereigns, was due to this silver alloy; but all such silvery gold coins are rapidly withdrawn now by gold refiners, who can profitably separate the silver. The very remarkable invention of Mr. F. B. Miller, of the new Melbourne mint, enables this separation to be effected with great ease, and at small cost, almost on the gold fields. It is only requisite to melt the silvery gold, and pass a current of chlorine gas into it, to obtain the silver in the state of chloride, which is readily separated from the gold and reduced to the metallic state. It is a further advantage of this simple process that all gold so treated is freed from accidental impurities, and rendered perfectly malleable and fit for coining. One of the great difficulties of mint masters, the brittleness of gold, has thus been entirely overcome. A full description of the process, as employed at the English, Australian, American, Norwegian, and other mints, will be found in the First Annual Report of the Deputy Master of the English Mint (p. 93), and in the Second Report (p. 33), or in the specification as printed by the Patent Office.

The Size of Coins.

There appear to be pretty well defined limits of size within which we should confine ourselves in the striking of money. Coins must not be so small that they can be easily lost, or can with difficulty be picked up. The rule seems to be that the coin should cover the whole area of contact between the points of the thumb and first finger; and though, of course, this area will differ with men, women, and children, we should err rather in excess than defect. On this ground I should condemn the English threepenny silver piece as too small, and, on the same ground, the Swedish ten-öre piece, the American one-dollar gold piece, the former Papal one-scudo piece, must be pronounced inconveniently small. The French five-franc gold piece of the later type, the English fourpenny piece, the Canadian five-cent piece, or the new silver piece of twenty pfennigs, now being introduced into the German empire, must be considered the smallest coins to be tolerated. The thickness of the coins, however, must be taken into account as well as the diameter. The moneys issued from the United States mint are thicker than usual, and though this tends to give some of the coins a clumsy appearance, yet they seem to me all the more convenient to use. The French have gone to the opposite extreme, the five-franc gold piece being very thin, and having a diameter of nearly seventeen millimetres, while the American dollar, which is more valuable, has a diameter of little more than thirteen millimetres. The maximum size of coins has probably been determined chiefly with regard to the practical difficulty of coining. The largest coin which has been very widely circulated is perhaps the Maria Theresa dollar, measuring 1·6 inches, or 41 millimetres, in diameter; the other most common species of dollar are somewhat smaller, such as the Spanish dollar of 1858, measuring 37 millimetres; the American dollar, 1846, the Spanish dollar, 1870, the Mexican dollar, 1872, measuring from 37 to 38 millimetres. The average diameter of the dollars which I have examined is $38\frac{1}{2}$ millimetres, or almost exactly an inch and a half. In their larger gold coins, the Americans maintain unusual thickness. Thus the double eagle, though in value equal to more than four pounds, has a diameter of only 34 millimetres, or $1\frac{1}{3}$ inch. The beautiful four-ducat piece of Austria has a larger diameter than the double eagle, though it contains less than half the quantity of fine gold.

The Wear of Coin.

Some attention must be given to the abrasion which coins suffer in use. In the case of gold coins the loss of metal thus occasioned is of importance, and leads, as we have seen (p. 111), to a gradual depreciation of the currency. As coins pass frequently from hand to hand, the amount of metal abraded will be nearly the same as regards each coin of the same type, and each year of circulation. The loss will be proportional to length of wear. Now the English law allows a sovereign to be legal tender so long as it weighs 122·5 grains, or more; and the difference between this and the full standard weight, or 0·774 grain, represents the margin allowed for abrasion. Now, from experiments described in a paper read to the London Statistical Society in November, 1868 ("Journal of the Statistical Society," Dec., 1868, vol. xxxi. p. 426), I estimated the average wear of a sovereign for each year of circulation at 0·043 grain (0·00276 gram). It would follow that a sovereign cannot in general circulate more than about eighteen years without becoming illegitimately light. This length of time, then, would constitute what may be called the *legal life* of a sovereign. It has since been shown by Dr. Farr, that certain considerations overlooked in my calculations would reduce this estimate of the legal life to fifteen years. Mr. Seyd, on the other hand, thinks that twenty years might be adopted as the legal age of the sovereign.

When we compare the currencies of different countries, it becomes evident that the rate of abrasion will depend partly upon the rapidity and constancy of circulation, partly upon the size and character of the coins. According to the inquiries of M. Feer-Herzog in Switzerland, the average loss of the twenty-franc piece amounts to 200 millionths of the full weight in each year, while with the ten and five-franc gold pieces, the corresponding amounts are 430 and 620 millionths. My own weighings of English gold show that the sovereign loses about 350 millionths in each year of wear, and the half-sovereign no less than 1120 millionths, or more than one-tenth per cent. per annum. As the English coins are heavier than the napoleon and half-napoleon, they should suffer less loss in proportion. M. Feer-Herzog attributes the excessive loss manifested by English money to the softer character of the English alloy of eleven-twelfths. This cause may contribute something to the effect observed, but it is probable that the greater rapidity of the circulation in England is the main ground on which so great a difference can be explained.

The rate of wear of a coin depends greatly, it will be seen, upon its size. A large coin, like an English crown, a French silver écu, or an American double eagle, suffers comparatively little wear, because the surface increases much less rapidly in proportion than the contents of the coin. The slight degree of abrasion of the various silver dollars may be one cause of their popularity in the East. Smaller silver money loses much more. Thus, according to experiments made at the mint in 1833, the loss per cent. per annum on half-crowns is about 2s. 6d., on shillings 4s., and on sixpences 7s. 6d., or decimally ·125, ·200, and ·375 per cent. respectively. This loss becomes considerable in the course of years, as may readily be seen in the case of worn sixpences. The average loss of weight of the old silver coins melted at the mint, seems to be about $16\frac{1}{2}$ per cent., but this loss is more than covered by the profit upon the issue of new silver coin. Experiments were made at the mint in 1798 upon the weight of English silver coins then in circulation. It was found that the deficiency amounted in crowns to 3·31 per cent., and in half-crowns, shillings, and sixpences respectively, to 9·90, 24·60, and 38·28 per cent. In the recent withdrawal of the old silver money of South Germany, it was found to have lost on the average about one-fifth part of its weight.

To reduce the loss arising from the wear of gold coin, it might seem to be desirable to issue large gold pieces. The Americans used to have a great circulation of eagles and double eagles, the latter especially being very handsome medal-like pieces. In former days many large gold coins, such as the carlino, dobraon, doubloon, quadruple pistole, and the double ryder were current. A serious objection, however, to such coins as a double eagle, one-hundred franc-piece, or five-pound piece, is that they can readily be falsified. Small holes can be drilled through them, and then concealed by hammering. The application of the file, the sweating bag, or cylinder, or of chemical reagents, would probably be safer with large than with small coins. In some cases a double eagle has been completely sawn into two flat discs, which were afterwards neatly soldered together again with a plate of platinum between to give the requisite weight. It might have been thought that the labour and skill required to effect such falsification would have been better remunerated in some honest employment; but, according to the reports of the Director of the United States

Mint, there is evidence to show that the practice is profitable. It is proposed to prevent this falsification by reducing the thickness of the double eagle, and also making it somewhat dish shaped; but it would be better to abandon the issue of such large gold money, as has long been done in England and France. Experience shows that sovereigns, napoleons, half-eagles, and gold coins of the same size are not fraudulently treated, nor are silver coins ever debased in the way described.

In order to diminish the abrasion of coins as far as possible, the design and legend should be executed with the least possible relief consistent with perfect definition, and the head of the monarch, or other personage, should not protrude. In this and most other respects the sharply defined flat design upon the English florin is much superior to the high rounded ornaments of the old crown, half-crown, and shilling. The French mints seem to be very successful in the execution of dies, all the coins, gold, silver, and bronze struck by them having flat yet admirably executed devices. Perhaps the most beautiful recent coin which I have seen is the new twenty-franc gold piece struck during 1874 for Hungary, the engraving of the die being excellent. The new Scandinavian gold pieces of five-specie dollars, or twenty kroner, are also well executed.

Methods of Counting Coins.

To count large quantities of coin by tale, piece after piece, is not only a tedious operation, but very uncertain as regards accuracy. Several methods have been devised to facilitate the operation. In mints, the Bank of England, and other establishments, where vast quantities of coin are treated, *counting boards* are used. Similar boards have, indeed, been used from time immemorial in some parts of India by money-changers and tradesmen. These consist of simple flat trays, with several hundred depressions regularly arranged, and of such a size that one coin will exactly fit into each depression. Handfuls of uniform coins are thrown on to the board, and shaken over it, until most of the holes are filled; the remaining holes are then filled up one after another by hand. The number contained upon the board is then known with infallible accuracy, and at the same time it is very easy to examine the coins, and detect any counterfeit, defective, or foreign pieces. By the use of such boards, bags of equal numbers of any coinage are readily made up with great certainty.

In English banks it is requisite to count out considerable sums in gold coin with rapidity for the payment of cheques over the counter, or to verify the number of sovereigns paid in on deposit. For this purpose balances are employed, with weights prepared so as to be equivalent to 5, 10, 20, 30, 50, 100, 200, and 300 sovereigns. Any sum which is a multiple of five sovereigns can thus be rapidly, and almost infallibly, weighed out in a few seconds, provided that the coins are not too old and worn. An error of a sovereign is sometimes possible in a large sum, on account of deficiency of weight. In the case of half-sovereigns, this process is seldom to be depended upon, owing to the very considerable lightness of the coins. This uncertainty in weighing is one of several serious inconveniences which arise from the defective state of our gold coinage.

Half sovereigns, however, and in fact all coins which are approximately equal to each other on the average, can be rapidly counted on the balance by the ingenious *method of duplication*. Any convenient number, for instance, fifty coins, being counted into one scale, an equal number may be made to balance them, without counting, in the other scale. The two equal lots being united, one hundred more coins may be made to counterbalance them, and by a second union we get two hundred coins. We may repeat this duplication, if the balance will bear the weight, and afterwards, using one lot of coins as the fixed weight, may go on counting out lot after lot equal to it in weight and number.

When neither balance nor counting board is available, coins may be counted out into little piles of ten, fifteen, or twenty. Placing these piles alongside each other on a flat board, it is easy to detect any inequality of height by the unassisted eye, or by a straight edge laid along the top. A mistake in counting will thus be generally made manifest.

Cost of the Metallic Currency.

Calculations of some interest may be made as to the cost which falls upon the public in one way or another, owing to the use of metallic money. Speaking first of the subordinate coins of silver and bronze, the government make a profit by their manufacture, owing to the reduced weight at which they are issued as tokens. Standard silver can usually be bought by the mint for 5s. per standard ounce. It is issued to the public at the rate of 5s. 6d. per ounce, so that the government receives a seignorage of at least nine per cent. on the nominal value of the coin issued. The average coinage of silver at the English mint during the last ten years has been £546,580, upon which the seignorage would be about £49,200 per annum. On the other hand, the mint has to buy back worn silver coinage at its nominal value, and in recoining such money there is a loss, which, on the average of the last ten years (1864-73) has been £16,700, leaving a net annual profit of £32,500, no account being taken of the cost of the mint establishment. At present the price of silver is not above 4s. 10d. per ounce, so that the seignorage is about 12 per cent., and the profit on coining silver proportionately greater.

We may look at this matter in another way, by regarding the seignorage as so much money funded to bear interest, to meet the cost of withdrawing the coin, when worn out, say thirty years subsequently. Now a pound bearing $3\frac{1}{4}$ per cent. compound interest, becomes in thirty years 2·61 pounds, so that the 9 per cent. of seignorage will have multiplied to 23·5 per cent. But the actual deficiency of weight of the silver coin withdrawn is, on the average, only $16\frac{1}{2}$ per cent., so that, without taking into account the considerable number of coins which must be lost, exported, melted, hoarded, sunk in the sea, or otherwise finally withdrawn from circulation, there is a profit on the issue of the silver coin under the present regulations.

In the issue of bronze money there has been, as before stated, a profit of £270,000, against which must be set off the possible, but uncertain, cost of recoining a light token currency at some future time.

The cost of the currency is made up of four principal items: the loss of interest upon the capital invested in the money, the loss by the abrasion of gold coins, the expenses of the mint, and lastly the casual loss of coins. The last item is of wholly unknown amount; the other items may be estimated as follows. We may, roughly speaking, assume the gold currency of the kingdom to consist of 84,000,000 of sovereigns and 32,000,000 of half-sovereigns, the total value being 100,000,000 sterling. The sovereigns lose annually on the average 0·043 grain each, giving an annual loss of about £30,000; the half-sovereigns lose 0·069 grain each, producing a loss of £18,000. The loss of interest, however, is a far more serious matter. The whole value of the metals employed in the currency is, roughly speaking, as follows:—

TECHNICAL MATTERS RELATING TO COINAGE. 165

Gold coin in circulation . . . . . 100 millions
Bullion in the Bank of England . . 15 ,,
Silver coin . . . . 15 ,,
Bronze coin . . . . 1⅛ ,,

            Total . . . . 131⅛ millions.

The interest on this sum at $3\frac{1}{4}$ per cent is no less than £4,262,000.

The cost of the mint establishment is about £42,000 annually. The following statement, then, shows the aggregate cost of the metallic currency so far as it can be estimated.

Loss of interest £4,262,000
Wear of coin   48,000
Mint establishment   42,000

                                    £4,352,000

From this amount ought to be subtracted the profit which the mint makes out of the seignorage upon silver and bronze coins; but we may set off this profit against the wholly unknown amount which the public loses by the accidental dropping of coins.

CHAPTER XIV.

INTERNATIONAL MONEY.

In a book upon money written in the present day, reference must certainly be made to the scheme put forward, and even the steps accomplished, towards a world-wide system of International Money. Much time will no doubt pass before such a notion is realized, and the recent retrograde action of the German government tends to retard so great an achievement of advancing civilization. Yet in all our changes and discussions of monetary matters we ought to bear in mind the eventual introduction of a uniform monetary system. We may surely look for a gradual amelioration in the relations of nations, though wars cannot yet be avoided. We have international copyright, extradition of criminals, maritime codes of signals, postal conventions, treaties for lessening the horrors of war. Nations have long since ceased to be isolated bodies wishing evil to all their neighbours; and as free trade becomes everywhere predominant, and communication by means of railway, steamboat, telegraph, post, and newspaper continually increases, we may look for the time when all people will seek to break down, as far as possible, the barriers between one family and another of the human race.

I will first of all state the advantages which may be expected to accrue from an international system of metallic money, and will then describe in succession the corresponding possible disadvantages, the progress which has already been made towards the simplification of monetary systems, the principal schemes set forth, and their comparative merits and demerits.

Advantages of International Money.

Short-sighted people have objected to all schemes of international money, that the object in view, if ever realized, would only save trouble to the comparatively few people who travel from nation to nation. This is the least of all the benefits which the uniformity of money would confer. I am disposed to put in the first place the immense good which would arise from facility in understanding all statements of accounts, prices, and statistics, when expressed in terms of a uniform measure of value. To the statistician it is almost intolerable to meet with tables of information, variously expressed in francs, pounds, dollars, thalers, metres, yards, ells, hundredweights, kilograms. The labour of statistical inquiry is sufficiently great without the preliminary labour of reducing great masses of figures to a common unit. To the merchant, or man of business, the variety of moneys and measures is equally perplexing. In many places the value of the currency is not certainly known, and only those who happen to have special knowledge of a locality, and the money and measures there employed, can venture to trade with it. The difference of monetary systems, again, renders calculations relating to the foreign exchanges very complex, so that profit falls to those who have acquired skill in calculations of the kind.

In the second place, the actual adjustment of the foreign exchanges would be rendered more prompt and perfect when the coin of one country could be transferred directly into the circulation of another country. One result of international currency would be that the precious metals would be held more in the form of coin. At the present time, what is coined by one country has often to be melted up and recoined by another, although to some extent the principal kinds of coin, English sovereigns, American eagles, French napoleons, Mexican dollars, are held by banks and bought and sold. With a single system of coins, all stocks of gold and silver would, as a general rule, be kept in the coined state, ready to go into circulation at any moment. Some small savings would accrue from the less amount of mintage required, though this is a very secondary matter. One of more importance is the lessened opportunities of profit which there would be for bullion brokers and others, who trade upon the difficulties of conducting the bullion traffic in the present state of things. Nor is the saving of trouble and loss to travellers a matter of indifference. As international communication increases, the number of travellers will increase, and we ought to break down, as far as possible, all factitious difficulties.

One benefit of international money which has been insufficiently noticed, is the improvement which its adoption would probably effect in the currencies of minor and half-civilized states. In many parts of the world there is still a mixture of coins of various and uncertain value; and as long as the principal nations coin money on totally different systems, the coins will circulate elsewhere and make confusion. Already for a long time the practically international currency of the Mexican dollar has been a matter of great convenience; and where it is the unit of value, merchants know on what basis they are making contracts. Now, if all the leading nations combined to issue coins of one uniform series of weight and sizes, these would by degrees form the currencies of non-coining states, and would effect a reform in the most remote parts of the world.

Disadvantages of International Money.

There are, no doubt, certain evils which might possibly arise from the circulation of money between nation and nation. One government, for instance, might coin money slightly inferior to the proper standard, and such money, once introduced, would, in virtue of Gresham's law, be difficult to dislodge. The French mint has been in fault in this respect. French gold coin, when carefully assayed, is found to have a fineness of 898 or 899 parts in 1000, instead of 900 parts. There is, indeed, a mint remedy of two parts, so that the coin was legally issued; yet the mint authorities have taken advantage of this remedy in an improper way. On the average, the coins issued by any mint ought to have almost the exact standard fineness, and the divergence allowed under the name of remedy is only intended to cover accidental faults of workmanship in particular coins, and not an intentional average divergence from the standard.

It is hardly to be supposed that a state issuing money under international obligations would wish to make a profit of one or two parts in a thousand in this way. To secure uniformity, it would be desirable for the assayers and officers of different mints to meet and agree upon a common standard process, and uniform trial plates. Experience does not show that one nation need distrust the faithfulness of another in matters of coining. We do not look upon Spain and Mexico as models of financial integrity, yet so faithfully used the mints of those countries to maintain the standard of weight and fineness in the issue of silver dollars, that these coins have for a hundred years past been received by tale almost without question in most parts of the world, and were at one time made current in England. The possibility of international currency is proved by the fact that, without any international treaties, the coins of several nations are recognized as a legal tender elsewhere. This is the case with English sovereigns, not only in the British colonies and possessions, but also in Portugal, Egypt, Brazil, and probably elsewhere. The napoleon has circulated freely in most parts of Europe. The ducat of Holland has also been a highly esteemed coin; and of the wide circulation of several species of dollars I have frequently spoken.

Conflict of Monetary Systems.

The chief difficulty in establishing an international money, arises from the fact that there are several great nations, the French, English, Americans, and Germans, each with its own system of money, which, from motives worthy and unworthy, it is unwilling to give up. There is no overpowering advantage which marks out any one of these systems on its own merits as distinctly the best. There is accordingly a balance of power which produces a dead lock. Each of the three first-named nations has much to say in favour of its own system. The French system, founded on the franc, is an eminently perfect decimal coinage, and has the prestige of being recognized as international money in Belgium, Switzerland, and Italy, besides being adopted with international currency as regards gold in Austria, and without it as regards silver in Spain, Greece, and some minor states.

The English may very properly urge that, though the subdivision of the pound is not to be recommended, the pound sterling is itself an excellent unit of value. It is the largest existing monetary unit, and on a gold basis, so that it seems to be peculiarly suitable for the growing wealth of nations. Though recognized only in a small corner of Europe, namely, Portugal, we must remember that Europe is rapidly ceasing to be the exclusive centre of trade and civilization. In the Australian, Polynesian, and African colonies are growing states which will make their might felt ere long, and they adhere to the pound. The world-wide extension of British commerce and British shipping makes the sovereign known in all the ports of the world.

On their part, however, the Americans might have much to say in favour of the dollar. It is decimally divided, and, as we shall see, in the most convenient manner. It corresponds to the coins which have for two or three centuries been most widely circulated and treated as units of account, so that there is much weight of experience in its favour. But, above all, it is firmly adopted as the money of a nation, which, as far as human wisdom can penetrate the future, is destined to be the most numerous, rich, and powerful in the world. That nation, which has arisen from the best stock of England, has absorbed much of the best blood of other European nations, and has inherited the richest continent in the world, must have an importance in coming times of which even Americans are barely conscious.

International Monetary Negotiations.

It is quite impossible that I should in this brief work give any sufficient sketch of the long series of discussions, meetings, congresses, associations, negotiations, and conventions which resulted in the actual establishment of an international money among the nations of western continental Europe. I must refer the reader, desirous of more information, to the excellent pamphlet of the eminent actuary, Mr. Frederick Hendriks, which first made the subject well known in England. It is called "Decimal Coinage; a Plan for its immediate Extension in England in connection with the International Coinage of France and other Countries," and was privately printed in 1866. Mr. Seyd's "Treatise on Bullion and the Foreign Exchanges" may also be consulted, and the *Journal des Economistes* is full of information on the subject.

The International Association for obtaining a Uniform Decimal System of Measures, Weights, and Coins, was founded in Paris in 1855, and the English branch carried on active operations. In 1858 the United States made proposals towards the assimilation of currencies. In 1860 and 1863 important international congresses were held at London and Berlin, and, at the latter one especially, important resolutions were adopted which we shall have to consider. It was, however, the close contiguity of the countries, Belgium, France, Switzerland, and Italy, and the fact that French gold, and even silver coin, could not be prevented from passing the frontiers, which forced the question forwards, and led in December, 1865, to an actual Convention for International Currency.

The report of the Congress of 1863 concerning currency is a highly important document. It points out the superior convenience of a gold standard, with a subsidiary coinage of silver and bronze; advocates uniform fineness of nine parts in ten for all standard coins; suggests a definition of weights of coins, on the metric system; and, finally, propounds a scheme by which the existing monetary units could be brought into simple relations with each other.

In 1870, a short time previous to the declaration of

war with Germany, France summoned a fresh Imperial Commission, presided over by the Minister of Commerce and the Minister President of the Council of State (M. de Parieu), to take evidence from all sides on the various questions connected with the standard and its bearing upon international coinage. No less than thirty-seven witnesses were examined, and the results of the inquiry, printed by the French government in two very large volumes in 1872, show that the majority of the witnesses and of the Commissioners were decidedly in favour of a single gold standard.

Owing to a purely accidental coincidence, the principal monetary units already closely approximate to simple multiples of the franc. The following table shows the present relative values of these units and the multiples to which it is proposed to make them exactly conform.

	Present value in francs.	Proposed value in francs
Franc	1	1
Florin (Austrian, silver)	2·47	2½
Dollar (American, gold)	5·18	5
Pound sterling . . .	25·22	25

It is only requisite to raise the florin 1·21 per cent., and to lower the dollar and pound sterling respectively 3·5 and 0·88 per cent., to establish very simple ratios between them. Thus, without any appreciable change of monetary systems, it would be possible to reduce statements from one mode of expression into another; moreover, the coins might themselves have international currency, the pound sterling serving as a twenty-five franc piece in France, and as a five-dollar piece in America, the American gold dollar reciprocally circulating as an écu in France, and a four-shilling piece in England.

The congress abstained from recommending any one unit for universal adoption, but urged that every nation, not possessing one of the four units named, should select that which pleased them best. Had this scheme been accepted by all nations in an intelligent and liberal spirit, we should ere now have probably seen our way clearly to the selection of the best unit. Since 1865, unfortunately, both the German empire and the Scandinavian kingdoms have made alterations not in accordance with these principles. A great assimilation of moneys has taken place, but it is in the direction of groups of national, rather than of international currencies, although, as has been demonstrated by Mr. Hendriks in several articles in the *Economist*, the new coins have many fresh and important points of contact and of agreement with the metrical and decimal systems, so that some real progress has actually been accomplished.

Decimalization of English Money.

Since Lord Wrottesley in 1824 proposed in parliament to adopt a decimal subdivision of the pound sterling, an immense amount of discussion has taken place upon various schemes for a new arrangement of our money. The advantages of several plans are so nearly balanced, and the difficulty of carrying any one into effect is so great, that no practical result has yet been achieved by half a century of debate. The two principal schemes, which perhaps need alone be noticed now, are the *Pound and Mil* scheme, and the *Penny and Ten-franc* scheme.

The former of these schemes reposes upon the fact that the farthing is nearly the thousandth part of the pound. Since 960 farthings make a pound, it would only be necessary to alter the farthing 4 per cent. to obtain the lowest decimal submultiple, to be called the *mil*. The penny would be five mils, like the French halfpenny or five centimes; as some have supposed, a new coin, in value 2·4d., would have to be introduced, as the hundredth part of the pound; but this is unnecessary, and the florin would be one hundred mils, and the half-sovereign five hundred mils. The great advantage of this method is, that it retains the pound as the principal unit, together with several other familiar coins. Against it has been urged, (1) the supposed fact that it excludes the most familiar of all coins, the shilling and sixpence, and (2) that the mil is somewhat too small a submultiple to begin with. This is, however, not necessarily the case. The shilling might remain, as coin of circulation, of the same weight, fineness, and value as at present, but would be translated, as coin of account, into fifty mils instead of forty-eight farthings, and the sixpence into twenty-five mils instead of twenty-four farthings. This subdivision is not more complex than the one successfully, and in the almost parallel forms of fifty and twenty *pfennige, centimes, lire, öre*, etc., pieces, carried out in the new coinages of Germany, Scandinavia, or of the monetary allies of France. As to the mil being too small a submultiple, it seems to be overlooked that it is $2\frac{1}{2}$ times as large as the initial submultiple of the French system, and $2\frac{1}{25}$ times as large as that of the new German system.

The second scheme was suggested by the late Professor Graham, and by Mr. Rivers Wilson, in their Report upon the Proceedings of the International Monetary Conference of 1867. It is founded upon the fact that the ten-franc piece is within $\frac{3}{4}d.$ of eight shillings, and only differs 4 per cent. from one hundred pence. Thus it would only be requisite to introduce a gold piece of ten francs, temporarily serving as a token for eight shillings, to obtain a link with the French system. The subsequent reduction of the penny by 4 per cent., and the replacement of the shilling by a franc or tenpenny-piece, would give us a truly decimal system. A great advantage of this proposal is, that it retains, almost unaltered, so familiar a coin as the penny, and makes it, as it is for the most part at present, the lowest money of account. It is, moreover, in close accordance with the French monetary system. The main difficulty is that it involves the abandonment of the pound, which becomes two and a half of the new unit; and that, of all our present coins, only the florin, penny, and halfpenny, would fall in conveniently. To convert sums of money from pounds sterling into the new currency, it would be requisite to multiply by the factor $2\frac{1}{2}$, which would be regarded by most people as a very troublesome process.

When the decimalization of English money was first proposed, the notion of international money had never been seriously entertained, and hardly indeed conceived. So much progress has now been made, that it is impossible to consider the one reform without reference to the other. The difficulty of making any change whatever is so great, that it would not be worth while to achieve a partial reform.

The Future American Dollar.

The most easy and important step which can now be taken towards an international money, consists in the assimilation of the American dollar to the five-franc piece. A great opportunity arises from the fact that the currency of the United States is now a variable paper currency. Considering the enormous fluctuations of value which have been experienced in the last ten years, it would be altogether needless scrupulosity to bring it back to the old standard, to the last degree of exactness. Every change of value of the currency, whether it be a fall or a rise, is so far injurious. Now the American dollar consists of 25·8 grains of gold, valued in English money at 49·316 pence. When gold is at 111 the paper dollar will be at a discount of 10 per cent., and will therefore be worth 44·384 pence, whereas the French dollar, or five-franc gold piece, weighs 24·89 grains, and is worth 47·58 pence. It would be obviously desirable, therefore, to make the new metallic dollar exactly of the same weight as the French one, and to commence specie payments when the greenback currency shall have risen to par with this coin. As regards all contracts made in paper, all current prices and charges, this change would involve no breach of faith whatever; it would in fact imply less change and breach of contracts than if the paper currency were reduced sufficiently to come to par with the old dollar.

The reduction of weight of the dollar would indeed lead to a repudiation of all gold contracts, including all bonds of the United States, railway companies, and other bodies payable in coin, unless provision were made to alter the terms of such contracts. This difficulty, however, could be overcome by simply enacting that each $103\frac{1}{2}$ of the new dollars shall be received and paid as equivalent to 100 of the old ones.

There is little doubt that the adhesion of the American government to the proposals of the Congress of 1863 would give the holding turn to the metric system of weights, measures, and moneys. It is quite likely that it might render the dollar the future universal unit. The fact that the dollar is already the monetary unit of many parts of the world, gives it large odds. In becoming assimilated to the French écu, American gold would be capable of circulation in Europe, or wherever the French napoleon has hitherto been accepted. It may seem unpatriotic in an Englishman to advocate a change which may lead to the defeat of the pound sterling, but I look upon any one scheme of unification as better than none. Whatever may be the ultimate results, I desire to see assimilation between the French and American systems adopted as soon as possible. For reasons subsequently stated, I consider the dollar so good a unit that it would be mere national prejudice to oppose it, were there a fair chance of its general adoption. Even if it were not generally adopted, it would be a great step in advance if Great Britain, America, and France were to agree to coin gold money identical in weight and fineness, which might circulate indifferently as sovereigns, five-dollar pieces, and twenty-five-franc pieces.

German Monetary Reform.

The new monetary system of the German empire is introducing a good money where all was before confusion. In a few years it will hardly be comprehensible to Germans that they had so long endured a state of the currency in which two, or even three or four, inconsistent series of coins were mingled without any method. In many respects the new system is all that could be desired. In place of the antiquated silver standard, gold is selected as the measure of value, the sole principal money, and unlimited legal tender. The unit of account is the mark, consisting of 6·1465 grains of gold of the fineness of 9 parts in 10. Its value is, therefore, about $11\frac{3}{4}d$. The principal coin will be the twenty-mark piece, weighing 122·92 grains, or 7·964954 grams, and containing 7·168459 grams of pure gold. There is also a ten-mark piece of exactly half the weight.

The subordinate coins of silver and nickel-copper are issued on the footing of the composite tender, or English system, being tokens. The seignorage to be levied on the German silver coins, will be 11·111 per cent., exceeding the amounts subtracted from the English and French silver money, which are about 9 and 7·784 per cent. respectively.

It cannot be too much regretted by all friends of progress that, in deciding upon the weight of the new mark piece, the German government should have studiously avoided assimilation to the French system. The sovereign contains 7·3224 grams of pure gold, the twenty-five-franc piece when coined will contain 7·2581, and the twenty-mark piece has been made to contain 7·1685. The only ground on which this precise weight could have been justified, is that three marks are approximately equal to one thaler. But so various was the coinage of the German states, that the field was open to the adoption of any system; and it is impossible to suppose that in so great a reform a difference of $1\frac{1}{4}$ per cent. would have been an insuperable obstacle to the adoption of international coinage.

Systems of Fractional Money.

A unit of value having been chosen, there are three competing methods according to which it might be subdivided, the *binary*, *duodecimal*, and *decimal*. The first system is carried out most perfectly in our avoirdupois weights, in which sixteen ounces make a pound;

but it is also freely employed in our monetary system, the sovereign being divided into half-sovereigns, crowns, and half-crowns, the shilling into sixpences and threepenny pieces; and the penny into halfpence and farthings. At the same time, the duodecimal method is represented in our money by the division of the shilling into twelve pence, of which the third part is still in circulation as the groat, or fourpenny piece, now being withdrawn.

Each system of subdivision has its own advantages, and there must always exist a kind of natural competition between them. They have thus competed from the earliest times. In ancient Italy the duodecimal system predominated to the south of the Apennines, while the decimal divison was in use to the northward. In Sicily the two methods were confused together. China has had a purely decimal system from an unknown epoch in antiquity. In England duodecimal and binary divisions have existed from very early times. It will be readily allowed that the binary system is most simple and natural, involving as it does the least possible factor above unity. The duodecimal system also has marked advantages, because it allows of division into several aliquot parts, involving the factor 2 twice over, and the next higher factor 3 once. Thus the shilling is divisible exactly into two sixpences, three fourpences, four threepences, and six twopences.

The decimal system is far less simple, and in some ways less convenient. Ten admits of only two factors superior to unity, namely, 2 and 5, and 5 is a more complex prime factor than appears in either of the previous methods. But the system has the supreme advantage of exactly falling in with our decimal system of numeration and calculation. Although probably not the best method which might have been selected, had selection been open to us, decimal numeration is firmly fixed among the institutions of the human race, as an hereditary habit, derived from the early practice of counting on the fingers. We have no choice but to accept the inevitable, and as all our arithmetical processes are conducted on the decimal method, there is an overwhelming advantage, as education and the use of writing advance, in making all our weights, measures, and coins conformable to the same system.

A perfectly and purely decimal system, indeed, would admit only the decimal multiples and submultiples, thus:—1000, 100, 10, 1, 0·1, 0·01, 0·001. But it is so troublesome to have to count out as many as ten coins, before coming to the next higher unit, that the rigour of the decimal divisions has always been relaxed. In the French system, the half and the double of each multiple are allowed to be represented by intermediate coins, the series being 1, 2, 5, 10, 20, 50, 100, 200, 500, etc. The American coinage is less simple and symmetrical, since it admits the half and quarter eagle, half and quarter dollar, the ten and five-cent pieces, and also a three-cent piece. I am inclined to prefer the French method, and to think that the American mint has issued too many denominations of coins.

Final Selection of the Unit of International Money.

I will conclude this chapter by some remarks on the reasons which should guide us in selecting the monetary unit to be finally established as the basis of a future universal money.

I attribute very little weight to arguments concerning the absolute amount of the rival units. It is said that as the wealth of nations increases, and the value of gold at the same time sinks, we need a larger unit. The pound is recommended on this ground as clearly superior to the franc. If we count in francs our figures will be twenty-five times as large as in pounds sterling. It seems to be forgotten that the same unit can never suit the extremely different sums which we have to express, so that we must use multiples or submultiples of the actual unit. Just as we use inches, feet, yards, furlongs, miles, or diameters of the earth's orbit, according to the magnitudes to be measured, so we vary the unit with money. If we are discussing a workman's weekly wages, we count in shillings; if we speak of a clerk's yearly salary, we speak of pounds; if the fortune of a merchant or banker is in question, we take notice only of thousands of pounds; in matters relating to the revenue of the kingdom or the national debt, we give our exclusive attention to millions of pounds. The Portuguese unit of account, called the *rei*, is worth only about the nineteenth part of an English penny, and is probably the smallest unit in the world. Practically, however, the milreis, or thousand reis, worth $53\frac{1}{3}d.$, becomes the unit. In the same way Indian merchants speak of lacs and crores of rupees. The French estimate their national debt in milliards of francs. No doubt it is puzzling to Englishmen to interpret exactly the meaning of a milliard of francs, but, to those accustomed to count in francs it is no more difficult than a million of pounds. Exactly the same considerations apply to units of weight; thus, though the French use so small an ultimate unit as one gram, or 15·43 grains, yet according to the magnitudes of the objects to be weighed, they use smaller or larger units, centigrams or milligrams on the one side, or decagrams and kilograms on the other. The absolute amount then of the ultimate unit seems to me to be entirely a matter of indifference in this point of view.

As regards the subdivision of the unit there are considerations of more importance. The subdivision ought of course to be decimal, and it ought to be so contrived that the lowest submultiple shall correspond to the smallest sum which is thought worthy of being recorded in mercantile transactions. Now the franc is divided into 100 centimes, so that the centime has a value of less than the tenth of a penny. Though bronze pieces of one and two centimes were coined to the amount of about 5 per cent. of the whole bronze currency, it is found that they hardly circulate. Even if they were used in the smallest retail transactions at baker's shops, they would not be entered in account books. Thus the lowest entry which a French accountant makes is five centimes, and the next lowest ten centimes, corresponding to our penny. A needless complexity is thus introduced into small accounts. It is indeed so inconvenient to have to call the smallest coin in general use *cinq centimes* that it is still common to speak of it as a *sou*, in spite of the ninety years during which the decimal system has existed in France. The Portuguese rei is so small a unit that it is not represented by any coin at all. It nevertheless has a place in Portuguese mercantile accounts, and thus needlessly adds a figure to all pecuniary statements.

In England the smallest coin in actual use is the farthing, but in accounts little notice is taken of farthings or halfpennies, so that the penny is the lowest money of account. The post-office, in the regulations of the savings bank business, refuses to recognize any coin less than the penny. But the penny is inconveniently related to the pound, the hundredth part of which is 2·4*d*., and the thousandth part about a farthing. Thus the decimal system applied to our pound would oblige us to record as the lowest money of account an inconveniently small coin, namely, the *mil*. In this respect, indeed, the pound and mil scheme is superior to the franc and centime system. Thus 12*s*. 6*d*. may be expressed as 625 mils; but in French money (at twenty-five francs to the pound) it would become 15·625. Taking the ten-franc piece as the principal unit, it would become 1·56 units, or 156 metrical pennies. In many cases it would require less figures to express a sum in pennies than in mils or centimes.

The American system is unexceptionable in this

respect. The dollar is divided into one hundred cents, each of which has the value of about one halfpenny. Although half-cents have been coined, and may be used in some trifling purchases, they need never be entered in ordinary accounts. The cent thus seems to me to correspond to the smallest sum which need be treated in accounts, so that money statements are reduced to the greatest possible simplicity. The question may well be asked whether the lowest coin actually recorded is not truly the unit, of which all other coins are multiples. Perhaps the best answer would be to say that the unit is indifferently the cent, or the dollar, or the eagle. In English money it matters not whether we regard the pound, or its twentieth part, or its two hundred and fortieth part, as the unit. The absolute amount of the unit, I repeat, is totally a matter of indifference, and the only point we have to consider is whether it, or any decimal part of it, corresponds to the smallest sum of which we need take account. In this respect the dollar is the best existing unit; but it might admit of discussion whether the double dollar, or ten-franc piece of gold, equal to eight shillings, or one hundred pence, would not be better. If the wealth of nations continues to grow, and the value of gold to fall, even the cent will be too small a coin to appear conveniently in accounts, and the penny will be a better lowest unit. In this case the hundred pennies, or the ten-franc piece, would become the best unit. The choice thus seems to me to lie between the five-franc and the ten-franc piece in gold as the ultimate unit of international money. In favour of the ten-franc piece it may be added, that it would make a convenient gold coin of the smallest size which it would be well to issue. The gold dollar and five-franc piece are too small, and suffer great abrasion.

CHAPTER XV.

THE MECHANISM OF EXCHANGE.

Having now sufficiently discussed the subject of metallic money, we pass on to consider the devices which naturally develop themselves in a highly organized commercial nation, for the purpose of economizing the precious metals, or even avoiding the use of coins altogether. No sooner have a people fully experienced the usefulness of a good system of money, than they begin to discover that they can dispense with it as a medium of exchange, and return to a method of traffic closely resembling barter. With barter they begin and with barter they end; but the second form of barter, as we shall see, is very different from the first. Purchases and sales continue to be made in terms of gold and silver coin, but equivalent quantities of goods thus estimated are made to pay for each other. If ownership in gold or silver intervenes at all, it is in the shape of *warrants* or *representative documents* with which gold can be procured, if desired, but which are seldom used to procure it.

At the outset we found that money performed at least two, and probably four distinct functions (Chapter III.);

and, in a simple state of industry, it is convenient that the same metallic substance should fulfil all these functions concurrently. But it does not follow that this union of functions is the best possible arrangement under all conditions. We shall find that gold or silver always continues to be the common denominator of value, but that these metals cease to a great extent to be the actual medium of exchange which is passed about between buyer and seller. In a later part of the book (Chapter XXV.) I shall further show that money may with great advantage be replaced in its function as a standard of value for long periods of time by a *Tabular Standard*.

Progressive Development of the Methods of Exchange.

Beginning with the primitive method of barter, a series of steps have been made towards a perfect and world-wide system of interchange of commodities, with the least possible use of the precious metals. We may classify the devices employed for avoiding the use of metallic money under five different heads, as follows :—

1. Replacement of standard money by representative money.
2. Intervention of book credit.
3. The cheque and clearing system.
4. Use of foreign bills of exchange.
5. International clearing system.

Representative Money.

Metallic money, as we have seen, immensely facilitates and, so to speak, lubricates the operation of exchange. But nations employing gold and silver money have usually discovered, in the course of time, that tokens of small metallic value, or even pieces of leather and paper of nominal value, might be passed from hand to hand as signs of the ownership of coins. That which replaces gold, or silver, or copper money, is at first of a purely representative character. But, when a community has become thoroughly habituated to the circulation of a currency of this character, it is often found possible to remove the basis of valuable metal, which it is supposed to represent, and yet to maintain the valueless bits of leather or paper in circulation as before. Thus arises the abnormal phenomenon known as an *inconvertible paper money*. Such a currency is, however, never accepted beyond the frontiers of the state recognizing it.

Merchants conducting large international transactions soon found out that great loss of interest and risk of loss of the whole money would arise, if they were to trade with actual specie. Hence they introduced the use, many centuries since, of *bills of exchange*, which are signs or certificates of debt, passed from hand to hand almost like representative money, and often accomplishing many acts of exchange by a single transfer of specie.

Cheque and Clearing System.

There is yet a more potent way of avoiding the actual use of a medium of exchange, without encountering any of the inconveniences of barter. Those who frequently traded with each other, both buying and selling, found that it was absurd to pay a sum of money for what was bought, and then receive it back for what was sold. It was sufficient to estimate in terms of money the values of the articles exchanged, and then pay the difference, if any, in actual cash. The practice having grown up of depositing the metallic money not immediately wanted with goldsmiths or bankers, for safe custody, it was gradually discovered that an order to pay money would serve instead of the money; and that, if two persons trade with the same banker, they need not in their mutual transactions handle the money at all. A transfer in the books of their common bankers will effect the payment of any balance of debt. Bankers can in like manner arrange their mutual accounts, and in this way there has been gradually developed in this country and in America a vast system, which I propose to denominate the *Cheque and Clearing System*, whereby all the larger internal transactions of the people are arranged by a mere settlement of accounts.

In this system London naturally becomes the monetary centre of the United Kingdom; but there is a further tendency to make London the banking centre of the world as regards all large and international transactions. It is found to be advantageous to deposit money in

London, or to obtain credit and make bills payable there, rather than elsewhere. By such a concentration of banking operations, London tends to become the seat of a *world-wide Clearing House*. Such are the principal steps in the development of the mechanism of exchange, and we proceed to consider them in detail.

CHAPTER XVI.

REPRESENTATIVE MONEY.

ALTHOUGH we now distinguish money according as it is metallic or paper money, because paper has in recent times been universally adopted as the material for representative money, yet it is well to remember that various other substances have been used for the purpose. We may pass, in fact, by gradual steps from the perfect standard coins, whose nominal value is coincident with their metallic value, to worthless bits of paper, which are yet allowed to stand for thousands, or even millions of pounds sterling.

Token money, which we considered in Chapter VIII. (p. 67), is in some degree representative money, because it derives its value, not so much from the metal it contains as from the standard coins for which it can be exchanged. There is no need that a promise should be always expressed by ink and paper. It may be still more durably recorded by a die upon a piece of metal. Accordingly, while the monarchs of England down to the end of Elizabeth's reign refused to debase their currency, as the notion seems to have been, by issuing such a poor metal as copper, the tradesmen supplied the want of pence by issuing tokens. These pieces were in the earlier centuries composed of lead, or latten, a kind of brass, or sometimes, it is believed, of leather. During the last century, again, they were issued in large quantities, chiefly in copper, and often bore an express statement that they served as promissory notes. Thus a well-executed piece, issued at Southampton in 1791, bears the inscription, "Halfpenny Promissory, payable at the Office of W. Taylor, R. V. Moody & Co." A token struck by the Flint lead works in 1813, states the promise in different terms, thus—"One Penny Token, One Pound Note for 240 Tokens." The variety of such promissory coins issued at one time or other is very great, and their study forms an important branch of numismatic science, as will be learnt by looking into such a work as Akerman's "London Tradesmen's Tokens." In quite recent years small money was found to be scarce in New South Wales, and some tradesmen issued copper or bronze tokens which circulated until the year 1870, when their further use was prohibited.

The ancients were well acquainted with the difference between a standard and a token currency. The iron money of the Lacedæmonians was probably standard legal tender, for it is described as being heavy and bulky, and yet of small value. The iron money of the Byzantines, on the contrary, was token representative money. We shall find in the following section that pieces of money of the same nature as bank-notes were also employed by several ancient nations.

Early History of Representative Money.

Ancient nations were unacquainted with the use of paper money, simply because they had no paper. But it would be a mistake to suppose that they did not employ representative money exactly on the same principles as we use bank-notes. Some few particulars on the subject have long been known, but a recent article by M. Bernardakis in the *Journal des Economistes* (vol. xxxiii. pp. 353-370) has added much to our knowledge, and made it quite clear that the ancients were more acute in matters of currency than we have given them credit for.

One of the very earliest mediums of exchange, as we have seen (p. 20), consisted of the skins of animals. The earliest form of representative money consisted of small pieces of leather, usually marked with an official seal. It is a very reasonable suggestion made by Storch, Bernardakis, and other writers, that when skins and furs began to be found an inconveniently bulky kind of money, small pieces were clipped off, and handed over as tokens of possession. By fitting into the place from which they were cut they would prove ownership, something in the same way that notched sticks, or tallies, were for many centuries used to record loans of money to the English Exchequer. We know by experience in the case of paper money, that if a people had become thoroughly accustomed to the circulation of these small leather tallies, they would in time forget their representative character, and continue to circulate them, when the government, or other holders of the skins themselves, had made away with the actual property. Such is no doubt the history of the leather money which long had currency in Russia.

It is impossible to ascertain what was the character of the leather money which, according to an obscure tradition, was in use at Rome before the time of Numa. There is no doubt that the Carthaginians had a representative leather currency, for Æschines the Socratic tells us that they used small pieces of leather wrapped round cores of unknown material, and then sealed up. Neighbouring nations refused to receive these curious pieces of currency, whence we may safely infer that their value was nominal.

It is however in China that the use of paper money was most fully developed in early times. More than a century before the Christian era, an emperor of China raised funds to prosecute his wars in a way which shows that the use of leather tokens was familiar to the people. The tokens having been made of the skins of white deer, he collected together into a park all deer of this colour which he could find, and prohibited his subjects from possessing any animals of the same kind. Having thus obtained a monopoly of the material, reminding one of the monopoly of the Bank of England in watermarked paper, he issued pieces of the white leather as money at a high rate.

In the middle of the thirteenth century, Marco Polo found a paper money in circulation in China, composed of the inner bark of a tree beaten up and made into paper, square pieces of which were signed and sealed with great formality. These notes were of various values, and were legal tender, death being the penalty imposed upon those who refused to receive them. Counterfeiters likewise incurred the same penalty. Another traveller, who visited China in the fourteenth century, gives a very similar account of the paper money then circulating, and adds that, when worn or torn, it could be exchanged for new notes without charge. It is needless to follow out the long and doubtful history of the subject in later times, many particulars of which will be found in the article of M. Bernardakis, or that of M. Courcelle-Seneuil on Papier Monnaie in the "Dictionnaire de l'Economie Politique." It may suffice to say that the history resembles that of most inconvertible currencies. The quantity of paper afloat increased so much under the Mongol dynasty as to cause great evils, and the Ming dynasty, continuing the issues, went so far as to prohibit the use of gold or silver money. The value of the paper fell so low, it is said, that one metallic cash was worth a thousand paper cash, reminding us of the present state of the paper currency in San Domingo. The result was a collapse and reaction in the fifteenth century.

Among other Asiatic nations, the Tartars and the Persians also understood the use of paper money, and Sir John Maundeville, who travelled in Tartary in the fourteenth century, gives the following account of the advantages which the Great Chan enjoyed in consequence. " This Emperour may dispenden als moche as he wile, withouten estymacioun. For he despendethe not, ne makethe no money, but of Lether emprented, or of Papyre. And of that money, is som of gretter prys, and som of lasse prys, aftre the dyversitee of his Statutes. And whan that Money hathe ronne so longe that it begynnethe to waste, than men beren it to the Emperoure's Tresorye; and than thei taken newe money for the olde. And that Money gothe thorghe out alle the contree, and thorghe out alle his Provynces. For there and beyonde hem, thei make no Money nouther of Gold nor of Sylver. And therefore he may despende ynow, and outrageously." Not a few great emperors and kings and even republics have imitated the Great Chan, and have spent their paper money, " ynow and outrageously."

Reasons for the Use of Representative Money.

It is well to analyse and state exactly the reasons which may be given for the introduction of pieces of representative money. Several motives may be detected, and they have been of different weight in different cases. The origin of the European system of bank-notes is to be found in the deposit banks established in Italy from four to seven centuries ago. In those days the circulating medium consisted of a mixture of coins of many denominations, variously clipped or depreciated. In receiving money, the merchant had to weigh and estimate the fineness of each coin, and much trouble, loss of time, and risk of fraud thus arose. It became, therefore, the custom in the mercantile republics of Italy to deposit such money in a bank, where its value was accurately estimated, once for all, and placed to the credit of the depositor.

The banks of Amsterdam and Hamburg were subsequently established on a similar system, and a full account of them will be found in Adam Smith's " Wealth of Nations," Book IV., Chapter III., and in Hewitt's " Treatise upon Money " (p. 121). The money placed to the credit of individuals in these banks was called *bank-money*, and commanded an *agio* or premium corresponding to the average depreciation of the coins. Payments were made by the merchants attending at the bank at a particular hour, and ordering transfers to be made in the bank books. The money paid was thus always of full value, and all trouble in counting and valuing it was avoided. The regulations of these banks were, however, in many respects complicated, and it is difficult to understand their purpose.

Inconvenience of Metallic Money.

Closely involved with the previous motive for the use of representative money is that of avoiding the trouble and risk of handling large amounts of the precious metals. In order to keep large sums of metallic money in safety a person must have strongholds and watchmen. The origin of banking in England has never been sufficiently investigated, but, so far as we know, it arose for the purpose of safe custody. While public and well-regulated deposit banks had existed for centuries in Italy, the only trace of such an institution in England was found in the mint in the Tower of London, whither merchants were accustomed to send their specie for safe keeping. Unfortunately, in 1640 King Charles I. appropriated as a loan £200,000 thus deposited, and the merchants, no longer trusting the government, and finding it dangerous to keep large sums of money in their own houses during the troubled times which followed, resorted to the practice of depositing their money with goldsmiths, who probably had vaults and guards suitable for the purpose.

As acknowledgments of the possession of such sums of money, the goldsmith gave receipts, and at first these documents were special promises, like dock warrants. The practice arose of transferring possession by delivery of these receipts, or "goldsmith's notes," as they were called. Such notes are frequently referred to in Acts of Parliament, and even as late as 1746 most of the London bankers continued to be members of the Goldsmith's Company. It is plain from the manner in which these notes were mentioned in some statutes that they had become general and not special promises—mere engagements to deliver a sum of money on demand, without conditions as to keeping a reserve for the purpose.

The Weight of Currency.

Even the weight of metallic money would be a sufficient reason for the use of representative documents in large transactions. In proportion as the legal tender is more bulky and inconvenient to carry about, is this motive more powerful. Thus, when the state of Virginia employed tobacco as the medium of exchange in the eighteenth century, the tobacco was placed in stores, and receipts on paper were handed about. Paper money was issued in Russia under Catherine II. in 1768, on the ground that the copper money, then forming the legal tender, was inconvenient. So much were these *assignats*, or notes, preferred, that they at first circulated at a premium of $\frac{1}{4}$ per cent.

In the present state of commerce, even gold money would be far too heavy to form a convenient medium for making large payments. M. Chévalier states that it would require forty men to carry the gold equal in value to the Regent Diamond. The average daily transactions in the London Bankers' Clearing House amount to about twenty millions of pounds sterling, which if paid in gold coin would weigh about 157 tons, and would require nearly eighty horses for conveyance. If paid in silver the weight would be increased to more than 2500 tons. For the conveyance and custody of very moderate sums in coin or bullion, individuals, or even large banks, resort to the aid of the Bank of England, whose officials are experienced in the matter, and have all facilities.

I find that a Bank of England note weighs about 20½

grains (1⅓ grams), whereas a single sovereign weighs about 123 grains, and the note may represent five, ten, fifty, a thousand, or ten thousand such sovereigns with slight differences in the printing. If we were obliged to handle a medium of exchange actually embodying value, it would, ere now, have been necessary to employ precious stones, or some metal much more rare and precious than gold. But the use of representative documents is becoming so general in the most advanced commercial countries, that the portability of metallic money is a question of very minor importance. Gold already acts in England only as change for notes, and the question will arise whether it will long be needed even for that purpose.

Saving of Interest.

A further and very potent motive for employing representative tokens or notes, consists in the saving of interest and capital, which is effected by substituting a comparatively valueless material in place of costly gold and silver. Whenever a nation is in great straits for want of revenue, there is a great temptation to treat the metallic currency as a treasure to be temporarily borrowed for the necessities of the state. The ancient Greeks understood this as well as the modern English, Italians, or Americans. Dionysius, on this ground, obliged the Syracusans to accept tin tokens in place of silver coins, worth four times as much in metallic value. In the book on Economics, attributed to Aristotle, we are told that Timotheus the Athenian persuaded the soldiers and merchants to receive copper money in place of silver, promising to exchange it for silver coins at the close of the war. The Clazomenians made a similar issue of token money avowedly for the sake of the interest thereby saved. Being unable to pay twenty talents due to some mercenary troops, they were under the necessity of paying four talents a year as interest. They fell upon the device of coining iron tokens to the nominal amount of twenty talents, which they obliged the citizens to take in place of silver coin. The silver thus obtained was used for the immediate discharge of the debt, and there was a spare annual revenue of four talents, formerly absorbed in the payment of interest, which now enabled them in a few years to redeem the token money. Closely parallel to this is the case of the Guernsey Market, which was built without apparent cost. Daniel le Broc, the governor of the island, determined to build a market in St. Peters, but not having the necessary funds, issued under the seal of the island four thousand market notes for one pound each, with which he paid the artificers. When the market was finished and the rents came in, the notes were thereby cancelled, and not an ounce of gold was employed in the matter. There is, however, no mystery in this advantage of paper money.

Daniel le Broc, by issuing his market-notes, drove an equivalent amount of gold out of circulation, and thus effected a kind of forced loan out of the metallic currency of the island, without paying any interest for it. A similar gain of interest accrues upon all paper notes so far as their amount exceeds the gold held in readiness to pay them. The private and joint stock banks of issue in England in this way enjoy the interest upon a sum of about six millions and a half sterling, the Scotch banks upon two millions and three quarters, and the Irish banks upon more than six millions. The issue of paper representative money is beneficial to all parties, provided that it be conducted upon a sound method of regulation, a subject upon which the greatest differences of opinion exist.

CHAPTER XVII.

THE NATURE AND VARIETIES OF PROMISSORY NOTES.

Before attempting to come to any conclusion as to the best mode of regulating the issue of promissory notes, we must carefully analyse the differences which may exist between one promise and another. What seems at first sight a very slight and subtle distinction, may be found to lead to important results. He who issues a representative or promissory document, engaging to give a certain quantity of a defined commodity in return for the document when presented, may really make any one of three distinct engagements.

1. He may promise to keep a certain identical article in his possession until it is called for.

2. He may engage to have in his possession a certain amount of commodity ready to meet the promissory notes, without distinguishing between portion and portion of a similar substance.

3. The undertaking may be merely to the effect that the required commodity shall be forthcoming when the note is presented, no covenant being made as to the quantity to be held in stock for the purpose.

Specific Deposit Warrant.

The most satisfactory kind of promissory document is the first, which is represented by bills of lading, pawn-tickets, dock-warrants, or certificates which establish ownership to a definite object. A bill of lading entitles the legal holder of it to certain cases or packages of goods, described by marks, numbers, dimensions, or otherwise. The ship-master signing such a bill is obliged to retain the identical cases committed to his care, until he delivers them up in return for the bill of lading at the close of his voyage. Dock-warrants are of the same character, being receipts for packages of goods deposited in the London or other dock warehouses. The holder of a dock-warrant has a *prima faci*· claim to the pipes of wine, bales of wool, hogsheads of sugar, or other packages named thereon. Transfer of the warrant by endorsement or otherwise, as required by law and custom, is accounted a transfer of the ownership of the goods. The important point concerning such promissory notes is, that they cannot possibly be issued in excess of the goods actually deposited, unless by distinct fraud. The issuer ought to act purely as a warehouse-keeper, and as possession may be claimed at any time, he can never legally allow any object deposited to go out of his safe keeping until it is delivered back in exchange for the promissory note.

General Deposit Warrant.

We pass to the case in which the issuer of a promissory document engages to keep on hand goods exactly equivalent in quantity and quality to what are specified thereon, without taking note of individual parcels. In many cases commodities are so homogeneous that there seems to be no need to distinguish parcel from parcel, or to restore the identical portion deposited. Thus the keeper of a pig-iron store in Glasgow receives large quantities of pig iron, of several brands, and issues corresponding warrants representing ownership therein. As no difference, however, is known to exist between different portions of iron of the *same* brand, it was the practice in former years not to allot one heap of pigs to each warrant, but simply to retain a stock of each brand equal in weight to the aggregate amount due on outstanding warrants. More recently a better system has been introduced, and each specific lot of iron has been marked and set aside to meet some particular warrant. The difference seems to be slight, but it is really very important, as opening the way to a lax fulfilment of the contract. Misunderstandings occasionally arise upon this point in other trades. For instance, a cotton merchant in Liverpool, a few years since, obtained a loan of money upon the security of cotton in his possession, and a court of law was subsequently called upon to decide whether he had mortgaged certain individual bales of cotton, and undertaken to retain them until the loan was repaid, or whether he had merely engaged to have in his hands an equal quantity of cotton of the same quality. I have heard that carrying and warehousing companies are sometimes careless about distinction of parcel and parcel. If they are continually conveying or holding portions of exactly the same goods, flour from the same miller, coal from the same seam, they will sometimes deliver out the required quantity of the same sort of goods, irrespective of its being the identical portion delivered to them for conveyance or safe custody.

Difference between a Special and a General Promise.

The great importance of the distinctions pointed out in the last section will be easily apparent. He who has made a special promise to give definite parcels of goods in return for particular individual papers, cannot issue any such promissory papers without holding corresponding goods. If he does so, he will be continually liable to be convicted of fraud or default by the presentation of a particular document. If the promises made by him, however, are only general ones, any promissory document can be met by any portion of commodity of the proper quality, and it will be necessary to present most or all of the documents in order to disclose default. The way is thus opened for the speculative issue of promissory notes. The receiver of deposits, finding that a large portion of the deposited commodity always remains on hand, may proceed to use it in trade, only keeping so much as may meet current demands. So long as he does fulfil promises no harm seems to be done; but experience proves that there will always be a certain proportion of persons who, in such circumstances, will not act so discreetly as to be in a position to redeem all their engagements.

Moreover, it now becomes possible to create a fictitious supply of a commodity, that is, to make people believe that a supply exists which does not exist. The possessor of a promissory note or warrant regards the document as equivalent to the commodity named thereon. It is only necessary then to print off, fill up, and sign an additional number of such notes in order to have a corresponding supply of commodity to sell. It is true that the issue of promises involves their fulfilment at a future day; but the future is unknown, and the issuer may believe that before the fulfilment is likely to be demanded the price of the commodity will have fallen. Thus, if pig-iron warrants could be issued in unlimited quantities (irrespective of the stocks actually in the stores at Glasgow), an unscrupulous band of speculators might perhaps make large profits by selling great quantities of iron for future delivery. After suddenly and excessively depressing the price of pig-iron they might succeed in gradually buying up enough at lower prices to meet the warrants when presented. This kind of "bear" operations has certainly been successful in other markets.

About ten years ago it became the practice to rig the market as regards the shares of particular joint-stock banking companies. A party would be formed, perhaps owning none of the shares of the selected company, and they would proceed to sell considerable quantities of the shares, hoping so to damage the reputation of the company and lower the value of the stock as to be able to buy up enough before delivery would be required. This noxious kind of speculation was checked by an Act of Parliament (30 Victoria, c. 29, 1867), which now requires the seller of bank shares to specify the numbers or the registered proprietors of the shares which he is selling for future delivery.

It might be urged, indeed, that there is a natural right belonging to all persons to make promises, if they can thereby benefit themselves. Any one can accept a bill, thereby promising to deliver money at a future day. It is quite common to make contracts involving the delivery of government stock, or of cotton or corn expected to arrive by sea, before delivery becomes due. But we must remember that all laws and all social relations are devised to secure the greatest good of the the greatest number. If a right to make all promises be recognized by law, it must be because the right is beneficial to society, and it is the recognition by law which makes it a right. If, on the contrary, it be found by experience that freedom of making and selling promises in a particular way gives scope to illegitimate speculation, or otherwise injures society more than it produces benefit, the law ought certainly to restrict this freedom and regulate the matter for the good of the community. The whole matter, in short, is one of expediency. It used to be held as a general rule of law, that any present grant or assignment of goods not in existence is without operation. Though the rule seems to be generally disregarded, there are many cases in which it might be advantageously enforced.

Pecuniary Promissory Notes.

Applying these considerations to the special matter of money, we find that pecuniary promises are nearly always of a general kind. He who undertakes to pay a sum of money on a future day, rarely specifies the individual coins which will be paid. In fact the Coinage Act, in defining legal tender, makes any sovereigns, shillings, and pence, duly coined and of proper weight, a discharge for a corresponding sum named in a contract. It is true that just as pipes of wine are warehoused in the London docks, cases of gold and silver bullion or, it may be, of foreign or English coin, are warehoused in the vaults of the Bank of England. In fact, imports of gold and silver, at whatever port in the kingdom they may arrive, are almost always sent up for delivery at the bullion office of the bank, which acts precisely as if it were a dock warehouse, and delivers the packages on production of the bills of lading. These bills of lading are specific promises, and may yet be passed by endorsement from one person to another. Such consignments of bullion, however, do not enter into the banking accounts.

A Bank of England note is neither more nor less binding upon the bank authorities than a bill

THE NATURE AND VARIETIES OF PROMISSORY NOTES. 213

of lading, but it does not specify the bag or box of money to be employed in paying it. Almost all other pecuniary engagements are in the same way general engagements. No banker could make any profit if he were obliged to put away the sovereigns deposited by a customer until that customer presented a cheque for them, nor would there usually be sufficient motive for desiring such a special pledge. The idea never enters into our heads in mercantile matters. Disputes, however, have occasionally arisen upon this point. Some people have a peculiar fancy for collecting particular coins, and an old lady, having formed a hoard of fourpenny pieces, died after bequeathing them to a relative. Although wishing to keep them out of respect to the old lady, this relative was in want of ready cash, and desired to realize their value; he thought to achieve both objects by pledging them with a pawnbroker. The broker readily received them, but after a time thoughtlessly used the groats as change. When the pawn-ticket was presented he considered that the tender of the equivalent sum in sovereigns and shillings was a sufficient discharge. Here, however, the pledge should have been held as a special one.

Now, if pecuniary promises were always of a special character there could be no possible harm in allowing perfect freedom in the issue of promissory notes. The issuer would merely constitute himself a warehouse-keeper, and would be bound to hold each special lot of coin ready to pay each corresponding note. But this is not the case, and much harm may arise from the excessive issue of promises to pay gold on demand. The gold market may be rigged as well as the iron or any other special market. One difference is that the gold market is the most extensive of all markets, so that a great many individuals or companies, each acting under the separate impulse of self-interest, must over-issue notes in order to produce any appreciable effect. A further difference is that gold, being itself the measure of value, the rise or fall in its price cannot be apparent except in the average fall or rise in the price of many commodities. This subject must be pursued in Chapter XXIV.

Principles of the Circulation of Representative Money.

In the last two sections of Chapter VIII. (pp. 80-85), we found that by analyzing the motives of individuals in receiving, holding, or paying away metallic money, we could arrive at certain laws of circulation, which were amply confirmed by experience. It was also pointed out that the same laws might be extended *mutatis mutandis*, to the mixed circulation of metallic and paper money. Habit is almost as powerful in supporting the use of representative money as of real metallic coins. Persons who have long been accustomed to pay away certain pieces of paper without loss, will continue to regard them as good currency until some rude shock is given to their confidence. This may go so far that a dirty bit of paper, containing a promise to pay a sovereign, will be actually preferred to the beautiful gold coin which it promises. The currency of Scotland is a standing proof of this

THE NATURE AND VARIETIES OF PROMISSORY NOTES. 215

assertion; and the same may be said of Norway, where until 1874, no gold at all was in circulation, and notes for one, five, or ten dollars formed the principal part of the currency.

There is one all-important point in which representative differs from metallic money; it will not circulate beyond the boundaries of the district or country where it is legally current or habitually employed. No doubt Bank of England notes are frequently carried abroad by travellers, and are in most places readily exchanged for the money of the locality; but they never circulate, and are treated as bills upon London, forming a convenient mode of remittance. They do not satisfy a debt from this to another country, but rather create it, an English bank-note, in the hands of a Paris banker, representing a claim which he has upon the Bank of England. The only money which can really be exported in payment of debts due to foreign merchants is standard metallic money. Hence paper money has exactly the same capacity for driving out standard money that light or depreciated coins possess.

In the case of inconvertible notes this has always been most obvious. As the quantity of such notes issued progressively increases, as almost always happens, coin must be exported, otherwise the currency would become excessive. But when most of the coin is gone, need of it begins to be felt for making foreign payments, and then the value of the paper falls below that of the coin which it is supposed to correspond to. Many persons begin to hoard the coins for the sake of anticipated profit, and nothing but paper is soon to be found in circulation. This effect of paper in driving coin out of use has been manifested over and over again, as in the time of the assignats of the French Revolution, the suspension of specie payments at the Bank of England between 1797 and 1819, and the late American war. One of the most recent and striking instances is to be found in Italy, where large quantities of beautiful gold and silver coins had been struck in the years 1862 to 1865, but all disappeared very rapidly from circulation as soon as the *cours forcé* of paper money was proclaimed.

CHAPTER XVIII.

METHODS OF REGULATING A PAPER CURRENCY.

WE may now proceed with advantage to consider the various methods on which the issue of paper money may be conducted. This question is perhaps the most vexed and debatable one in the whole sphere of political economy; but, by carefully adhering to the analysis of facts, we may perhaps get a view of the subject free from the great perplexities in which it is commonly involved. The elementary principles of the subject are not of a complex character; and if we hold tenaciously to those principles, we may perhaps be saved from that dangerous kind of intellectual vertigo which often attacks writers on the currency.

The state may either take the issue of representative money into its own hands, as it takes the coining of money, or it may allow private individuals, or semi-public companies and corporations, to undertake the work under more or less strict legislative control. We will afterwards briefly consider the relative advantages of government and private issues, but in either case we may lay down the following series of methods according to which the amount of issue may be regulated, and the performance of the promises guaranteed.

1. *The Simple Deposit Method.* The issuer of promissory notes may be obliged to keep a stock of coin and bullion constantly on hand, equal in amount to the aggregate of the uncancelled notes, each of which, being instantly paid on presentation, will produce a corresponding decrease of the reserve.

2. *The Partial Deposit Method.* Instead of being obliged to keep the whole of the precious metals deposited in his vaults, the issuer may be allowed to invest a fixed amount in government funds, or other safe profitable securities.

3. *The Minimum Reserve Method.* The issuer may be bound to have on hand under all circumstances a fixed minimum amount of coin and bullion.

4. *The Proportional Reserve Method.* The reserve may be made to vary with the amount of outstanding notes, being, say, at least one-third or one-fourth of the total.

5. *The Maximum Issue Method.* Permission may be given to issue notes not exceeding in the aggregate a fixed amount, prohibitory penalties being imposed upon any breach of this restriction.

6. *The Elastic Limit Method.* A limit may be assigned to the aggregate amount of notes, as in the last method, but the penalties on the excessive issue may be intentionally made so light, that the issuer will under some circumstances prefer to pay the penalty rather than restrict his issues.

METHODS OF REGULATING A PAPER CURRENCY. 219

7. *The Documentary Reserve Method.* The reserve of property which the issuer is required to keep may consist not of gold or silver coin or bullion, but of government funds, bonds, shares, or other documentary securities.

8. *The Real Property Reserve Method.* Instead of merely documentary property, the issuer may be allowed to treat various property, such as land, houses, ships, railway shares, etc., as his reserve of wealth to meet engagements.

9. *The Foreign Exchanges Method.* Some important bank may be allowed to issue convertible notes on the understanding that it will not increase the amount in circulation so long as the foreign exchanges are against the country, and render the export of specie profitable.

10. *The Free Issue Method.* The business of issuing promissory notes may be left open to the free competition of all individuals, free from any restrictions or conditions, except such laws as apply to all commercial contracts and promises.

11. *The Gold Par Method.* Paper money may be issued, bearing the appearance of promissory notes, but inconvertible into coin. The issue being restricted as long as any premium on gold is apparent, the paper money may be thus maintained equal in value to the coin which it nominally represents.

12. *The Revenue Payments Method.* Inconvertible paper money may be freely issued, but an attempt may be made to keep up its value by receiving it in place of coin in the payment of taxes.

13. *The Deferred Convertibility Method.* Notes may be issued promising to pay metallic money at some future day, either definitely fixed or dependent upon political or other contingent events.

14. *The Paper Money Method.* Lastly, those who coin apparent promissory notes may be entirely absolved from the performance of their promises, so that the notes circulate by force of habit, by the command of the sovereign, or in consequence of the absence of any other medium of exchange.

Although I have, in the above statement, enumerated no less than fourteen distinct methods of managing the issue of paper currency, it is by no means certain that other methods have not been employed from time to time. There may be, in fact, an almost unlimited number of devices for securing the performance of promises, or for rendering the performance unnecessary. Moreover, these methods may be combined together in almost unlimited variety. The reserve may be required to be partially in the form of specie, and partially in documentary securities, or real property. A banker may be allowed to issue a certain fixed amount of notes without any condition as to reserves, and to issue further notes on the Deposit Method.

It would obviously require a very large volume to enter at all in an adequate manner upon a description of these methods, their relative advantages or defects, and the ways in which they have been combined and carried into effect at different times and places. I must therefore confine myself in this small book to a very concise discussion of this most extensive subject.

1. *Simple Deposit.*

This method is perfectly represented by the ancient deposit banks in the Italian commercial republics, by the banks of Amsterdam and Hamburg, or by the London goldsmiths, so long as they only acted as safe keepers of the specie committed to their care. Notes issued on this system have a purely representative character, like dock warrants or pawn tickets, as I have already fully explained. The performance of promises is rendered certain so far as legislation can provide for it. The amount of such a currency will vary exactly like that of a metallic currency, and there can be no fear of paper replacing specie, and driving it out of the country, because the specie must be in the vaults of the issuing bank before the notes are issued.

At the same time the advantages of the method are comparatively slight, because the use of paper representatives merely saves the abrasion of coin, and the trouble and risk of carrying it about and counting it. The community loses the interest of the whole sum held in pledge, and this forms by far the largest part of the cost of the currency, as we have seen (p. 164). The coin, too, may be safer in the hands of the people. When lying apparently useless within the reach of an arbitrary government, it often proves an irresistible temptation. Charles I. seized the money in the Tower.

When the French invaded Holland in 1795, a large part of the specie supposed to be deposited in the vaults of the bank of Amsterdam was not forthcoming, having been secretly lent to the Dutch East India Company, and the city authorities. The Russian government diligently collected a bank reserve in the citadel of St. Petersburg, which was under the cognizance of members of the Exchange, until the troubles of 1848 forced the emperor to assume the control himself. In innumerable instances governments, including the English government in 1797, have made use of bank deposits, under the form of suspending specie payments.

2. *Partial Deposit.*

The Bank of England, under the Bank Charter Act of 1844, perfectly represents this method. For each additional five-pound note which is put forth out of the issue department, gold to the weight of 616·37 grains must be deposited in that department. The whole amount of gold, however, retained in the vaults is less by £15,000,000 than the outstanding notes, this constant difference being covered by documentary securities, and by a sum of about eleven millions which the bank lends to the government without interest. Under this arrangement we secure all the advantages of the simple deposit system, while the community gains the interest amounting to about £445,000, of which the government receives £188,000 per annum. The character of the contract between the government and the bank is of too intricate a nature to be readily fathomed or described, but it substantially amounts to the government borrowing the larger part of the fifteen millions of deposits, and allowing the bank to use the rest to cover the cost of printing and managing the note circulation. I shall treat of this system again in Chapter XXIV. The Partial Deposit method is the basis of the new law concerning the issue of notes in the German empire, in combination with the Elastic Limit method, which possibly constitutes an improvement.

3. *Minimum Reserve.*

One mode of guaranteeing the payment of notes, which might be suggested, would consist in obliging the issuers to keep on hand a stock of specie, which is never to be allowed to fall below a certain fixed amount. This would be like recommending a man to avoid impecuniosity by always keeping a shilling in his pocket. The fact that the minimum amount must be kept in the vaults renders it unavailable for meeting demands when they come. There can be no use in such a reserve unless there be a power exercised by the legislature or executive government, of arbitrarily suspending the operation of the law when there is a run upon the banks.

4. *Proportional Reserve.*

The issuer of promises to pay money on demand may be required to keep a reserve of coin never less than, say, one-fourth of the whole outstanding notes.

This is analogous to the method on which the National Bank currency of the United States was lately regulated, and it is, perhaps, better to enforce the keeping of a certain amount of reserve than to leave the matter entirely to the discretion and good faith of the individual issuers. As the banker sees his reserve running down nearly to the legal limit, he will be compelled to use additional caution, in order to avoid a breach of the law. But if the untoward state of trade and credit causes any large portion of the outstanding notes to be presented, the legal tender reserve will be diminished in a greater proportion than the amount of notes, which is larger in absolute quantity. If there be 100,000 dollars of outstanding notes, and 40,000 dollars reserve, then it is obvious that the presentation of 20,000 dollars of notes will reduce these numbers respectively to 80,000 dollars of outstanding notes, and 20,000 dollars of reserve; and if the law required the reserve to be one-fourth part of the liabilities, no more notes could be paid. Thus, from the moment that the banker allows his reserve to touch the legal minimum, it becomes unavailable to him, except by a breach of law, and it may be said that the law is of little use except when broken. This system, in fact, reduces itself, when it comes into operation at all, to the Minimum Reserve method last described. The banker cannot touch his reserve just when he most wants it, and the deadlock thus occasioned was acutely felt in the United States during the panic of 1873.

This method of regulation has, moreover, little or no effect in removing the motives for an extension of the circulation. The greater part of the value of every additional note kept in circulation is a gratuitous addition to the loanable capital of the bank, and bears interest as long as it can be kept afloat.

5. *Maximum Issue.*

To allow a bank or banks to issue in the aggregate a certain fixed amount of promissory notes, and no more, appears to me quite consistent with the principles of political economy. It saves interest upon a certain portion of the circulating medium, and supplies a convenient and economical currency. At the same time, the notes issued cannot drive gold out of the country beyond a fixed amount. It is strongly urged by Mr. R. Inglis Palgrave and others, that the limitation is arbitrary, and that the people want more money; but it is always open to them to use metallic money instead. The limitation imposed is not upon money itself, but upon the representative part, and though we thereby forego the increased saving of interest upon enlarged issues, this loss may be balanced by the freedom from any risk of producing a fictitious abundance of gold. This system is sufficiently illustrated in the 170 banks of England which are still allowed to issue notes. Sir Robert Peel provided, in the Act of 1844, that they might continue to issue, without any condition as to reserve, the same quantity of notes as they had issued on the average of twelve weeks preceding a day named. If any bank exceeded the amount thus determined it was to be fined a sum of money equal to the average excess of the month; and sworn returns of their circulations were required from all issuing banks.

6. *Elastic Limit.*

The above is the best name which I can find for a new method of regulation which has just been adopted in the Bank Act of the German empire. So far as regards the issue of bank-notes the banking organization of Germany will substantially resemble that of England. The new Imperial Bank, and such of the state or other banks which conform to the requirements of the law, will have the right of issuing notes not backed by gold to the aggregate sum of 385 millions of marks. They may apparently issue any further quantity of notes in exchange for a deposit of gold to an equal value. So far the method is precisely that of the *partial deposit* already described (p. 222). Observing, however, that the English Bank Charter Act has on several occasions been violated to prevent a panic, the German legislature has provided that more bank-notes may be issued, provided that a tax of 5 per cent. be paid thereon. It is intended in this way to make it unprofitable for any bank to exceed the normal limits. It seems likely that this provision will work well, and form an improvement on our method. The English government, indeed, has always deprived the Bank of England of the interest on any excess of notes which it issued during a suspension of the Bank Act, but the German law makes the limit of issue elastic in all cases, so as to avoid the danger of panic.

7. *Documentary Reserve.*

It might seem enough in order to ensure the convertibility of notes, that the bankers issuing them should prove their possession of abundant funds, in the form of government stocks, bonds, exchequer bills, rentes, or even good mercantile bills, sufficient to establish the perfect solvency of the firm. If a considerable margin be left, it may seem impossible that the notes should not ultimately be paid. To argue in this way, however, is to forget that bank-notes are promises to pay gold or legal tender metallic money *on demand*, and that to pay the notes ultimately is not to pay them on demand. With such a reserve, payment can only be made in any large quantity by selling the stocks and bonds for metallic money; but it is just when there is a scarcity of gold and silver, that notes are presented for payment. No doubt good government funds and good bills can always be sold at some price, so that a banking firm with a strong reserve of this kind might always maintain their solvency. But the remedy might be worse for the community than the disease, and the forced sale of the reserve might create such a disturbance in the money market as would do more harm than the suspension of payment of the notes. Payment of notes on demand implies the possession of adequate gold and silver, and if there be not sufficient bullion and coin in the country, no paper documents, or promises to pay at a future day, can take their place.

8. Real Property Reserve.

Many currency theorists have held, that in securing the repayment of notes we need not restrict ourselves to a single commodity gold, but may mortgage for the purpose, land, houses, or any kind of fixed real property. The celebrated scheme of John Law was of this nature. In his remarkable tract on "Money and Trade Considered, with a Proposal for Supplying the Nation with Money," published in 1705, he suggests that commissioners should be appointed to "coin" notes "to be received in payments where offered," that is, I presume, as legal tender. He sets forth three alternative modes of issuing these notes on land security, the first and simplest being to lend them to landowners at the ordinary interest, to the extent of one-half or two-thirds of the value. He endeavours to provide against depreciation of the notes by taking care that the prices are always estimated in silver money.

The assignats of the French Revolutionary Government represented land *assigned*, namely, portions of the confiscated estates of the Church. They were to be received back and cancelled as the lands were bought by the public; but, as the price of the land was not fixed, no proportion was established between land and paper, and no amount of land could prevent the assignats from falling as they did to one two-hundredth part of their original value. In the subsequent issue of *Mandats*, an attempt was made to fix the price of land in mandats, but this scheme also failed. The inconvertible land mortgage notes, issued by Frederick the Great to recruit his treasury exhausted by wars, were of somewhat the same nature, but bore interest.

Land is doubtless one of the best kinds of security for the ultimate repayment of a debt, and is therefore very suitable when money is lent for a long time. But representative bank-notes purport to be equivalent to gold payable on demand, and nothing is less readily convertible into gold on an emergency than land. In this respect a reserve of real property is worse than a reserve of exchequer bills or consols.

This method of providing paper money has generally been advocated on the ground that the quantity of money in circulation might thus be greatly increased, and the wealth of the nation augmented. It could readily be shown, however, that an increase of the money in circulation will lead to a reduction in its value. In any given state of industry only a certain quantity of circulating medium is needed, and were the notes really convertible into definite quantities of land or any other substantial commodity, the excess of notes would ultimately be presented for payment. To suppose that the currency could be made equal in aggregate value to any large part of the lands of the country is evidently absurd.

9. *Regulation by the Foreign Exchanges.*

A theory was very much in favour among bank directors at the beginning of this century that a paper currency could be regulated merely by watching the rates of the foreign exchanges, and restricting the issue when the lowness of the rates and the export of specie showed a depreciation of the paper. This was one of the methods proposed in opposition to the celebrated Bullion Report, and a summary of the interminable discussions on the subject will be found in Mr. Macleod's Treatise on Banking, Vol. II. Chapter IX.

Regulation by the foreign exchanges is much better than no regulation at all, but if perfectly carried out it would give exactly the same results as the deposit method, and is only a loose and indirect way of reaching the same end.

10. *Free Issue System.*

There is a school of economists, both in this country and America, who uphold the expediency of allowing all persons to issue as many promissory notes payable on demand as they can get other persons to accept. They call this system the Free Banking system, but incorrectly, because it is no necessary function of a banker to issue promissory notes, and a great many banks exist in England without any power of issue. This subject will be further discussed in a subsequent chapter, and I will only add here that under the system of unrestricted issue, a banker is bound by law to pay a note issued by him, but is left entirely at his own discretion to keep such balance of specie for the purpose as he may think proper. As a general rule, no doubt, notes thus issued will be paid; but, having regard to the great fluctuations of commerce, which are becoming more, rather than less marked, there will occur periods when a pressure for payment of notes will be made. Experience abundantly shows that a certain number of individuals will calculate too confidently on their good fortune, and fail to carry out their promises and intentions when the critical time arives.

11. *The Gold Par Method.*

Assuming an inconvertible paper currency to be issued, and to be entirely in the hands of government. many of the evils of such a system might be avoided if the issue were limited or reduced the moment that the price of gold in paper rose above par. As long as the notes and the gold coins which they pretend to represent circulate on a footing of equality, they are as good as if convertible. Since the beginning of the Franco-Prussian war, the Bank of France appears to have acted successfully on this principle, and the inconvertible notes were never depreciated more than about $\frac{1}{2}$ or 1 per cent. in spite of the vast political and financial troubles of France. But this is one of the very few cases in which inconvertible paper currency has not been seriously depreciated. During the restriction of specie payments in England, gold was bought and sold at a premium varying up to 25 per cent., yet Fox, Vansittart, and other leading men of the time, declared it to be absurd to suppose that paper was depreciated. So unaccountable are the prejudices of men on the subject of currency that it is not well to leave anything to discretionary management.

12. *Convertibility by Revenue Payments.*

In many instances governments have tried to maintain the value of a paper circulation by engaging to receive it as taxes, or even rendering its use for this purpose obligatory. The Russian government when issuing assignats received them at a fixed rate in place of copper coin, and required that at least one-twentieth part of every payment was to be thus paid. The French assignats of the Revolution were also received at the public treasuries. This would be a fair method of securing stability of value on two conditions :—(1) that the taxes or charges were themselves levied according to a fixed tariff; and (2) that the quantity of notes issued was kept within such moderate limits that any one wishing to realize the metallic value of the notes could find some one wanting to pay taxes, and therefore willing to give coin for notes. It is very unlikely, however, that these conditions could ever be fully and conveniently realized in practice.

The United States greenback currency was made receivable for all United States stamps, and was also to be received in payment of all taxes and dues in sums of certain assigned amounts, excepting Customs dues. But the fact that some notes are thus withdrawn will not prevent depreciation, if they be soon paid out again with additions required to meet the pressing expenditure of a government.

In a small way postage stamps are becoming used as currency in several countries. They were extensively used in the earlier years of the American war as the well-known fractional currency. They are now a recognized medium of payment in England, being repurchased by most postmasters at a discount of $2\frac{1}{2}$ per cent. if presented in a piece of two or more undivided stamps. Independently, however, of repurchase, stamps are so continually being cancelled by use in postage, that their value can hardly be lowered by excess of quantity. They form a convenient and costless form of remittance for very small sums, say from a halfpenny to five shillings, and little or no objection can be made to their occasional use as change, in place of pence. They would, however, form a very bad currency if circulated to any great extent.

13. *Deferred Convertibility.*

It is a common resource for insurrectionary or belligerent governments in want of funds to issue documents promising to pay cash after their successful establishment. When interest proportional to the time is also promised, these notes must be regarded rather as bonds. Of such nature were those issued by Kossuth in New York to form a Hungarian fund, to be paid after the erection of an independent Hungarian government. Similar bonds were signed by the notorious Walker, as President of the provisional government of the republic of Nicaragua. By far the best instance of this kind of currency is furnished by the Confederate States treasury notes, the early issues of which were made payable six months after the ratification of a treaty of peace with the United States, and further issues were to be payable two years after such treaty.

All such documents may be considered as bills of very long date and of very uncertain value. The public spirit of a people in time of war often enables them to be put afloat, and the need of currency keeps them in circulation for a time, but their value undergoes violent variations, and there are few instances in which such bills have been eventually paid.

14. *Inconvertible Paper Money.*

Finally we come to the undisguised *paper money* issued by government and ordered to be received as legal tender. Such inconvertible paper notes have in all instances been put in circulation as convertible ones, or in the place of such, and they are always expressed in terms of money. The French mandats of 100 francs, for instance, bear the ambiguous phrase "Bon pour cent francs." The wretched scraps of paper which circulate in Buenos Ayres, are marked " Un Peso, Moneda Corriente," reminding one of the time when the peso was a heavy standard coin. After the promise of payment in coin is found to be illusory the notes still circulate, partly from habit, partly because the people must have some currency, and have no coin to use for the purpose, or if they have, carefully hoard it for profit or future use. There is plenty of evidence to prove that an inconvertible paper money, if carefully limited in quantity, can retain its full value. Such was the case with the Bank of England notes for several years after the suspension of specie payments in 1797, and such is the case with the present notes of the Bank of France.

The principal objections to an inconvertible paper currency are two in number.

1. The great temptations which it offers to over issue and consequent depreciation.

2. The impossibility of varying its amount in accordance with the requirements of trade.

Over Issue of Paper Money.

It is hardly requisite to tell again the well-worn tale of the over issue of paper money which has almost always followed the removal of the legal necessity of convertibility. Hardly any civilized nation exists, excepting some of the newer British colonies, which has not suffered from the scourge of paper money at one time or other. Russia has had a depreciated paper currency for more than a hundred years, and the history of it may be read in M. Wolowski's work on the finances of Russia. Repeated limits were placed to its issue by imperial edict, but the next war always led to further issues. Italy, Austria, and the United States, countries where the highest economical intelligence might be expected to guide the governments, endure the evils of an inconvertible paper currency. Time after time in the earlier history of the New England and some of the other states now forming parts of the American Union, paper money had been issued and had wrought ruin. Full particulars will be found in Professor Sumner's new and interesting "History of American Currency." Some of the greatest statesmen pointed to these results; and Webster's opinion should never be forgotten. Of paper money he says, "We have suffered more from this cause than from every other cause or calamity. It has killed more men, pervaded and corrupted the choicest interests of our country more, and done more injustice than even the arms and artifices of our enemy."

The issue of an inconvertible money, as Professor Sumner remarks, has often been recommended as a convenient means of making a forced loan from the people, when the finances of the government are in a desperate condition. It is true that money may be thus easily abstracted from the people, and the government debts are effectually lessened. At the same time, however, every private debtor is enabled to take a forced contribution from his creditor. A government should, indeed, be in a desperate position, which ventures thus to break all social contracts and relations which it was created to preserve.

Want of Elasticity of Paper Money.

A further objection to a paper money inconvertible into coin, is that it cannot be varied in quantity by the natural action of trade. No one can export it or import it like coin, and no one but the government or banks authorized by government can issue or cancel it. Hence, if trade becomes brisk, nothing but a decree of the government can supply the requisite increase of circulating medium, and if this be put afloat and trade relapse into dullness, the currency becomes redundant, and falls in value. Now, even the best-informed government department cannot be trusted to judge wisely and impartially when more money is wanted. Currency must be supplied, like all other commodities, according to the free action of the laws of supply and demand.

Some persons have argued that it is well to have a paper money to form a home currency, which cannot be drained away, and will be free from the disturbing influences of foreign trade. But we cannot disconnect home and foreign trade, except by doing away with the latter altogether. If two nations are to trade, the precious metals must form the international medium of exchange by which a balance of indebtedness is paid. Hence each merchant in ordering, consigning, or selling goods must pay regard not to the paper price of such goods, but to the gold or silver price with which he really pays for them. Gold and silver, in short, continue to be the real measure of value, and the variable paper currency is only an additional term of comparison which adds confusion.

CHAPTER XIX.

CREDIT DOCUMENTS

Much mystery has been created on the subject of money by those who assert vaguely that credit can replace coins, and that we have only to print sufficient bills and other promissory documents in order to have an abundant circulating medium. Credit has been said to multiply property and to perform all kinds of prodigies. When we analyze its nature, however, credit is found to be nothing but the deferring of a payment. I *take credit* when I induce my creditor to consent to my paying a month hence what might be demanded to-day; and I *give credit* when I allow my debtor in the same manner to put off the liquidation of his debt. Thus credit involves, as Locke very accurately said, "the expectation of money within some limited time." The debts, indeed, may consist of a definite quantity of any commodity. I may have to pay corn, pig iron, palm oil, cotton, or any other staple article, but, generally speaking, debts are debts of legal tender money.

Measurement of Credit.

In order to measure and define exactly the amount of credit which is given or received, and to estimate the present value of a debt, we must take into account at least five distinct circumstances, which are as follows:—

1. The amount of money to be received.
2. The probable interval of time elapsing before its receipt.
3. The probability that it will then be paid.
4. The rate of interest likely to prevail in the mean time.
5. The legal liabilities which it creates or involves.

Writers upon currency have been too much accustomed to mass together all kinds of credit documents, taking no account of the important results which may follow from very slight legal or customary differences. No doubt every kind of promise to pay money has a certain value, but the degree in which it may be made available to facilitate exchange varies exceedingly according to circumstances.

Bank-notes.

What we call a bank-note is a promissory note, issued by a banker, and binding him to pay the sum named therein to the bearer immediately upon demand. The note is transferable by delivery, so that the holder is like the holder of a coin, the owner *primâ facie*, and as such can claim the fulfilment of the promise at any moment, within reasonable hours, without inquiry. The failure of the banker to pay the note when presented does not create any liability between the persons through whose hands the note had previously passed, so that the note is continually employed, like metallic money, in settling debts and removing liabilities. It is most important to observe that a bank-note being payable on demand bears no interest, and is never bought at a discount, except when the ultimate payment is doubtful. Hence the holder of a note has, like the holder of ordinary coins, no motive in keeping it, except to make future purchases. If a man has more notes than he expects to pay away in the next week or two, he will do best to deposit them in a bank, where they will be safer and at the same time bear interest. There is thus an inherent tendency in notes to circulate like coins, and to be kept down in amount to the lowest quantity consistent with the accomplishment of retail purchases.

Cheques.

A cheque payable to bearer is an order addressed to a banker, requiring him to pay the sum named to the bearer of the cheque on demand. Like a bank-note, it bears no interest, and is transferable from hand to hand without any formality, so that the holder is *primâ facie* the owner. If there be no doubt at all as to the credit both of the drawer and of the bank on which the cheque is drawn, it is difficult to see why a cheque should be inferior to a bank-note as representative money, except

CREDIT DOCUMENTS. 241

that it is usually drawn for an odd sum. In some places cheques have been so used, and in Queensland at the present time, in the absence of coins and notes, the settlers pay their men in small bank cheques, which are received at the stores, and thus become the circulating medium of the colony. Obvious objections to this use of cheques may be pointed out.

It is impossible to be acquainted with the cheque forms of all banks, the signatures of those who draw them, and the credit of the drawers. If the public were in the habit of daily receiving and paying cheques without minutely inquiring into their validity, immense facilities would be given to the perpetration of fraud. Forgery would be easy but hardly requisite, since it would be better to obtain possession of a cheque book, and then fill up cheques for amounts exceeding the deposits in the banker's hands. Every one accepting a cheque thus receives it at the risk of fraud or bankruptcy on the part of the drawer. There is, moreover, the possibility of failure of the bank on which it is drawn; for it is a well-understood point of law, that if the holder of a cheque does not present it in "reasonable time," that is before the close of business hours on the day following the receipt of the cheque, he loses his claim against the drawer, if the bank on which it is drawn should happen to fail. The reason obviously is that the drawer loses the deposit which he left in the banker's hands to meet the cheque, and should not suffer from the holder's want of diligence.

The salutary effect of this law and of other conditions is, that cheques do not circulate in this kingdom in place of money, but are usually presented within one or two days of receipt. Hence they come to serve as mere instruments of transfer of money, and involve no considerable length of credit. Nothing can be gained by holding an ordinary cheque, for there is no interest, and something may be lost. Beyond the mere trouble of presentation, then, there is no motive to prevent a holder from at once getting coin or bank-notes for his cheque which, though paying no interest, are safer. Or still better, he may deposit the sum at his bankers, get a low interest in the mean time, and draw a new cheque of his own when he wishes to pay the money away again. Experience shows that the latter is the most satisfactory course, the money being usually safer and more available in the hands of a good banker than elsewhere, and usually paying interest all the time. On this foundation is erected the extensive system of payment which will be described in the next chapter, and which may be called *the Cheque and Clearing System.*

There are, indeed, many varieties of cheques. Bankers' cheques are those drawn by one banker upon another, and are used as a means of remittance. If both the bankers concerned are of perfect credit, and the form and signature can be verified, such cheques seem to me to be in no way inferior to bank-notes as representative money. If two perfectly well-known banks were to arrange to draw cheques upon each other for convenient even amounts, and to issue these to their customers, it would effect a successful evasion of the law against the unlimited issue of notes. So great however is the force of habit, or the respect for law, that no such attempt is made, and bankers' cheques are presented almost as promptly as any others.

Certified cheques, as employed in the New York trade, are a still nearer approach to a bank-note, for they are cheques which have been marked by the bankers on which they are drawn, as sure to be paid on presentation. Either the banker in certifying the cheque has funds belonging to the drawer which he can retain to meet it, or else he pledges his own credit that he will meet the cheque in any case. Such cheques are really promissory notes of the banker, and I can see no reasons why they should not circulate as freely as bank-notes, except that they are drawn for odd sums, and present few safeguards against forgery. The cheques of the Cheque Bank, which will be subsequently considered (Chapter XXII.), are equivalent to certified cheques, as they cannot be issued except against deposits which are retained until the cheque is presented.

Of late years the practice has become very general of making cheques payable to order instead of to bearer, and of crossing them so as to necessitate their presentation through a banker. The order may, indeed, be discharged by an open endorsement, which renders the cheque again payable to bearer, but there remains the possibility of a forged endorsement, concerning which difficult points of law have arisen. A general crossing need not interfere appreciably with the circulation of a cheque, but when crossed specifically for presentation through a particular bank, the cheque becomes practically an order to credit a particular individual, who keeps his account in that bank, with the sum of money named.

Bills of Exchange.

A bill of exchange is an order to a person to pay money to the legal holder of the document on a day indicated therein. If payable at sight, a bill does not apparently differ from a cheque or draft to order, except that it will be usually drawn upon persons of less credit than well-known bankers. If not payable at sight, the length of time intervening between the day named for payment and the day of issue may vary from a day or two upwards, and the money cannot be demanded in the mean time. Hence a bill generally bears interest, or rather is only bought at such a discount as will enable it to be held to maturity without loss. To estimate the liability of loss, some estimate must be formed of the rate of interest likely to prevail in the mean time, and the value of the bill will thus vary according to a multitude of circumstances. Bills of exchange may be made payable to the bearer, but as a general rule they are payable to a specified person, and transferred by endorsement to other specified persons. Thus every party concerned with a bill incurs a certain liability, which is not removed until it is duly paid. In several respects, then, a bill may differ from coined money, which bears no interest, and discharges instead of creating liability when tendered in payment of debts.

Interest-bearing Documents.

It is extraordinary that few writers on currency have remarked the deep difference between commercial documents which bear interest and those which do not. On this point turns the possibility of their forming representative money. For it is an essential characteristic of coin that it yields no profit by keeping it in the pocket or the safe. I may be obliged to keep money ready to pay debts, but in the mean time I lose the interest which I might receive by investing the sum in the funds, in bills, bonds, or even as a bank deposit. Hence money must be considered as a commodity which, as Chevalier says, is *in a constant state of supply and demand.* Every one is always trying to part with it in a profitable purchase, and keeps as little in hand as possible. The same is even more true of bank-notes, cheques, circular notes, bills at sight, and a few other kinds of documents, all of which are payable on demand at any moment, so that no amount of interest can be assigned to them. Except so far as the payment may be doubtful, or the possession of the documents may involve the holder in legal difficulties, these documents have the characteristics of coin, and the amount held is kept down to the lowest convenient figure. Interest-bearing documents, on the contrary, are held in as large quantities as possible, because the longer they are held the more interest accrues. It is the principal business of every banker to hold a portfolio full of good bills, which really represent the investment of capital in industry. Government bonds, or bonds issued by public companies and corporations, do not differ from commercial bills except in the fact that they have very long, or even interminable, usance, and that the interest is paid at definite intervals. Such bonds represent the sinking of capital in fixed undertakings, and are therefore held as property by individual investors. They may be bought and sold for money, but are not money themselves. They rather necessitate than replace the use of money, since currency must have been paid at the first investment, and is repaid by degrees at the periodical terms fixed.

A number of schemists have urged from time to time, that, in addition to our ordinary currency, there ought to be an *interest-bearing currency*. The first small issue of the French assignats bore interest, and about twelve years ago the United States government tried a similar experiment, which was soon discontinued. Persons have proposed to coin the whole National Debt into money, so that instead of some 160 millions of metallic and paper currency we might have more nearly a thousand millions. Mr. E. Hill has published a form of bank-note entitling the holder to one hundred pounds on demand, and to interest at the rate of $3\frac{1}{3}$ per cent. up to the time when it is presented, the amount of interest being tabularly stated on the form. It is obviously impossible, however, that any government should issue such notes, because whenever the current rate of interest rose above $3\frac{1}{3}$, and the value of the note accordingly fell below par, a profit would be made by presenting the notes for payment. Thus the government issuing such notes would have to keep a large quantity of coin in reserve to meet them, and would at the same time be paying interest on the whole of the notes. Thus there would be a loss of interest upon the whole reserve of coin.

The English government has rendered the National Debt as transferable as possible by authorizing, in terms of the Act of 33 and 34 Victoria, chapter 71, the issue of stock certificates. These certificates resemble the bonds of the United States and other governments. They have coupons for the payment of interest, and when not filled up with a name are transferable by delivery like bank notes. They are issued in exchange for Three per Cent Annuities for even sums of not less than £50 and not more than £1000; and if the right to an annuity could be passed from one person to another as currency, these certificates would allow of its being done. But it is understood that a comparatively small amount of such certificates has ever been applied for. They are, I believe, used to some extent by bankers and others, who have to hold sums of money invested in the funds for short periods, and can save the cost of transfers by the use of certificates. The public at large are found to prefer the old method of registering their stock in the books of the Bank of England.

Definition of Money.

Much ingenuity has been spent upon attempts to define the term *money*, and puzzling questions have arisen as to the precise kinds of credit documents which are to be included under the term. Standard legal tender coin of full weight is undoubtedly money, and as convertible legal tender bank-notes are exactly equivalent to the coined money for which they may at any moment be exchanged, it has often been considered that these also may be included. But inconvertible notes are often made legal tender by law, and can discharge in inland trade all the functions of money. Are they not then to be included? The question will next arise whether cheques may not be as good as money.

All such attempts at definition seem to me to involve the logical blunder of supposing that we may, by settling the meaning of a single word, avoid all the complex differences and various conditions of many things, each requiring its own definition. Bullion, standard coin, token coin, convertible and inconvertible notes, legal tender and not legal tender, cheques of several kinds, mercantile bills, exchequer bills, stock certificates, etc., are all things capable of being received in payment of a debt, if the debtor is willing to pay and the creditor to receive them; but they are, nevertheless, different kinds of things. By calling some money and some not, we do not save ourselves from the consideration of their complex legal and economical differences. Bullion is evidently not coin, but can be turned into it at little or no cost, and will make foreign payments almost as well as coin. Token coins are not standard coins, and will not make foreign payments, but are legal tender for small sums, and may be readily exchanged for standard coin at little or no loss. Bank of England notes are not exactly coin, but can be readily turned into coin by those who dwell near the Bank of England, and are received as equivalent to coin by other persons. Cheques are not coin, but orders to receive it on demand, and are valuable in proportion to the probability that the sum will be received. Accepted bills are an engagement to pay coin at a day named; if we overlook the possible failure of the acceptor to pay them, they are, as it were, deferred money. A certificate of consolidated stock entitles the holder to an annuity, that is, to quarterly sums of money.

We get back, in short, to that with which we started. Standard legal tender coin is that in which all commercial transactions and documents are expressed, but according to infinitely various circumstances, the receipt of the money is more or less probable, more or less deferred, more or less involved in legal complexities, and also variable in amount, as interest is or is not to be received in addition. All other commercial property, mortgage deeds, preference shares and bonds, and ordinary shares, resolve themselves into more or less probability of receiving coin at future dates; and thus we pass insensibly from the golden sovereign in hand to the most flimsy chance of receiving gold which is still like the bird in the bush.

The word *cash* is used with exactly the same ambiguity

as *money*. Originally cash meant that which was *encaissé*, *i.e.* put into the chest or till. Strictly speaking, it should consist of actual specie, and the word is used in some English banks to include only coin of the realm. But I find by actual inquiry that bank cashiers use it with every shade of meaning. Some take Bank of England notes to be cash. Good cheques upon a bank paid into that bank are evidently as good as cash. Others go so far as to include cheques upon other banks of the same town, and even country bank-notes are sometimes included in cash. The question is evidently one of degree, and cannot be settled except by the general adoption among cashiers of some one arbitrary line of definition.

In ordinary life we use a great many words with a total disregard of logical precision. Who shall decide, for instance, what objects are to be included under the names *building* and *house?* Let the reader attempt to decide which of the following objects is to be considered a house, and why?—namely, stables, cow-houses, conservatories, sheds, lighthouses, tents, caravans, hulks, sentry-boxes, ice-houses, summer-houses, and parish pounds. The difficulty is exactly analogous to that of deciding what is money or cash.

CHAPTER XX.

BOOK CREDIT AND THE BANKING SYSTEM.

CONSIDERABLE economy of the precious metals arises, as we have seen, from passing about pieces of paper representing gold coin, instead of the coin itself. But a far more potent source of economy is what we may call the Cheque and Clearing System, whereby debts are, not so much paid, as balanced off against each other. The germ of the method is to be found in the ordinary practice of *book credit*. If two firms have frequent transactions with each other, alternately buying and selling, it would be an absurd waste of money to settle each debt immediately it arose, when, in a few days, a corresponding debt might arise in the opposite direction. Accordingly, it is the common practice for firms having reciprocal transactions, to debit and credit each other in their books with the debt arising out of each transaction, and only to make a cash payment when the balance happens to become inconveniently great. An insurance broker is one who acts as a middleman between the owners of ships and the underwriters who insure them in shares. He has therefore to make many small payments to underwriters, for the premiums on policies, and at intervals has to receive back the indemnity for any insured vessel which has been lost. It is the common practice to avoid cash payments; the broker credits the underwriters with the premiums and debits him with losses, and only pays or receives the balance when large.

To represent the highly complex system of book credit which is organized by the bankers of a large kingdom, we shall have to employ a method of diagramatic notation. I will therefore remark that the simplest case or type of book-credit is represented by the formula

$$P \longrightarrow Q.$$

Each of the letters, P and Q, indicates a person or a firm, and the line indicates the existence of transactions between them. Only in special cases, however, will this direct balancing of accounts render the use of cash or of a more complex system unnecessary. Generally speaking, there will be a tendency for a surplus of goods to pass in one direction, so that money must pass in the opposite direction. The manufacturer sells to the wholesale dealer, the latter sells to the retailer, and the retailer to the consumer. By the intervention of the banker, however, the transactions of many different individuals, or even of many branches of trade, are brought to a focus, and a large proportion of payments can be balanced off against each other.

Single Bank System.

To obtain a clear notion of the way in which bankers help us to avoid the use of money as the medium of exchange, we must follow up the rise of the system from the simplest case to the complete development of the complex organization now existing in the United Kingdom. Let us imagine, in the first place, that there is an isolated town having no appreciable dealings with other parts of the world, and possessing only a single bank, in which each inhabitant has deposited all his money. If any person a, then, wishes to make a payment to b, he need not go to his banker, draw out coin, and carry it to b, but may hand to b a cheque requiring the banker to pay the coins to b, if needed. But if b makes payments in the same way, he will not need to draw out any coin. It would be a mere formality for b to receive the coin due from a, and then pay it back over the counter to the credit of his account with the same banker. The payment is made by merely writing the sum of money to the debit of a's account, and to the credit of b's account. If b wishes to make another payment to c, a similar record in the banker's ledger will accomplish the business. However many other traders, d, e, etc., there may be, their mutual transactions may be settled in the same way, without their seeing a single coin. We may represent this elementary banking organization by the following diagram,

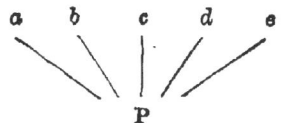

in which it is obvious that P represents the single banker, and a, b, c, d, e, his customers. The deposit banks of Amsterdam and Hamburg form perfect illustrations of this arrangement.

So long as we regard only the internal transactions of a town, then, a stationary amount of coin, lying untouched in the bank, will allow the whole to be accomplished. If the traders never require to make payments to a distance the metallic money might be dispensed with altogether. But since any of the customers a, b, c, etc., may want his money, the banker ought to keep at least as much as will meet possible demands.

System of Two Banks.

As a second case, let us suppose that there is a town which is able to support two banks. Some of the inhabitants keep their money in one bank and some in the other, but all whom it is requisite to consider have an account with one or the other. In the diagram,

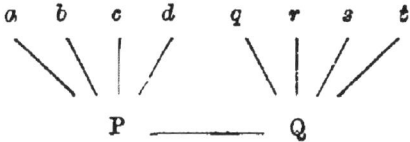

let P and Q be the two bankers, a, b, c, d, being customers of P, and q, r, s, t, customers of Q. Now, the mutual transactions of a, b, c, d, will, as before, be balanced off in the books of P, and similarly with the customers of Q. But if a has to make a payment to q, the operation becomes somewhat more complex. He draws a cheque upon P, and hands it to q, who may, of course, demand the coin from P. Not wanting coin, he carries the cheque to his own banker, Q, and pays it in to his account in place of coin. It is the banker, Q, who will now have to present the cheque upon P, and it might seem as if the use of coin would be ultimately required. There will be other persons, however, making payments in the town in the same manner, and the probability is very great that some of these will result in giving P cheques upon Q, and some in giving Q cheques upon P. The two bankers, then, will be in the position of the two traders before described (p. 251), who have a running account. At the worst the payment to be made in coin will be only the balance of what is due in opposite directions; but as this balance will probably tend in one direction one day, and in the opposite direction the next day, the balance need only be paid when it assumes inconvenient proportions.

Complex Bank System.

A large commercial town usually possesses several or many banks, each with its distinct body of customers. The mutual transactions of each body will, as before, be balanced off in the books of their common bank, but the larger part of the transactions will now be cross ones, resulting in a claim by one banker upon another. The probability is very great, indeed, that each banker will have to receive, as well as to pay, each day; but it does not follow that he will pay to the same as those who are going to pay to him. The complexity of relations becomes considerable; thus among fourteen banks there are $\frac{14 \times 13}{2}$ or 91 different pairs which may have mutual claims, and among fifty banks there would be no less than 1225 pairs. The result is, that P might happen to have a considerable balance to pay to Q, and yet might be going to receive about the same sum from R or S. The actual carrying about of coin under such circumstances would be absurd, because a manifest extension of the book-credit system at once meets the difficulty. The several banks need only agree to appoint, as it were, a *bankers' bank,* to hold a portion of the cash of each bank, and then the mutual indebtedness may be balanced off just as when a bank acts for individuals. In the figure we see four banks, P, Q, R, S, each with its own body of customers, but brought into connection with each other by the bankers' bank, X.

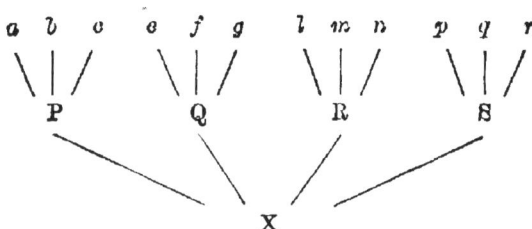

P need not now send a clerk to present bundles of cheques upon Q, R, and S, but can pay them into the central bank, X, where after being placed to the credit of P and sorted out, they will be joined to similar parcels

BOOK CREDIT AND THE BANKING SYSTEM. 257

of cheques received from Q, R, S, and finally presented at the banks upon which they are drawn. Thus all the payments made by cheques will be effected without the use of coin, just as if there were only a single bank in the town. What each bank has to pay each day will usually be balanced pretty closely by what it has to receive. Such balance as remains will be paid by a transfer in the books of X, the bankers' bank.

It is not precisely true that there is in any English town a bankers' bank, which thus arranges the payments between banks. The accountants' part of the work is carried out by an institution called the Clearing House, managed by a committee of bankers, and the Bank of England is employed to hold the deposits of the bankers, and make transfers which close the transactions of each day. The organization of the Clearing House will be described in the next chapter.

Branch Bank System.

It is impossible to avoid perceiving that the organization of the English bank system is undergoing a complete transformation, and is approximating to that which has existed for a century or more in Scotland. Instead of a great number of small, weak, disconnected banks, there is arising, by amalgamation and extinction of the weaker ones, a moderate number of important banks, each possessing numerous branches. The Scotch banks have long had many branches, and at present each of the eleven great banks has on the average 78 branches, the lowest number being 19, and the highest 125. Already a few of the English banks have equally extensive ramifications. Thus the London and County Bank, and the National Provincial Bank, which have especially developed the branch system, have respectively 148 and 137 branches; the Manchester and Liverpool District Bank has 50 branches and sub-branches. The Irish banks also adopt the same system, and the National Bank of Ireland has about 114 branches and sub-branches. It is interesting to observe that in Australia, too, the banking system has taken a similar form, and a comparatively small number of strong banks, such as the Bank of New South Wales, or the Bank of New Zealand, leave no rising village without its branch.

Now, the close connection which exists between the head office and each of the branches of an extensive bank leads to a great clearing off of claims. The diagram on p. 256 again serves to represent this relation, X being the head office, P, Q, R, S, branch banks, and a, b, c, etc., customers. If a pay m with a cheque on P, the cheque will be paid into R, credited to m, forwarded by post direct to P, and debited to a. The head office, being informed of this transaction in the usual daily statement, will close the business by transferring the sum from the account of P to that of R. Much accountants' work seems to arise, but it is work of mere routine which costs little. Cash remittances are seldom necessary, because each branch settles accounts only with the head office, so that many sums will be credited and debited during each week, and the balance will usually be small. The head office, in fact, acts in every way like a clearing house, or bankers' bank.

The question naturally arises, indeed, how will the branches of one bank transact business with those of another bank? The solution, however, is simple; for unless the branches happen to be in the same town, or for other reason, in close relation with each other, they will communicate through their head offices. A cheque upon any branch of the London and County Bank received by a branch of the National Provincial Bank, will be presented through the head office of the latter at the Clearing House upon the head office of the former.

Bank Agency System.

Another important feature of the banking system is the extensive organization of agencies. A large bank has various business to be transacted in each of the principal commercial towns of the kingdom, and if it has no branches in these towns employs a banker in each town to act as its agent. This agent-bank collects cheques, bills, notes, etc., payable in the district, cashes drafts drawn against them, retires bills according to instructions, and does almost all that a branch bank would do, the main difference being that the remuneration for this work consists of a commission. Each agent-bank has a running account with its principal, so that to a certain extent each important bank and its agencies form a clearing system analogous to that of a head bank and its branches.

London Agency System.

By insensible degrees there has grown up in England an all-comprehensive and most perfect system of relations between the provincial and London city banks. Every banker in the United Kingdom, without, I believe, any exception, employs one or other of the great London city banks to act as agent. There are twenty-six city clearing banks which thus undertake agencies, and on an average, each of these banks represents at least twelve country banks; but the number varies very much, and some country banks have two London agent-banks.

This agency system leads at once to a clearing of transactions, because, if any two country banks have the same London agent, all their mutual adjustments of accounts can be made by transfers in the books of the agent. The diagram on p. 256 applies for a third time, and X represents the city agent, having running accounts with P, Q, R, S, the country banks. The whole of the customers of all the banks, having the same London agent, are thus brought into close relation, though they may live in the most distant parts of the country. Each of the city banks may be regarded as a bankers' bank and a clearing house on a small scale.

Country Clearing System.

Only one further step is required to complete the system of connections between each bank in the kingdom and all other banks. Every country bank, as we have seen, has a running account with some city bank, and all the city banks daily settle transactions with each other through the Clearing House. It follows that a payment from any part of the country to any other part can be accomplished through London. In the following diagram, let P, Q, R be country banks having the

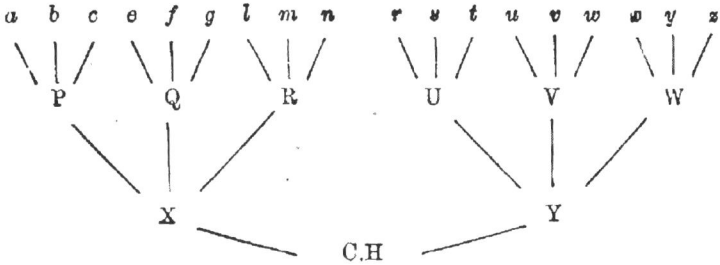

London agent, X, and U, V, W, other country banks having the London agent, Y. If a, a customer of P, wishes to pay r, a customer of U, he transmits by post a cheque upon his banker, P. The receiver, r, pays it into his account with U, who having no direct communication with P, forwards it to Y, who presents it through the Clearing House on X, who debits it to P, and forwards it by the next post. Nothing can exceed the simplicity and perfection of this arrangement.

It will be readily seen, too, that sums of money passing between London banks, or rather cleared off in the Lombard Street Clearing House, will frequently be the balances of extensive running accounts between country banks and their agents and correspondents.

So long as the balance of accounts between any two banks does not assume large proportions, it need not be paid in cash at all, except for special reasons. When a balance has to be paid, and the banks happen to have the same London agent, it is only requisite for the debtor bank to direct their London agent to transfer so much money to the credit of the other country bank. If they have different London agents, and P, in the last diagram, desires to pay a balance to U, it is done by directing X to credit Y, the agent of U. The credit note effecting this payment passes through the Clearing House amid a mass of other documents representing payments in one direction or the other, and will, in general, become an insignificant item in the general clearing. If it can be said to be paid in cash at all, it is in the form of a final transfer in the books of the Bank of England, as we shall see. Great as are the transactions daily settled in the London Clearing House, they are after all only those which have not been previously cleared off by any more direct communication, and they often represent the balances of multitudinous transactions which never pass through London at all.

CHAPTER XXI.

THE CLEARING-HOUSE SYSTEM.

By means of the London agency system, the banking transactions of the country are, as we have seen, brought to a focus in the city of London. The settlement of the reciprocal claims of the twenty-six principal city banks is therefore a business of the utmost magnitude and importance, representing as it does the completion of the business of no small part of the world. In a room of moderate dimensions, entered from a narrow passage running from the post-office in King William Street across to Lombard Street, debts to the average amount of nearly twenty millions sterling per day are liquidated without the use of a single coin or bank-note. In the classic financial neighbourhood of Lombard Street, and even in this very chamber, the system of paper commerce has been brought nearly to perfection. The early history of the London Clearing House is buried in obscurity, and it is much to be desired that those who are acquainted with the principal incidents in its progress should put them on record before it is too late.

The Clearing House appears to have been first created just a century ago. About the year 1775 a few of the city bankers hired a room where their clerks could meet to exchange notes and bills, and settle their mutual debts. The society was of the nature of a strictly private club, the public knowing nothing about it, and the transactions being conducted in perfect secrecy. Mr. Gilbart tells us that, even in this form, it was regarded as a questionable innovation, and some of the principal bankers refused to have anything to do with it. By degrees, however, the convenience of the arrangement made itself apparent, more bankers were admitted to the society, and a distinct committee and set of rules were formed for its management. Although it remains to the present day a private and voluntary association, unchartered, and in fact unknown to the law, the Clearing House has steadily grown in importance and in the publicity of its proceedings.

Several important extensions of the clearing work have been made in the last twenty-five years. After the rise of the London Joint Stock Banks, subsequent to 1833, they were for a long time refused admittance to the Clearing House; but in June, 1854, they were at last allowed to join the association. The Bank of England long remained entirely outside of the confederation, but more recently it has become a member, so far as regards the presentation of claims upon other banks. The West End banks of London are still beyond its sphere, partly, perhaps, because their distance stands in the way of the working of the system. They are thus in the position of provincial banks, and can clear through city agents like provincial banks.

Before the year 1858 the business of the Clearing House was restricted to the exchange of cheques and bills actually drawn on the clearing bankers. Country bankers receiving cheques drawn upon other distant country banks were in the habit of remitting them direct by post, the paying bank effecting the payment by directing their London banker to pay the amount to the London agent of the receiving bank. In the year 1858, at the suggestion of Mr. William Gillett, but chiefly by the exertions of Sir John Lubbock, the country clearing system was organized. The country banker, instead of posting many cheques every day to all parts of the kingdom, sends them in a single parcel to his London agent, to be presented through the Clearing House on the London agents of the paying banks. This exchange is made, as we shall see, at different hours of the day, but the results are summed up in the general balance of the day's transactions.

Transaction of Business at the London Clearing House.

There are three clearings daily at the Lombard Street House. The morning clearing opens on ordinary days at 10.30; drafts are received not later than 11, and the work must be closed at noon. The country clearing then begins, drafts being received until 12.30, and the clearing closed at 2.15. The heaviest clearing, however, is that of the afternoon, which begins at 2.30.

The bustle and turmoil of the work grow to a climax at four o'clock, the runners rushing in with the last parcels of drafts, up to the moment when the door is finally closed. On the fourth day of each month, when the heaviest work occurs, the hours are extended, the House opening at nine o'clock.

The Clearing House is a plain oblong room, with rows of desks in compartments round three sides, and down the middle. A small office for the two superintendents stands at one end. Each bank sends as many clerks to the House as may be requisite for the rapid completion of the work, and some banks have as many as six clerks. The cheques and bills to be presented by any one clearing banker, say the Alliance Bank, upon any other clearing banker, are entered at home in the "Out-clearing book," and are then sorted into twenty-five parcels, one of which is to be presented on each of the other clearing banks. On reaching the Clearing House, these parcels are distributed round the room to the desks of the clerks representing the several paying banks, who immediately begin to enter them in the "In-clearing books" in columns bearing at the head the name of the presenting bank. After being entered, the drafts are, as soon as possible, forwarded to the banking house for examination and entry in the bank books. Any cheques or bills refused payment are called "returns," and can generally be sent back to the Clearing House the same day, and entered again as a reverse claim by the bank dishonouring them on the banks which presented them. At the close of the day the clerks of the Alliance Bank are able to add up the whole of the claims which have been made upon them by the other twenty-five banks, and they learn from the out-clearing book the amount of the claims which the Alliance Bank is making on other banks. The difference is the balance which the Alliance Bank has either to pay or receive as the case may be. These balances being communicated to the superintendents of the House are by them inserted in a kind of balance sheet. When finally added up, the debtor and creditor sides of the sheet should exactly balance, because every penny to be received by one bank must be paid by another.

In former years the balance due by or to each bank was paid in bank-notes, and in the year 1839, average daily transactions to the amount of about three millions were cleared by the use of £200,000 in bank-notes, and £20 in coin, or about one-fifteenth part of the debts liquidated. More recently a suggestion of the late Charles Babbage was carried into effect, and the balances were paid by drafts upon the Bank of England, in which bank each city banker deposits a large part of his spare cash.

One ingenious minor arrangement in the London Clearing House is the division of the whole list of twenty-six bankers into three groups, in such a way that one of the clearing clerks of the Alliance Bank corresponds with one group of the other banks, a second clerk with the second group, and so on. Thus when a comparison or correction of accounts is made between any two banks, it is known precisely which clerk must answer to the questions called across the room.

Although the rapid and effective way in which the settlement is carried out in the London Clearing House must always excite surprise, it is quite open to question whether improvements are not needed. The room did not seem to me large enough for the convenient and wholesome transaction of such vast and increasing work. Although some banks employ as many as six clerks, the pressure is very great at times. The facility which these clerks acquire by practice in making and adding up entries is very great, but the intense head work performed against time, in an atmosphere far from pure, and in the midst of bustle and noise arising from the corrections shouted from one clerk to another across the room, must be exceedingly trying. Brain disease is occasionally the consequence.

The question must arise, too, whether the privilege of clearing is to be for ever restricted to twenty-six principal city banks, when there are certainly many other banks existing or being founded which need the convenience of access to the House. In New York the clearing circle, as we shall see, is much wider. At present the minor London banks are forced to employ the clearing bankers as agents, or to forego the advantages of the Clearing House altogether. It is hardly just or possible that a narrow monopoly of the sort should be maintained for ever.

Manchester Clearing House.

Though the London Clearing House is entirely the birthplace of the system, and the spot where the work has been organized on the largest scale, it does not follow that it is in every respect the most suitable for imitation in commercial towns of less magnitude. At least two English provincial towns, Manchester and Newcastle, have established local clearing houses. The bankers of Liverpool, also, I am told, have recently arranged a private system of clearing among themselves; and it is possible that the bankers of other towns may have taken a similar step without the fact becoming generally known. Through the kindness of some members of the committee, I have received full information as to the working of the Manchester Clearing House. The business seems to have been arranged, chiefly, I believe, by Mr. E. W. Nix, with great success, and it may be useful to describe the arrangements in detail, as they would be very suitable for adoption in many English, foreign, or colonial towns, which will doubtless before long establish clearing houses.

In the Manchester Clearing House the work is performed entirely upon loose forms, and not in account-books, as in London. Though these forms may seem rather numerous and elaborate, they greatly assist in the accurate and orderly settlement of the balance. The clearing clerk, before leaving his bank, sorts out the drafts, which he has to deliver, into thirteen parcels, one for each of the thirteen other banks, and then fills up thirteen lists, one for each parcel, in the Form No. 1 shown below, each cheque being represented only by the amount of money expressed in it. A copy of the list is entered in one of the books of the bank provided for the purpose.

Form No. 1.

MANCHESTER BANK CLEARING.

Mem. of Cheques delivered by

to

_____Clearing.   _____187

Adding up each such list, he inserts the totals in one of the left-hand columns of the Form No. 2. He thus obtains a complete abstract of all the claims he holds upon other banks, and adding up the columns ascertains the aggregate "Out-clearing."

Form No. 2.

MANCHESTER BANK CLEARING.

_____ 187

OUT.			IN.	
First Clearing.	Second Clearing.		First Clearing.	Second Clearing.
		Adelphi		
		Bank		
		Consolidated		
		County		
		Cunliffe's		
		District		
		Heywood		
		Joint Stock		
		King Street		
		Lancashire		
		National Provincial		
		Salford		
		Sewell		
		Union		
		Total		
		Balance		

On reaching the Clearing House, the clerk walks round the room and lays on the desk belonging to each other bank the parcel of cheques and the corresponding list already described. In the course of a little time thirteen similar parcels and lists will be laid on his own desk by the clerks of other banks, and as they come in he compares the list with the cheques, verifies the addition, and if all be correct, enters the amount in one of the right-hand columns of the second form, against the name of the bank presenting the drafts. These parcels are called the "*In-clearing*," and represent all the claims of other banks upon the one in question, so that when all the thirteen amounts are entered, and the columns added up, the clerk learns the aggregate which his bank will have to pay.

At Manchester two clearings are held each day. The first at 11.15 a.m. is a preliminary one only, and no payment of balances is made. As soon as the columns for the first clearing are filled up, the clerk returns to his bank with the in-clearing parcel of cheques and drafts presented upon the bank. These documents are immediately examined by the proper officials in order to detect any which may be irregular, fraudulent, or, for want of funds, or other reasons, must be dishonoured. At the Clearing House the clerk has already made a first rough inspection, and returned any documents which were obviously irregular, but no draft is considered to be finally accepted until one hour after the clearing is over. The returned drafts are comparatively few, and, as soon as detected, are forwarded direct to the bank presenting them.

The second clearing takes place at 2.15 p.m. and is

conducted just as in the morning. The second columns of the out- and in-clearing, in Form 2, having been filled and summed up, the totals of the first columns are added in, and the clerk learns the sum that has to be paid, and at the same time to be received, by his bank. The difference is the balance which he has either to receive or pay. These totals and the balance he copies into the following brief form, No. 3, which he hands to the inspector of the Clearing House.

Form No. 3.

CLEARING RETURNS.

Messrs.

Out-Clearing £ : :
In-Clearing £ : :
Balance . . . £ : :

Date_____ 187

The inspector now proceeds to verify the balances by inserting the amounts in Form No. 7, given on the next page, in an abbreviated form, only four of the names of the banks being inserted, to save space. In these forms the names of the banks are given in the briefest manner, and the Branch Bank of England is called simply "Bank."

Form No. 7.

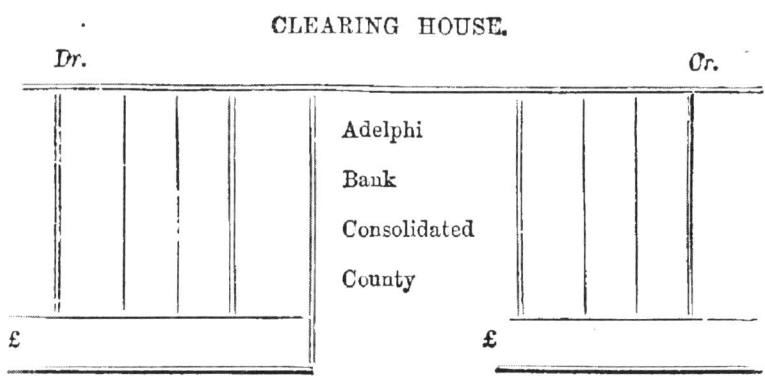

It is evident that the total which some of the banks have to receive on balance must equal what the others have to pay, because every cheque has been added in twice, once in favour of, and once against, some bank. If the debtor and creditor columns of the seventh form, being added up, fail to balance, some error of account must have been committed, and all the work is submitted to careful re-examination until the error is detected. When all is correct, it remains only to effect the payments, which is done by means of credit and debit notes, directing transfers in the books of the Branch Bank of England, to or from the accounts of the clearing bankers. The payments are made, indeed, to and from the Clearing House, as a kind of fictitious entity; but as its payments and receipts each day exactly balance, the Clearing House requires no separate ledger account, except for small current expenses, or inconsiderable errors.

To effect the transfer the clerk of each paying bank fills up the double form, No. 4, as follows:—

Form No. 4.

SETTLEMENT AT THE CLEARING HOUSE.	SETTLEMENT AT THE CLEARING HOUSE.
Manchester, _____ 187	BANK OF ENGLAND,
To the Cashiers of the BANK OF ENGLAND,	*Manchester,* _____ 187
Be pleased to TRANSFER from our Account the sum of _____	*A* TRANSFER *for the sum of* _____
and place it to the Credit of the Account of the Clearing Bankers, and allow it to be drawn for by any of them (with the knowledge of the Inspector, signified by his countersigning the Drafts).	*has this evening been made at the Bank, from the Account of Messrs.* _____ *to the Account of the Clearing Bankers.*
	For the Bank of England,
£	£

The coupon on the left-hand side is a draft to be signed by the clerk, if he has authority for the purpose, or else to be carried by him to his principals to be signed, and then paid into the Bank of England. It directs the cashier to credit the Clearing House with the balance, and debit the sum to the paying bank in question. The authorized official of the Bank of England signs the corresponding form on the right hand, when the payment is made, as a receipt for the sum on behalf of the Clearing House.

When, on the other hand, the balance is in favour of a bank, Form No. 5, printed on green paper for the sake of easy discrimination, comes into use. It sufficiently explains itself.

Form No. 5.

SETTLEMENT AT THE CLEARING HOUSE.	SETTLEMENT AT THE CLEARING HOUSE.
Manchester, _____ 187	BANK OF ENGLAND,
To the Cashiers of the BANK OF ENGLAND,	*Manchester,* _____ 187
Be pleased to CREDIT our Account the sum	*The Account of Messrs.* _____
£ _____	*has this evening been* CREDITED *with the Sum*
	of _____
out of the money at the Credit of the Account of the Clearing Bankers.	*out of the money at the Credit of the Account of the Clearing Bankers.*
	For the Bank of England.
£ _____	£ _____

There remains then only the question of the returned cheques. Even these do not require cash payment. The balance at the close of the day is paid only provisionally, and those cheques which have to be dishonoured are returned within an hour to the bank presenting them. Unless the irregularities be explained away, or removed, the presenting cashier then signs the following form, No. 6, which is an acknowledgment that so much money too much was received by him at the last clearing. This form is included by the bank dishonouring the cheques, in its out-clearing parcel, and the matter is rectified in the balance of the next clearing.

Form No. 6.

MANCHESTER BANK CLEARING.

Manchester, _____ 18

We shall Credit _____

in next clearing, on presentation of this slip, £ _____
as below, for unpaid cheques.

For _____

£ _____
,, _____
,, _____

The settlement in the Manchester Clearing House is often effected in less time than it would take to read this account of the method, and the work goes on with noiseless ease, strongly contrasting with the turmoil of the London House. No doubt, the amounts cleared are comparatively insignificant in Manchester, the average daily sums being, in the years 1872, 1873, and 1874, respectively £226,160, £237,150, and £247,930, or little more than one-hundredth part of the daily transactions in the Lombard Street House.

The Manchester Clearing House is managed by a committee of bankers, of which the chief agent of the Bank of England in Manchester is the chairman, and the superintendence of the clearing work is conducted by an official of the Bank of England. Thus the Bank, while naturally taking precedence, harmoniously co-operates with the local bankers.

New York Clearing House.

The New York Clearing House was established in October, 1853, and has become a most important institution, embracing 59 banks, as compared with 26 in London, and settling transactions hardly, if at all, inferior in amount to those of the London house. The general method of settling the business is necessarily much the same as that already described, but it seems to be in some respects better arranged than in London. The work is carried on in a fine large Exchange Room, and there is proper accommodation for the manager and his clerks, instead of the small glass box in which the inspectors sit in the Lombard Street room.

Each New York bank has one settling clerk in the Exchange Room, besides a messenger, who brings and delivers the parcels of cheques and bills. The settling clerks sit in a series of desks arranged in an oval form in the middle of the spacious room, and the exchanges are effected by an equal number of messengers simultaneously walking round the desks, delivering the parcels of "out-clearing," and receiving those of "in-clearing," or as they are called in New York the *Credit* and *Debit Exchanges*. An account of the institution will be found in Gibbon's work on "The Banks of New

York." There are said to be no less than fifteen provincial clearing-houses in the principal cities of the United States, so that the clearing system would seem to be more developed there than in the United Kingdom.

Extension of the Clearing System.

Until within the last few years there existed only two bankers' clearing houses, those of Lombard Street and New York, but much progress has recently been made in extending a similar system to other places, and even to other branches of business. The Manchester Clearing House was established in July, 1872, and Newcastle has a similar establishment. On the continent only a single city has yet adopted the method. In Paris about eighteen bankers have formed an association, called a "Chambre des Compensations," which is located in the Place de la Bourse, and balances the reciprocal claims of these firms much in the manner of the English clearing houses. In France, Germany, and other continental countries the use of the banker's cheque is much less developed than in England and America. In Germany a person wishing to remit a hundred pounds will often collect the actual coins, seal them up in a bag with five seals, and register them at the post-office. Thanks to the excellent system of government *Postes* existing in Germany, this method of remittance is sufficiently safe. But it is evident that where the monetary arrangements of a country are of such a kind there is no need of a clearing house.

The method of balancing claims needs by no means to be restricted to the business of banking. As, indeed, the monetary transactions of any locality come to a focus in the banks, the principal clearing will always be in the hands of bankers. But wherever a set of traders have numerous reciprocal claims, they may find it desirable to set up their own clearing house. As long ago as 1842, it occurred to Robert Stephenson and Mr. K. Morison, that the principle of the City Clearing House might be advantageously applied to settling the very complicated accounts arising between the railway companies, which have *through* booking arrangements. The work constantly carried on in the great house full of accountants at Euston Square is vastly more complicated and various than that of a bankers' clearing house; but the final result is to ascertain how much each railway company is indebted to each other one. The balance due to or from each company is then paid by a transfer at the bankers.

Within the last twelve months an attempt has been made, unsuccessfully as yet, to introduce the general use of cheques into Liverpool, where great sums of money are constantly passing, especially in the cotton market. For reasons which it would be difficult to trace out satisfactorily, the Liverpool merchants and bankers have never adopted the use of cheques to the same extent and in the same way as in other commercial towns. Many firms in Liverpool still refuse to receive payment by cheques, and only a year or two ago it was a common practice for a Manchester firm to send a clerk to Liverpool by railway with a bundle of bank-notes to make payments. At present, as I am informed, bank bills payable at sight, and forwarded by post, are substituted for Bank of England notes.

A Liverpool stock or cotton broker, wanting to make a payment, draws money out of his bank in notes and gold, and his clerks carry it about the town. Every evening a great number of small cash-boxes, containing large sums of money, are deposited at a well-known silversmith's shop, opposite the Town Hall, for safe custody during the night. A great amount of capital is thus kept lying idle, and it is surprising that the bankers do not secure this sum, as an addition to their deposits, by removing every obstacle. At present the practice is to charge $\frac{1}{8}$ or $\frac{1}{4}$ per cent. commission, whereas the actual cost of the accountants' work by which the bank transfers are accomplished is almost nominal in regard to large transactions.

An important extension of the clearing principle was effected by the establishment, in 1874, of the London Stock Exchange Clearing House, which undertakes to clear, not sums of money, but quantities of stock. As stock brokers settle their transactions only once a fortnight, or in consols once a month, it naturally arises that, in the intervals, the same broker will usually have bought the same kind of stock for one client and sold it for another. The very same stock may have passed through several different hands, and the same brokers may have had reciprocal dealings with each other. Instead, then, of actually making transfers of stock for each transaction, and paying by cheques which greatly swell the business of the Lombard Street Clearing House on settling days, a plan has been arranged, according to which each member of the Clearing House prepares a statement of the net amount of each stock which he has to receive from or deliver to each other member. The manager of the house, after verifying these accounts, which should balance in the aggregate, directs the debtor members to transfer quantities of stock to the creditor members in such a way as to close all the transactions. It will be noticed that, for pretty obvious reasons, the transfers are made in the stock exchange, directly from broker to broker, and not to the manager of the Clearing House, as in banking transactions. A separate clearing has, of course, to be made in each kind of stock. It is found that the quantities actually transferred do not exceed 10 per cent. of the whole transactions cleared, and the cheques drawn are diminished on settling days as much as ten millions sterling.

Still more recently the Cotton Brokers' Association of Liverpool, although unable to apply the system of clearing as yet to their money transactions, have arranged a clearing system for the settlement of business connected with sales of cotton "to arrive." Under the new arrangement the first seller and the last buyer come into contact, and all intermediate business, which sometimes occasioned much dispute and delay from contracts involving many middle-men, will be, as it were, cancelled by the Clearing House. The business, indeed, is being extended, so that all contracts, declarations, and payments will be effected through the agency of the association.

It may very well admit of question whether we have at all reached the limit of the advantageous application of the clearing principle. From bankers' transactions it has been extended to railways, stock exchange, and cotton brokers' business. It is conceivable that any other body of merchants, brokers, publishers, or others who have frequent pecuniary claims upon each other, might have a clearing meeting once or twice a week. Suggestions to this effect have already been made, and I am told that in the Glasgow iron market, a settlement day for the clearing of mutual transactions has been established.

Advantages of the Cheque and Clearing System.

Returning to the subject of the bankers' Clearing Houses, it is to be remarked concerning the vast system of relations which now exists between English banks, that it has grown spontaneously, uninvented, unauthorized by the legislature, and only recognized by the judges when firmly established as a matter of business custom. No Act of Parliament has been passed to facilitate the operations of clearing, and it is only by an understanding between the banks, that the presentation of cheques and bills through the Clearing House, or their settlement by the payment of a balance, is regarded as legally valid.

The advantages of the system are evidently of enormous magnitude. All the larger payments are made with a minimum of risk, loss of time, trouble, or use of the precious metals. While the cheque representing a payment is travelling about the country, the money which it is transferring is reposing in the vaults of some bank, or rather, not being needed in the operation at all, is lent or sent out of the country, so that its interest is saved. We found in p. 165 that the loss of interest upon the metallic money now circulating or stored up in the United Kingdom, amounts to between four and five millions annually. If payments were now made by coin only, many times as much metallic money would be needed.

The security with which the payments are effected is also an element of importance. Specie when transmitted in large sums, is always a temptation to thieves, and has usually to be accompanied by one or more guards. Through the agency of banks, whether by crossed cheques or credit notes, the largest payments may be made with almost absolute immunity from risk. The cheques, bills, and other documents transferred in the clearing houses are, as a general rule, so crossed or endorsed as to be of no value to any one but the legal owners, and in any case are regarded by thieves as "duffer," with which they dare not meddle.

Proportion of Cash Payments.

It is surprising to find to what an extent paper documents have replaced coin as a medium of exchange in some of the principal centres of business. In the *Statistical Journal* for September, 1865, Sir J. Lubbock published some particulars concerning the business of his bank during the last few days of 1864. Transactions to the amount of £23,000,000 were effected by the use of coin and documents, as shown in the following statement:—

	PER CENT.
Cheques and Bills passed through the Clearing House	70·8
Cheques and Bills not cleared	23·3
Bank of England Notes	5·0
Coin	·6
Country Bank-notes	·3
	100·0

The sums of money paid in by town customers amounted to £19,000,000, and when analysed gave the following results:—

	PER CENT.
Cheques and Bills	96·8
Bank of England Notes	2·2
Country Bank-notes	·4
Coin	·6
	100·0

It is not for a moment to be supposed that these figures represent the average use of coin in banking transactions. The proportional amounts of different kinds of money and commercial documents used in different parts of the country, in different tra'es, or in banks of different size and character vary widely. It is much to be desired that bankers and others who have the facts before them should publish more copious information on the subject. In Manchester the use of Bank of England notes appears to be much more extensive than in London. Mr. R. H. Inglis Palgrave gave in the *Statistical Journal* for March, 1873 (p. 86,, an estimate prepared for him by Mr. Langton, the Managing Director of the Manchester and Salford Bank, of the proportion of cash payments made in that bank. It appears that coin and notes formed 53 per cent. of the total turn-over in 1859, 42 per cent. in 1864, and only 32 per cent. in 1872, so that a rapid decrease has been going on. But we find that in 1872 the amount of notes was still large, the turn-over of customers' accounts being thus composed:—

	PER CENT.
Cheques, Bills, etc.	68
Bank-notes	27
Coin	5
	100

I have endeavoured to form some notion of the comparative amounts of cheques and bills which are cleared off at successive points in the organization of the banking system. It is very desirable that we should learn what proportion the transactions of the Clearing House bear to the whole transactions of the banks of the kingdom. There would not be much difficulty in forming a fair estimate if we had from one or more banks in each of the principal towns a statement of the comparative amounts of cheques dealt with in various manners. According to information kindly furnished to me by the authorities of one of the principal banks of Manchester, I find that, during the months July to October, 1874, the cheques and bills on demand presented on or through the bank were disposed of as follows:—

	PER CENT.
Cheques paid in Coin and Bank-notes over the Counter	34·2
Cheques on Selves paid to Credit of Account	25·4
Cheques presented through Manchester Clearing House	22·5
Cheques and Bills on demand on London presented through London Clearing House	10·8
Cheques on Country Bankers presented through the London Clearing House	3·5
Cheques on Country Bankers presented direct	3·6
	100·0

Although considerable trouble has been spent in the preparation of this account, it seems doubtful whether the items are complete and correct, and I give it more as a specimen of the kind of information which is much wanted than as a reliable statement.

Cases to which the Clearing System is inapplicable.

It will now be sufficiently apparent that, so long as trade is reciprocal, the cheque and clearing system can arrange all exchanges without the use of coin. The values of goods are estimated and expressed in terms of gold, which acts as the common denominator of value, but metallic money ceases to be the medium of exchange. The banking organization effects what I have heard Mr. W. Langton describe, as *a restoration of barter*. But it happens in some cases that transactions are not reciprocal, and cannot be made to balance. In certain trades there is a permanent *set* of the goods in one direction. In the Manchester cotton trade, for instance, the manufacturers in purchasing cotton from the Liverpool merchants, pay with cash or short credits. The goods when completed are often shipped again at Liverpool for foreign consignees at long credits, but are not generally purchased by the Liverpool merchants. Consequently, while the Manchester manufacturer owes the Liverpool merchant for the whole cost of the raw material, and for the shipping charges and freight upon the goods sent abroad, there are no equivalent claims of Manchester merchants against Liverpool. The foreign consignees of the goods pay for them by bills upon London. Now if the Manchester manufacturers held their funds in Manchester, and the Liverpool merchants their funds in Liverpool, there would have to be a constant current of money from London to Manchester, and from Manchester to Liverpool, whence it would go abroad to pay for the raw material. This inconvenient state of things is remedied to a certain extent, as we shall see in Chapter XXIII., by making London the head-quarters and clearing house both of home and foreign transactions.

But there is always a liability that claims expressed in metallic money, and actually capable of being demanded in that shape at the option of the owner, will sometimes be pressed. In certain states of trade, or under certain contingent circumstances, the holders of cheques require gold, and bankers who have become accustomed to consider metallic reserves as almost superfluous, find themselves suddenly in a difficult position. Such, as we shall see in Chapter XXIV., is the real cause of the present instability of the English money market.

CHAPTER XXII.

THE CHEQUE BANK.

THE Cheque and Clearing System, so far as we have hitherto considered it, is mainly restricted to the arrangement of considerable payments. No one can enjoy its advantages unless he keeps a banking account, and for this purpose he must be able to command a certain sum of money, and must have a sufficiently good position and credit to be entrusted by a banker with a cheque book. The result is that the larger part of the population is entirely outside the banking system, and must either use coin, postage stamps, or post-office orders in making payments.

A very ingenious attempt is now being made to extend the area of banking to the masses by the institution of the Cheque Bank. When preparing materials for this book, I was so much struck by the way in which this new bank seems to be adapted to complete the cheque and clearing system in a downward direction, that I applied to Mr. James Hertz, the able inventor of the scheme, for information upon the subject, and have been enabled to inquire minutely into it.

The weak point of the present ordinary cheque book is, that a person once getting a book full of blank cheques, can fill them up for any amounts, irrespective of the balance against which they are supposed to be drawn. Here is an opening for easy fraud, if cheques were generally received from strangers without inquiry. The Cheque Bank proceeds on the new principle of issuing cheques which can be filled up only to limited amounts, as shown by printed and indelible perforated notices upon the forms. These cheques, too, are only to be had in exchange for the utmost sum for which they can be drawn, which sum is retained as a deposit until each corresponding cheque has been presented. It follows that each cheque, when duly filled up and signed by the owner, is as good as a bank-note issued against a documentary reserve. It is true that cheque books or forms may be lost or purloined, and then fraudulently signed and issued; but, being drawn to order and crossed, these documents are very dangerous to meddle with in a criminal manner, and, in the only instance in which fraud has yet been attempted, swift punishment followed.

Relation of the Cheque Bank to other Banks.

We have seen how much has been accomplished by establishing relations between banks, as branches, agents, or correspondents of each other. The Cheque Bank carries out a similar system to the utmost extent by establishing relations with almost all the banks of the United Kingdom, as well as with most foreign banks of importance. Already 984 English, Irish, or Scotch banks, have entered into relations with the Cheque Bank, and 596 colonial or foreign banks cash the cheques. One advantage of this arrangement is, that the sphere of the cheque system can be greatly extended without any equal increase of trouble and risk. Whenever a bank opens a new account with an individual, that account has to be kept apart in the ledger, and constantly watched. But a bank can sell Cheque Bank cheques to any amount, without opening separate accounts with the purchasers, and may also pay such cheques when presented without risk. The Cheque Bank thus aims at becoming a great institution of accountants, operating for the most part through other banks, but relieving them of much of the risk and trouble of small transactions. The Bank of England is a bankers' bank in the sense that it holds the reserves of other banks, and makes those final payments of cash which close the general balance of transactions. The Cheque Bank seems to be a bankers' bank in the opposite sense of making deposits in all other banks and employing them as agents.

A peculiar feature of the Cheque Bank is that it entirely abstains from using, or even holding, the money deposited. All money received for cheque books is left in the hands of the bankers, through whom they are issued, or transferred to other bankers, as may be needed for meeting the cheques presented. The interest paid by these bankers will be the source of profit, and as the money thus lies in the care of the most wealthy and reputable firms in the kingdom, it could not be lost in any appreciable quantity, except by the break-down of the whole banking system of the country. It would hardly be true to say that these cheques correspond to notes issued on the deposit of government funds, because each agent-bank can use at its own discretion the portion of the funds of the Cheque Bank in its possession. Nevertheless, as the portion in the hands of any one bank will usually be a small fraction of the whole, and there is, moreover, a guarantee fund of consols in the background, the system of issue is more closely analogous to that of a documentary reserve than any other.

The Cheque Bank as a Monetary Agent.

The Cheque Bank appears to aim at becoming the medium for the accomplishment of an immense mass of small payments. Small pensions and annuities, small dividends, small disbursements by officers of departments, by agents, clerks, or even domestic servants are made through it. A book of the Cheque Bank cheques can be safely trusted to almost any servant or agent who can write, and the cheque when presented forms a record of the way in which he has applied the money. No one can venture in like manner to give signed blank cheques to a servant, as they may be filled up for unlimited amounts, and the Cheque Bank cheques are evidently better than a sum of metallic money, which may be more readily misapplied, purloined, or lost.

The recipient of such cheques finds them one of the most convenient possible forms of remittance, because they will be cashed by almost any banker, and will therefore be received as cash by any person who has acquired sufficient knowledge of their nature. Thus the Cheque Bank seems to be capable of replacing with great advantage the money-order system of the English Post-Office.

To procure a post-office order it is requisite to apply at an office and wait while certain forms are being filled up. A definite office of payment must be selected, and the receiver of the order can obtain payment, as a general rule, only by applying personally at the office, and giving the name of the sender. Even if a person cannot afford to purchase a book of Cheque Bank cheques, he can, in towns where agencies are established for the purpose, buy single cheques filled up for any odd sum with less formality than at the post-office, and these cheques are payable not at one office, but at almost any bank in the United Kingdom and in most foreign towns. They can afterwards be restricted in payment, if desired, to any particular bank. The cost of remittance by cheques will on the average be lower than by money orders, since the Post-Office makes charges for inland orders, increasing from 1d. for sums under 10s. to 1s. for a £10 order, with much higher charges for orders to be paid in certain colonies or foreign countries. The Cheque Bank cheque costs only one penny and one-fifth of a penny in excess of the sum remitted, and of this charge the penny is for the government stamp duty and represents so much public revenue.

The government can have no reason for opposing the Cheque Bank, because if successful it must earn for the Chancellor of the Exchequer a large annual revenue. The money-order system, on the other hand, in spite of the higher charges, is understood to yield no profit, and is rather a burden upon the department. It is said that the issue of every money order involves the filling up of eight or nine forms, and the amount of labour rendered requisite swallows up the revenue. It is a very striking instance of the comparative inefficiency of government industry, except in special cases, that a single banking company can bring into use a form of remittance available in all parts of the world, and far cheaper than post-office orders, and yet pay duty upon their transactions.

The Cheque Bank also aims at becoming a collecting as well as a paying agency. Any public institution needing to collect a subscription, for instance, has only to procure a "paying-in" form, or credit note, and the sum inserted therein will be received by any of the numerous banks in relation. Thus small debts and subscriptions may be readily collected without trouble or expense in any part of the country.

Payment of Wages by Cheques.

The managers of the Cheque Bank hope to substitute their cheques for the coin now used by manufacturers in payment of wages. If this could be accomplished it would be convenient rather than otherwise to bankers, who are weekly called upon to furnish large sums in gold and silver coin, and have the trouble and cost of holding and counting a sufficient stock. Now, if a master in paying his men presented them with small cheques, or, perhaps better still, with cheques for even sums, and the balance in silver, the cheques would be cashed by shopkeepers, and would be deposited by them in the banks, or might even be bought back in large sums by the masters for further use. It was at one time the practice of great railway contractors to issue tally checks in the form of one, two, or five-shilling cards, which were paid to their workmen, and circulated among the publicans and tradesmen of the neighbourhood, until taken back by the contractor in wholesale. Such cheques constituted true representative money, but would be of doubtful legality. The Cheque Bank cheques might serve the same purpose, and have been declared legal, but it is yet very doubtful how far the wholesome practice of immediately presenting ordinary cheques will stand in the way of the continued circulation of other cheques, for which there is no need of immediate presentation. Time after time we have found that habit and custom exercise an immense and very unmanageable influence in monetary affairs, and it will probably take a long time to teach the public to look upon a cheque as a safe document to keep.

The Cheque Bank as a Savings Bank.

Already the Cheque Bank serves as a savings bank into which persons may put surplus money for security, receiving as an acknowledgment the cheque forms by which it can be drawn out or paid away with ease. No interest, however, is paid on such deposits. It seems to me, however, that the bank, if successful in its present aims, might readily become the most admirable of savings banks. Instead of issuing cheques payable at any moment, it might issue through its agent-banks, deposit receipts, bills, or, what comes to much the same thing, post-dated cheques, the interest to be paid at the time of deposit as a discount at the rate of 2 or $2\frac{1}{2}$ per cent. This receipt could be retained, transferred by endorsement, or again discounted by the Cheque Bank. If retained until maturity it would become payable like a cheque at any bank in relation with the Cheque Bank. The money deposited in this way might be invested in consols at $3\frac{1}{4}$ per cent., and the cost of the documents and accountants' work, being slight, might leave a fair margin of profit.

The Post-Office Savings Bank system as established by Mr. Gladstone is an admirable institution; it has been very successful, and has done great service in increasing providence. But it is troublesome and costly in working, and leaves no profit to the state. Already the Scotch banks serve almost in the capacity of savings banks by receiving small fixed deposits; and it is well worthy of consideration whether, by the assistance of the Cheque Bank, almost all the English banks might not be converted into savings banks, to the advantage of every one.

Results of the Cheque Bank System.

I have thought it quite suitable to this book to enter somewhat minutely into the actual and possible work done by the Cheque Bank, because, if successful, the institution opens an indefinite sphere for financial improvement. The institution is, indeed, at present a mere experiment, undertaken at the risk of shareholders, and it can only succeed by offering conveniences to the public and the body of bankers. It may succeed in some of its schemes, and not in others, but in any case it will tend to replace coin payments by cheque payments, to be balanced off in the general London clearing. The profits of the bank depend upon the very small charge of $\frac{1}{5}$ of a penny for each cheque, and the interest on deposits. The amount of deposits remaining undrawn depends upon three circumstances: (1) the time before the cheque is utilized; (2) the time it is in circulation, or travelling about, and (3) the difference between the sum drawn and that deposited. The average duration of circulation, I am informed, was lately ten days, but many cheques have already been out a year.

I should add that, in describing with some detail the operations of the Cheque Bank, I have no interest in the success of the institution other than a strictly scientific interest. In any case it is a most ingenious innovation, and if successful cannot fail to benefit the community in a high degree, adding a new feature to a banking system already wonderfully organized.

CHAPTER XXIII.

FOREIGN BILLS OF EXCHANGE.

In early times foreign trade consisted in the direct exchange of commodities. A caravan set out with a variety of manufactured articles, across the deserts of Arabia or Sahara, and came back with the ivory, spices, and other valuable raw produce obtained by barter. In later times the merchant loaded his own ship and sent her forth on an adventure, trusting that his ship-master would sell the cargo to advantage, and, with the proceeds, bring back another cargo to be sold to great profit at home. Trade was thus evidently reciprocal, and what was sent out paid for what was brought back, so that little or no money was kept idle in the mean time.

Wherever this direct reciprocal exchange did not exist it was necessary either to transmit metallic money, or to devise some mode of transferring debts. Now the transmission of money not only causes the loss of interest during the interval of transit, but leads to the expense of guarding it, and the liability of total loss. Many centuries ago, accordingly, it was discovered that the use of paper documents would economize, if not altogether render needless, the use of metallic money in foreign trade.

Origin and Nature of Bills of Exchange.

Even the Romans appear to have been acquainted in a slight degree with the system of foreign bills of exchange; but it is to the early Italian, and especially the Jewish merchants, that we owe the development of the practice. The history of the subject is buried in much obscurity, but there is evidence that, as early as the fourteenth century, the use of bills of exchange was fully established. The forms of the bills, and the laws and customs relating to them, were then much the same as in the present day.

A bill is nothing but an order to pay money addressed by the drawer to the drawee, or person on whom it is drawn, specifying the amount to be paid, the time of payment, and the person to whom it is to be paid. Whenever a bill is drawn, it is to be presumed that a debt is due from the drawee to the drawer. When presented to the drawee and accepted by him, this acceptance is an acknowledgment of the existence of the debt. The bill, although drawn in favour of a particular person, is transferable by endorsement, and thus represents a negotiable claim to receive money at a future date in a distant country. Hence it is capable of being transmitted in discharge of another debt of equal amount.

England buys every year from America a great

quantity of cotton, corn, pork, and many other articles. America at the same time buys from England iron, linen, silk, and other manufactured goods. It would be obviously absurd that a double current of specie should be passing across the Atlantic Ocean in payment for these goods, when the intervention of a few paper acknowledgments of debt will enable the goods passing in one direction to pay for those going in the opposite direction. The American merchant who has shipped cotton to England can draw a bill upon the consignee to an amount not exceeding the value of the cotton. Selling this bill in New York to a party who has imported iron from England to an equivalent amount, it will be transmitted by post to the English creditor, presented for acceptance to the English debtor, and one payment of cash on maturity will close the whole circle of transactions. Money intervenes twice over, indeed, once when the bill is sold in New York, once when it is finally cancelled in England; but it is evident that payment between two parties in one town is substituted for payment across the whole breadth of the Atlantic. Moreover, the payments may be effected by the use of cheques, or the bills when due may themselves be presented through the Clearing House, and balanced off against other bills and cheques. Thus the use of metallic money seems to be rendered almost superfluous, and, so long as there is no great disturbance in the balance of exports and imports, foreign trade is restored to a system of *perfected barter*.

Trade in Foreign Bills.

It is an unnatural supposition that every importer of goods will meet with an exporter of goods to the same amount, so that two transactions will exactly balance each other. But there are many merchants in Liverpool indebted to American merchants, and many American merchants indebted to others in Liverpool. Hence there will be a continual supply of bills of various amounts, and a continual demand, and it becomes a profitable business for certain houses to deal in the bills, purchasing bills from those who can draw and selling to those who wish to remit.

Large firms of merchants often have houses both in America and in England, or a firm in one country has agents or correspondents in the other with whom they keep a running account. Not uncommonly, the very same firm may be both importing and exporting, so that a direct balancing of their accounts will be so far effected. The remaining balance need only be paid from time to time as opportunity offers. Thus, in foreign as in home trade, book credit serves in a great degree to economize the use of money. Only when there is a derangement of the balance of trade, and one country owes to another a preponderating debt of large amount, need specie be transmitted.

It is out of the question that I should, in this small treatise, attempt to enter into the intricacies of the Foreign Exchanges, which have been so admirably treated by Mr. Goschen, in his "Theory of the Foreign

Exchanges." The general principle of the subject is, that bills of exchange drawn on any particular place constitute a new kind of article, subject to the laws of supply and demand. Any circumstance diminishing the supply, or increasing the demand, raises the price of such bills, and *vice versâ*. The price being raised, there is additional profit on any transaction which allows a new supply of bills to be drawn. The export of any kind of goods in greater quantities tends to restore the balance, but, if requisite, coin or bullion can be sent at a certain cost, and bills drawn against it. Thus the cost of transmitting specie is the limit to the premium on bills. Gold and silver being everywhere considered a desirable possession, and being also very portable, form, as remarked at the outset, the natural currency between nation and nation. If a country were to be absolutely denuded of specie, and had foreign debts to pay, forced exportation and sale of the next most generally desirable and portable commodity would be the only resource, and the premium on bills might vary to almost any extent from par. Thus it is seen that, in an economical point of view, gold and silver differ from other merchandise not in kind but in degree.

The World's Clearing House.

It might seem that in the use of cheques internally, and of bills of exchange in foreign trade, we have reached the climax in the economy of metallic money; but there is yet one further step to make. We found that so long as all the merchants of a town keep their cash with the same banker, they have no need to handle the money at all, but can make payments by transfers in the books of their banker. Let us imagine, then, that merchants all over the world agreed to keep their principal accounts with the bankers of any one great commercial town. All their mutual transactions could then be settled among those bankers. An approximation to such a state of things exists in the tendency to make London the monetary head-quarters of the commercial world, and the general clearing house of international transactions.

All that is needed to secure economy of money is centralization of transactions, so that there may be the wider scope for the balancing of claims. Before the elaborate system of English provincial banking grew up, considerable economy was effected by the practice of "drawing upon London." In every country town many persons wanted to transmit money to London, and others wanted to draw money from the same place. To vast private trading transactions with the capital and principal commercial towns was added the whole of the payments connected with the collection and expenditure of the public revenue. In each country town some prominent trader discovered that profit was to be made by selling bills on London to those who wished to remit, and buying with the proceeds the bills of those who had claims upon banks or firms in London. The capital thus becoming the monetary centre, it was often convenient to make payments to other towns by bills upon

London. Each person wanting to remit was more likely to get a bill upon London with ease than upon any other place, and it was likely that the creditor would prefer such a bill to one upon a town with which he had no relations. It is obvious that if every important trader in England kept his principal cash with a city banker, the use of bills on London would have enabled all the commercial transactions of England to be centred in, and cleared through the books of these bankers and the Clearing House.

Centralization of Financial Transactions in London.

There is a similar advantage in centralizing foreign transactions in London. In the absence of any general centre each two commercial towns must settle their mutual transactions directly and separately. A merchant will be receiving bills upon the bankers and merchants of many other towns. There is a double inconvenience in this. The supply and demand for bills upon comparatively small places must be comparatively small and variable, and the bills will be drawn upon minor firms, of the soundness of which it will not be easy to get satisfactory information. Many firms, too, in the present day have houses in several parts of the world, and it would be more convenient that their mutual transactions should be brought to a centre somewhere, just as the transactions of branch banks are brought to a centre in the head office. Thus there arises a tendency to prefer bills drawn upon well-known London banks, or other great London firms, whose credit is known all over the world, and *ceteris paribus*, such bills will command a readier acceptance in the exchange market. Persons having to draw bills will get a better price if they can draw upon London, which they can do by opening an account with a London firm, and arranging that remittances due to them shall be deposited to their credit in London. It comes to pass that a merchant in America, Australia, or India, will prefer to receive money in London rather than anywhere else. Everyone wishing to remit money can then do so in the form of a bill upon the holders of these funds in London, and the fund will be recruited from time to time by similar bills received and transmitted to London for collection.

This tendency to the centralization of financial business in London is much promoted by the fact that the largest mass of cheap loanable capital exists there. The general rate of interest in New York is at least 2 per cent. higher than in London, so that a trader who has credit enough to obtain loans in London, will make a profit by borrowing there rather than in New York. Thus, instead of first depositing money in London, and afterwards drawing against it, the more usual and profitable form of the transaction is to get a credit there, that is, leave to draw against a banker, making subsequent remittances to recoup the banker accepting and paying the bills. As regards continental trade, Paris, Berlin, Vienna, Hamburg, and Amsterdam are of course highly important centres, but recent wars have occasioned a considerable transfer of financial business to London. Moreover, the great foreign trade of England, reaching into every quarter of the globe, and the many distant colonies and dependencies which naturally have financial relations with the capital of the empire, tend to give London a unique position.

Representation of Foreign Bankers in London.

The result of this centralization of banking transactions in London, is that colonial and foreign bankers find it very desirable to have agents, or even head offices in London. At the present time there are no less than 60 important colonial and foreign banks which have their own London offices or houses. These include the principal Australian, New Zealand, and Indian banks, and a number of minor banks, established by English capitalists to cultivate the trade of the minor states of Europe, South America, China, and the East. In addition to the above 60 banks, there are fully 1000 foreign and colonial banking houses in correspondence with London bankers, so that almost every town in the world which can maintain a bank at all, has the means of correspondence with some member of the London banking system. The foreign bankers vary greatly in the importance of their transactions, and some of them would, according to English ideas, be considered merchants rather than bankers; but, in the aggregate, their transactions must be exceedingly large. It must almost inevitably follow that transfers of money will be more and more made through London. Just as this city is the link of connection between each English country banker and each other one, so it may, and probably will by degrees, become the link between the most distant parts of the world. But the greater becomes the profitable burden of financial business thrown upon Lombard Street and Threadneedle Street, the more it behoves us to take care that our currency system is maintained upon the soundest possible basis. It is requisite, too, that our bankers, financiers, and merchants should regulate their operations with a thorough comprehension of the immense system in which they play a part, and the risks of derangement and failure which they encounter by over-severe competition. No one doubts that alarming symptoms have during recent years presented themselves in the London money market. There is a tendency to frequent severe scarcities of loanable capital, causing sudden variations of the rate of interest almost unknown thirty years ago. I will therefore in the next chapter offer a few remarks intended to show that this is an evil naturally resulting from the excessive economy of the precious metals, which the increasing perfection of our banking system allows to be practised, but which may be carried too far and lead to extreme disaster.

CHAPTER XXIV.

THE BANK OF ENGLAND AND THE MONEY MARKET.

WE commenced the study of money with the barter of ordinary commodities, and money appeared in the first place as some common commodity handed about as a medium of exchange. By degrees, however, the subject assumed a greater and greater degree of complexity. The metals took the place of other commodities as currency, and delicate considerations began to enter concerning token and standard coins. From metallic representative money, we passed to paper representative money, and finally discovered that, by the cheque and clearing system, metallic money was almost eliminated from the internal exchanges of the country. Pecuniary transactions now present themselves in the form of a room full of accountants, hastily adding up sums of money. But we must never forget that all the figures in the books of a bank represent gold, and every creditor can demand the payment of the metal. In the ordinary state of trade no one cares to embarrass himself with a quantity of precious metal, which is both safer and more available in the vaults of a bank. But in international trade, gold and silver are still the media by which

Expansion of Trade.

No one doubts that in the last thirty years there has been an immense expansion in the trade of this and most other countries. If, as is very commonly done, we take the foreign trade as a test of the general advance of industry, we find that the total declared real value of British and Irish produce exported from the United Kingdom was, in 1846, about 58 millions sterling. In 1866 it amounted to 189 millions, or more than three times as much. In the mean time the bank-note circulation had remained almost unchanged, and such alteration as there was, consisted in a decrease. The total circulation of bank-notes, English, Scotch, and Irish, was, in 1846, 39 millions, and in 1866, 38½ millions. I believe, however, that the best test of the progress of trade, both internal and external, is furnished by the out-put of coal, the mainspring of our wealth. Now, in 1854 the total quantity of coal raised was about 65 millions of tons, and the note currency 38 millions; in 1866 the coal raised had increased to 101½ millions of tons, or by 56 per cent., while the note currency still remained almost as before, namely, 38½ millions. Between 1866 and 1874, indeed, there was a remarkable increase in the circulation, the amount of which rose to

balances of indebtedness must be paid, and serious consequences may arise from any disproportion between the amount of transactions carried on, and the basis of gold upon which they are settled.

£43,912,000, or by 14 per cent., but the production of coal had in the mean time risen to 127 millions, an increase, compared with 1854, of 95 per cent.

Competition of Bankers.

It is quite apparent, therefore, that the tendency is to carry on a greater and greater trade upon an amount of metallic currency which does not grow in anything like the same proportion. The system of banking, too, grows more perfect in the sense of increasing the economy with which money is used. The competition of many great banks, leads them to transact the largest possible business with the smallest reserves which they can venture to retain. Some of these banks pay dividends of from 20 to 25 per cent, which can only be possible by using large deposits in a very fearless manner. Even the reserves consist not so much of actual coins or bank-notes in the vaults, as of money employed at call in the Stock Exchange, or deposited in the Bank of England, which again lends the deposits out to a certain extent.

Now the larger the trade which is carried on, the larger will be the occasional demand for gold to make foreign payments; and if the stock of gold kept in London be growing comparatively smaller and smaller, the greater will be the difficulty in meeting the demand from time to time. Such is, I believe, the whole secret of the growing instability and delicacy of the money market in this country. There is a larger and larger quantity of claims for gold, and comparatively less gold to meet them, so that every now and then there is a natural difficulty in paying claims, and the rate of interest has to be suddenly raised to induce those who have gold to lend it, or to induce those who were demanding it to forego their claims for a time. Most people, it is true, attribute all these troubles, either to the much-abused gentlemen who meet weekly in the parlour of the Bank of England, or to Sir Robert Peel, who established the note issue of the Bank upon the partial deposit system already described (p. 222).

The Bank Charter Act of 1844.

At all times, during the last two hundred years, there has been some currency topic upon the anvil. In early days it was the scarcity of silver coin, the South Sea Bubble, or the price of the guinea. Later on came the restriction of specie payments, the bullion report, the one-pound note question, and the joint stock banks. Since 1844, however, all currency theorists have concentrated their attentions upon the Bank Charter Act of that year, and, while endlessly differing about the nature of the remedy, have been unanimous in attributing all kinds of evils to a settlement of our currency, which I believe to be a monument of sound and skilful financial legislation.

The Acts of 1844 and 1845 placed a fixed limit upon the amount of notes which can in this country be issued without an equal deposit of gold. At present (April,

1875) the Bank of England can issue, without gold, fifteen millions; the private and joint stock banks of England are individually restricted to fixed amounts, which, added together, make about £6,460,000, while the Scotch banks can, in a similar manner, issue notes to the amount of £2,750,000, and the Irish banks to the amount of £6,350,000, making in all about $30\frac{1}{2}$ millions. In addition to this the Bank of England, and the Scotch and Irish banks, can issue as many more notes as they have deposits of bullion or coin; and in the year 1874, the extra amount thus issued was about $14\frac{1}{2}$ millions. Let it be never forgotten, that no restriction is thus placed upon the sum total of the currency of the country; for the original legal tender of the country is the coined sovereign of 123·274 grains of gold, and every one who has the gold can readily turn it into sovereigns. The objectors to the Bank Charter Act urge that we want more currency, but they cannot really mean more metallic currency. We must not look to changes in the law to increase the amount of specie in the country, and, as I have remarked, any one can get sovereigns if he has the needful gold. This metal, again, is only to be had, in the absence of gold mines, by that state of foreign trade which brings it, and does not drain it away again. The principal currency, in short, must be regarded as a commodity, the supply of which is to be left to the natural action of the laws of supply and demand. The unrestricted issue of paper representative notes produces an artificial interference with these natural conditions.

The Free-banking School.

What the currency theorists want, then, is not more gold, but more promises to pay gold. The Free-banking School especially argue that it is among the elementary rights of an individual to make promises, and that each banker should be allowed to issue as many notes as he can get his customers to take, keeping such a reserve of metallic money, as he thinks, in his own private discretion, sufficient to enable him to redeem his promises. But this free issue of paper representative money does not at all meet the difficulty of the money market, which is a want of gold, not of paper; on the contrary, an unlimited issue of paper would tend to reduce the already narrow margin of gold upon which we erect an enormous system of trade. Here we reach the critical point of the whole theory of currency. There is also a school of currency writers, formerly represented in England by Ricardo and Tooke, who hold that it is impossible to over-issue convertible paper money. Arguments to this effect have been recently urged with great ability by Mr. R. H. Inglis Palgrave, in his work entitled "Notes on Banking," and his wide acquaintance with the subject should lend much force to his opinions. But there is, to my mind, an evident flaw in their position.

Possibility of Over-issue.

When prices are at a certain level, and trade in a quiescent state, a single banker is, no doubt, unable to put

THE BANK OF ENGLAND AND THE MONEY MARKET.

into circulation more than a certain quantity of bank-notes. He cannot produce a greater effect upon the whole currency than a single purchaser can by his sales or purchases produce upon the market for corn or cotton. But a number of bankers, all trying to issue additional notes, resemble a number of merchants offering to sell corn for future delivery, and the value of gold will be affected as the price of corn certainly is. We are too much accustomed to look upon the value of gold as a fixed datum line in commerce; but, in reality, it is a very variable thing. The tables of prices analysed by me in the *Statistical Journal* for June, 1865, show that between 1822 and 1825 there was an average rise of prices to the amount of 17 per cent.; and between 1844 and 1847, and 1852 and 1857, the average rises were respectively 13 and 31 per cent. Such variations of prices mean that the value of gold is itself altered in the inverse ratio; and these variations are produced mainly by extensions of credit. Every one who promises to pay gold on a future day, thereby increases the anticipated supply of gold, and there is no limit to the amount of gold which can thus be thrown upon the market. Every one who draws a bill or issues a note, unconsciously acts as a "bear" upon the gold market. Everything goes well, and apparent prosperity falls upon the whole community, so long as these promises to pay gold can be redeemed or replaced by new promises. But the rise of prices thus produced turns the foreign exchanges against the country, and creates a balance of indebtedness which must be paid in gold.

The basis of the whole fabric of credit slips away, and produces that sudden collapse known as a commercial crisis.

Now, what is true of credit generally, is still more true of the special form of credit involved in bank promissory notes. These purport to be payable in gold coin on demand, so that they are taken by every one as equivalent to the coin. Even bills of exchange can be paid in notes, and as regards internal trade, no difficulty would be felt in maintaining credit so long as promises to pay gold circulate instead of gold. But foreigners will not hold such promises on the same footing; and, if the exchanges are against us, the metallic, not the paper, part of the currency will go abroad. It is at this moment that bankers will find no difficulty in expanding their issues, because many persons have claims to meet in gold, and the notes are regarded as gold. The notes will thus conveniently fill up the void occasioned by the exportation of specie; prices will be kept up, prosperity will continue, the balance of foreign trade will be still against us, and the game of replacing gold by promises will go on to an unlimited extent, until it becomes actually impossible to find more gold to make necessary payments abroad.

Professor Cliffe Leslie, writing in *Macmillan's Magazine* for August, 1864, correctly pointed out, as I think, that speculative credit often raises prices for a time above their natural range. Representative credit, on the other hand, by which I suppose he means notes issued against the actual deposit of metal, obviously forms no augmentation of the currency, and can have no effect in raising prices above the level which would exist under a purely metallic system.

The actual exhaustion of the bullion of a country is no mere ideal event, for it is what occurred in this country in 1839, under the free system of note issue. The Bank of England had parted with almost the whole of its bullion and was only saved from bankruptcy by the ignominious expedient of a large loan from the Bank of France. The narrow limits of this book evidently restrict me from entering into historical and statistical illustrations, but it may be said, that the collapse which followed the crisis of 1839 induced severer distress and depression of trade than has ever since been known in this country. We now carry on industry and commerce many times greater than in 1839, and there is nothing to indicate that either the bank directors or the commercial classes are more cautious or farseeing than they then were. On the contrary, competition, speculation, and the bold erection of the widest affairs upon the narrowest basis of real capital is more common than ever. Knowing as we do the very narrow margin of real metal upon which our many great banks conduct their business, it is impossible to entertain for a moment the notion of allowing the paper currency of the country to rest upon the discretionary reserves of such competing bankers.

The Right of Coining Bank Notes.

According to the view which I adopt, the issue of notes is more analogous to the royal function of coinage than to the ordinary commercial operation of drawing bills. We ought to talk of *coining notes*, as John Law did; for though the design is impressed on paper instead of metal, the function of the note is exactly the same as that of a representative token. As to the right to issue promises, it no more exists than the right to establish private mints. For our present purposes that alone is right which the legislature declares to be expedient to the community at large. As almost every one has long agreed to place the coinage of money in the hands of the executive government, so I believe that the issue of paper representative money should continue to be practically in the hands of the government, or its agents acting under the strictest legislative control. M. Wolowski, in his admirable works on banking, has maintained that the issue of notes is a function distinct from the ordinary operations of a banker; and Mr. Gladstone has allowed that the distinction is a wholesome and vital one. Bankers enjoy the utmost degree of freedom in this country at present, in every other point, so that it is wholly a confusion of ideas to speak of the unrestricted emission of paper representative money as a question of free banking.

Professor Sumner and others have objected to the Bank Charter Act, that it cannot be regarded as a scientific settlement of the currency question, inasmuch as no other nation had adopted the same principles. Quite lately, however, the German Imperial government has adopted the main principle of a partial deposit, adding to it the liberty of increasing the issues under a tax of 5 per cent., an arrangement which I have described under the name of the Elastic Limit System (p. 226). This provision appears to be designed to avoid the suspension of the law during times of crisis, and it is quite possible that we might with advantage introduce a similar modification into our own currency law. But the fine or tax upon the excessive issue ought surely to be much more than 5 per cent., and in this country should certainly not be less than 10 per cent.

Scotch and English Banking.

It is common, indeed, to point to the Scotch banks as a proof that a perfectly sound currency may be furnished by banks acting on their own unfettered discretion. Up to 1845, the twelve or thirteen Scotch banks certainly did possess the right of freely issuing notes down to one-pound notes, and only in one or two cases did bankruptcy occur. All this I grant, holding that Englishmen and Americans, and natives of all countries, may well admire the wonderful skill, sagacity, and caution with which Scotch bankers have developed and conducted their system. There is no doubt, too, that Scotch bankers are guiding the course of development of the banking system in England, India, the Australian colonies, and everywhere, with conspicuous success. If we were all Scotchmen, I believe the unlimited issue of one-pound notes would be an excellent measure. But when we compare the Scotch and English banking systems, we discover a profound difference. In Scotland there exist only *eleven* great banks, which take good care that there shall not be a twelfth great bank. The undoubted monopoly which they possess is, however, used with great moderation and wisdom, and by an immense ramification of branches (p. 258), every village has its banks, and every poor man may have his bank deposit, if he will save a few pounds. In England and Wales we have 267 private and 121 joint stock banks, or, in all, 388 banking firms, including in these numbers the London banks, but not including any of the numerous branch banks. There is, no doubt, a tendency to approximate to the Scotch system by the amalgamation of smaller banks. Still many new banks are from time to time started, and the competition between them is of the keenest character. The high dividends expected by the shareholders can only be earned by bold trading on small reserves, and every commercial man is aware that the money market is becoming more and more sensitive.

Cash Reserves of Bankers.

It is important, but very difficult to decide, what is the amount of real cash held by the bankers of the United Kingdom in readiness to meet their liabilities. Many banks publish balance-sheets professing to show the reserve of ready money. I have already remarked (pp. 248-250) upon the ambiguity which attaches to the words *money* and *cash* as commonly used; and, when we inquire into the nature of the banker's ready money, it is found to consist in a great degree of money invested in government securities, deposited with other bankers, especially the Bank of England, or held "at call," that is, lent to speculators who invest it in negotiable securities. From the published balance-sheets we thus get no indication of the real metallic reserve of the country, available for the payment of foreign debts.

Mr. R. H. Inglis Palgrave, in his important "Notes on Banking," published both in the *Statistical Journal*, for March, 1873 (Vol. xxxvi. p. 106), and as a separate book, has given the results of an inquiry into this subject, and states the amount of coin and Bank of England notes, held by the bankers of the United Kingdom, as not exceeding four or five per cent. of their liabilities, or from one twenty-fifth to one twentieth part. Mr. T. B. Moxon, of Stockport and Manchester, has subsequently made an elaborate inquiry into the same point, and finds that the cash reserve does not exceed about seven per cent. of the deposits and notes payable on demand. He remarks that even of this reserve a large proportion is absolutely indispensable for the daily transactions of the bankers' business, and could not be parted with. Thus the whole fabric of our vast commerce is found to depend upon the improbability that the merchants and other customers of the banks will ever want, simultaneously and suddenly, so much as one-twentieth part of the gold money which they have a right to receive on demand at any moment during banking hours.

Remedy for the Sensitiveness of the Money Market.

The present state of things in England is not to be cured by any legislation. No government can save those from trouble who will make unlimited transactions in gold, without a sure prospect of finding the gold when wanted. It is absurd to suppose that any single establishment like the Bank of England, itself becoming hardly more important than some of the great city banks, can prop up the whole fabric of English commerce.

The only measure which can restore stability to the London market, or prevent it from becoming more and more sensitive, is to secure by some means the existence of more satisfactory cash reserves, either in actual coin, or in Bank of England notes, representing deposits of coin in the Bank vaults. It would be of comparatively little use, however, for some banks to become more prudent and self-denying, while others are allowed to stretch their resources to the utmost possible point, and outbid the more prudent banks in the rates of dividend they can pay. Combined action, therefore, seems requisite, somewhat in the manner suggested by Mr. Bagehot, as regards the city bankers.

As the Bank of England pays no interest upon the eight millions which it on the average of the last four years holds as the deposits of the London bankers, there seems to be no sufficient reason why the Bank should be allowed to make a profit out of so large a sum. If held by a committee of the depositing banks it would be equally safe, almost equally available, and might, moreover, by the investment of a portion in government stock, yield a profit to the depositors. It may be asked, Why not leave each bank to hold its own reserve in its own vaults? But there would then be no security against some banks running their reserves dangerously low, and trusting to extrinsic aid in times of difficulty. One objection which I should make to the scheme as put forth is, that government stock should not be allowed to form any part of the ultimate reserve. When loanable capital is very scarce, such stock can only be converted into actual bullion by forced sales which depreciate the funds, shock public confidence, and drain away money from those who would in some other channel have employed it in the money market. Unless government stocks be sent abroad, their sale cannot possibly increase the stock of gold in the country. A cash reserve ought to be composed of *cash*, and although it may be very convenient to bankers to use this word in a loose and ambiguous manner, it ought not to mean, in speaking of the ultimate reserves of the country, anything but gold coin or bullion, or warrants, actually issued against coin or bullion, on the deposit system previously considered.

It has been pointed out, moreover, in an able article in the *Bankers' Magazine* for February, 1875, that the proposed scheme would be very insufficient if carried out merely by a narrow circle of city bankers. The association should include, in one way or another, all the more important banks in the three kingdoms. The vast trade of the country cannot be placed upon a sound basis until the force of public opinion among bankers imposes upon each member the necessity of holding a cash reserve bearing a fair proportion to the liabilities incurred. It matters little who holds the reserve, provided it actually does exist in the form of metal, and is not evaporated away by being placed at call, or deposited with other banks which make free use of it. In the absence of some common action among bankers, it is certain that the sensitiveness of the money market will increase, and it is probable that commercial crises will from time to time recur, even exceeding in their violence and disastrous consequences those whose history we know too well.

CHAPTER XXV.

A TABULAR STANDARD OF VALUE.

AT the outset it was observed that money, besides serving as a common denominator of value, and as a medium to facilitate exchange, was usually employed likewise as the standard of value, in terms of which contracts extending over long series of years are expressed. In letting land on long or perpetual leases, in lending money to governments, corporations, and railway companies, it is the general practice to make the interest and capital repayable in legal tender gold money. But there is abundance of evidence to prove that the value of gold has undergone extensive changes. Between 1789 and 1809, it fell in the ratio of 100 to 54, or by 46 per cent., as I have shown in a paper on the Variation of Prices since 1782, read to the London Statistical Society in June, 1865. From 1809 to 1849 it rose again in the extraordinary ratio of 100 to 245, or by 145 per cent., rendering government annuities and all fixed payments, extending over this period, almost two and a half times as valuable as they were in 1809. Since 1849 the value of gold has again fallen to the extent of at least 20 per cent.; and a careful study of the fluctuations of prices, as shown either in the Annual Reviews of Trade of the *Economist* newspaper, or in the paper referred to above, shows that fluctuations of from 10 to 25 per cent. occur in every credit cycle.

Corn Rents.

The question arises whether, having regard to these extreme changes in the values of the precious metals, it is desirable to employ them as the standard of value in long lasting contracts. We are forced to admit that the statesmen of Queen Elizabeth were far-seeing when they passed the Act which obliged the colleges of Oxford, Cambridge, and Eton, to lease their lands for corn rents. The result has been to make those colleges far richer than they would otherwise have been, the rents and endowments expressed in money having sunk to a fraction of their ancient value.

I believe that there is no legal impediment in the way of a landlord leasing his lands at present for a corn rent, or an iron, or coal, or any other rent. All that the law requires is that the contract shall be perfectly definite, and of exactly determinate meaning, so that the kind of commodity intended, and the quantity of that commodity, shall be exactly ascertainable. But the law, in defining legal tender money, provides against misapprehensions concerning money payments, whereas there is no security that mistakes and difficulties will not arise in taking other commodities as the matter of rents. Moreover any single commodity, such as corn or coal, undergoes considerable fluctuations from year to year, and as regards periods of ten or twenty years, might prove not to be so good a standard as silver or gold. Commodities which are comparatively steady in value on the average of long periods may be subject to great temporary variations of supply or demand.

A Multiple Legal Tender.

The question thus arises whether the progress of economical and statistical science might not enable us to devise some better standard of value. We have seen (pp. 136-143) that the so-called double standard system of money spreads the fluctuations of supply and demand of gold and silver over a larger area, and maintains both metals more unchanged in value than they would otherwise be. Can we not conceive a multiple legal tender, which would be still less liable to variation? We estimate the value of one hundred pounds by the quantities of corn, beef, potatoes, coal, timber, iron, tea, coffee, beer, and other principal commodities, which it will purchase from time to time. Might we not invent a legal tender note which should be convertible, not into any one single commodity, but into an aggregate of small quantities of various commodities, the quantity and quality of each being rigorously defined? Thus a hundred pound note would give the owners a right to demand one quarter of good wheat, one ton of ordinary merchant bar iron, one hundred pounds weight of middling cotton, twenty pounds of sugar, five pounds of tea, and other articles sufficient to make up the value. All these commodities will, of course, fluctuate in their relative values, but if the holder of the note loses upon some, he will in all probability gain upon others, so that on the average his note will remain steady in purchasing power. Indeed, as the articles into which it is convertible are those needed for continual consumption, the purchasing power of the note must remain steady compared with that of gold or silver, which metals are employed only for a few special purposes.

In practice, such a legal tender currency would obviously be most inconvenient, since no one would wish to have a miscellaneous assortment of goods forced into his possession. He who wanted corn, would have to sell to other parties the iron, beef, and other things received along with it; gold, or other metallic money, would doubtless be used as the medium in these exchanges. This scheme would, therefore, resolve itself practically into that which has been long since brought forward under the title of the Tabular Standard of Value.

Lowe's proposed Table of Reference.

Among valuable books, which have been forgotten, is to be mentioned that by Joseph Lowe on "The Present State of England in regard to Agriculture, Trade, and Finance," published in 1822. This book contains one of the ablest treatises on the variation of prices, the state of the currency, the poor-law, population, finance, and other public questions, of the time in which it was published, that I have ever met with. In Chapter IX. Lowe treats, in a very enlightened manner, of the fluctuations in the value of money, and proceeds to propound a scheme, probably invented by him, for giving a steady value to money contracts. He proposes that persons should be appointed to collect authentic information concerning the prices at which the staple articles of household consumption were sold. In regard to corn and sugar authoritative returns were then, and have ever since been, published in the *London Gazette*, and there seemed to be no difficulty in extending a like system to other articles. Having regard to the comparative quantities of commodities consumed in a household, he would then frame a *table of reference,* showing in what degree a money contract must be varied so as to make the purchasing power uniform. In principle the scheme seems to be perfectly sound; but Lowe did not attempt to work out the practical details, and his plan involves needless difficulties.

Poulett Scrope's Tabular Standard of Value.

A very similar scheme was independently proposed, about eleven years later, by Mr. G. Poulett Scrope, the well-known writer on geology and political economy. In a very able but now forgotten pamphlet, called "An Examination of the Bank Charter Question, with an Inquiry into the Nature of a Just Standard of Value"

(London, 1833), Mr. Scrope suggests (p. 26) that a standard might be formed by taking an average of the mass of commodities which, even if not employed as the legal standard, might serve to determine and correct the variations of the legal standard. The scheme was also described in Mr. Scrope's interesting book on the Principles of Political Economy, published in the same year (p. 406), and in the second edition of the same book, called "Political Economy for Plain People," issued two years ago, (p. 308). The late Mr. G. R. Porter, without referring to previous writers, gave the same scheme in 1838, in the first edition of his well-known treatise on "The Progress of the Nation," (Sections III. and IV. p. 235). He added a table showing the average fluctuations of fifty commodities monthly during the years 1833 to 1837.

Such schemes for a tabular or average standard of value appear to be perfectly sound and highly valuable in a theoretical point of view, and the practical difficulties are not of a serious character. To carry Lowe's and Scrope's plans into effect, a permanent government commission would have to be created, and endowed with a kind of judicial power. The officers of the department would collect the current prices of commodities in all the principal markets of the kingdom, and, by a well-defined system of calculations, would compute from these data the average variations in the purchasing power of gold. The decisions of this commission would be published monthly, and payments would be adjusted in accordance with them. Thus, suppose that a debt of one hundred pounds was incurred upon the 1st of July. 1875, and was to be paid back on 1st July, 1878; if the commission had decided in June, 1878, that the value of gold had fallen in the ratio of 106 to 100 in the intervening years, then the creditor would claim an increase of 6 per cent in the nominal amount of the debt.

At first the use of this national tabular standard might be permissive, so that it could be enforced only where the parties to the contract had inserted a clause to that effect in their contract. After the practicability and utility of the plan had become sufficiently demonstrated, it might be made compulsory, in the sense that every money debt of, say, more than three months' standing, would be varied according to the tabular standard, in the absence of an express provision to the contrary.

Difficulties of the Scheme.

The difficulties in the way of such a scheme are not considerable. It would, no doubt, introduce a certain complexity into the relations of debtors and creditors, and disputes might sometimes arise as to the date of the debt whence the calculation must be made. Such difficulties would not exceed those arising from the payment of interest, which likewise depends on the duration of the debt. The work of the commission, when once established and directed by Act of Parliament, would be little more than that of accountants acting according to fixed rules. Their decisions would be of a perfectly *bonâ fide* and reliable character, because, in addition to their average results, they would be required to publish periodically the detailed tables of prices upon which their calculations were founded, and thus many persons could sufficiently verify the data and the calculations. Fraud would be out of the question.

The only real difficulty which I foresee, is that of deciding upon the proper method of deducing the average. According to the method which I should advocate, a considerable number of commodities, say 100, should be chosen with special regard to the independence of their fluctuations one from another, and then the *geometrical average* of the ratios in which their gold prices have changed would be calculated logarithmically. This is the method which I employed in my pamphlet on the "Serious Fall in the Value of Gold, etc." and in the paper on the Variations of Prices since 1782, previously referred to (p. 323). A somewhat similar method had been previously employed by Mr. Newmarch. In the annual Commercial History and Review of the *Economist* newspaper, there has, for many years, appeared a table containing the Total Index Number of prices, or the arithmetical sum of the numbers expressing the ratios of the prices of many commodities to the average prices of the same commodities in the years 1845–50. Whatever method were adopted, however, the results would be better than if we continued to accept a single metal for the standard, as we do at present.

The space at my disposal will not allow me to describe adequately the advantages which would arise from the establishment of a national tabular standard of value. Such a standard would add a wholly new degree of stability to social relations, securing the fixed incomes of individuals and public institutions from the depreciation which they have often suffered. Speculation, too, based upon the frequent oscillations of prices, which take place in the present state of commerce, would be to a certain extent discouraged. The calculations of merchants would be less frequently frustrated by causes beyond their own control, and many bankruptcies would be prevented. Periodical collapses of credit would no doubt recur from time to time, but the intensity of the crises would be mitigated, because as prices fell the liabilities of debtors would decrease approximately in the same ratio.

CHAPTER XXVI.

THE QUANTITY OF MONEY NEEDED BY A NATION.

It might seem natural that one most important point for discussion in an Essay on Money would be the quantity of money required by a nation. Nothing would seem more desirable than to decide how much each person needs of paper, gold, silver, or bronze currency, so that the government might take care to provide sufficient for every one. In almost every country great complaints have from time to time been made as to the scarcity of the circulating medium, and the urgent need of more. All the evils of the day, the slackness of trade, falling prices, declining revenue, poverty of the people, want of employment, political discontent, bankruptcy, and panic, have been attributed to the want of money, the remedy suggested being in former days the setting of the mint to work, and in later times the issue of paper money.

The true answer to all such complaints is that no one can tell how much currency a nation requires, and that to attempt to regulate its quantity is the last thing which a statesman should do. In almost every case the apparent scarcity of currency arises from unskilful management of the metallic currency, bad regulation of paper representative money, illegitimate speculation, or some unsoundness in commerce which would be aggravated by a further increase of the paper currency. We shall find that to ascertain how much money is needed by a nation is a problem involving many unknown quantities, so that a sure solution can never be obtained.

Quantity of Work to be done by Money.

To decide how much money is needed by a nation, we must, firstly, determine the quantity of work which money has to do. This will be proportional, *ceteris paribus*, to the number of the population; twice the number of people, if equally active in trade and performing it in the same way, will clearly want twice as much money. It will be proportional, again, to the activity of industry, and to the complexity of its organization. The more goods are bought and sold, and the more often they pass from hand to hand, the more currency will be needed to move them. It will be proportional, again, to the prices of goods; and if gold falls in value, and prices are raised, more money will be needed to pay the debts increased in nominal amount.

Few of the quantities concerned in such considerations are known. We know the number of the population approximately, and the amount of foreign trade, but the quantities of goods bought and sold in inland trade are almost entirely unknown. It is needless to dwell on this side of the question, as our knowledge is still more defective in other respects.

Efficiency of the Currency.

By the efficiency of the currency we mean the average number of exchanges effected by each piece of money in a unit of time, such as a year. The aggregate work done by money will be measured by its quantity multiplied into the average number of times which each coin or note passes from hand to hand during the year. Now we know very imperfectly what is the quantity of currency in most countries, and we know nothing at all as to the average rapidity of circulation. Some coins, especially small silver or bronze coins, may pass several times in the course of a day. Other coins or notes may be kept in the pocket for weeks, or may be laid by for months and years. I have never met with any attempt to determine in any country the average rapidity of circulation, nor have I been able to think of any means whatever of approaching the investigation of the question, except in the inverse way. If we knew the amount of exchanges effected, and the quantity of currency used, we might get by division the average number of times the currency is turned over; but the data, as already stated, are quite wanting.

There is no doubt that the rapidity of circulation varies very much between one country and another. A thrifty people with slight banking facilities, like the French, Swiss, Belgians, and Dutch, hoard coin much more than an improvident people like the English, or even a careful people with a perfect banking system like the Scotch. Many circumstances, too, affect the rapidity of circulation. Railways and rapid steamboats enable coin and bullion to be more swiftly remitted than of old; telegraphs prevent its needless removal, and the acceleration of the mails has a like effect. A decrease in the circulation of country bank-notes in England, in 1842, was attributed to the effect of the penny postal reform in facilitating presentation of notes by post.

Effects of the Cheque and Clearing System.

Far more important than these considerations is the fact that, where an extensive banking system exists, only a portion of the exchanges are actually effected by money. I do not lay much stress upon the use of bills of exchange as replacing money, because the degree in which they are so used must be comparatively limited, and they are rather articles bought and sold with money than money itself. But we have traced out step by step the way in which the cheque and clearing system enables debts to be balanced off against each other, so that the money is never touched at all, and only intervenes as the unit of value in which sums are expressed. Almost all large exchanges are now effected by a complicated and perfected system of barter. In the London Clearing House, transactions to the amount of, at least, £6,000,000,000 in the year are thus effected, without the use of any cash at all, and, as I have before explained, this amount gives no adequate idea of the exchanges arranged by cheques, because so many transactions are really cleared in provincial banks, between branches, agents, or correspondents of the same bank, or between banks having the same London agents.

If our knowledge of the amount of transactions in England is highly imperfect, we know still less of the way in which payments are effected in other countries. The New York Clearing House transactions are very extensive, as we have seen, and there is an elaborate banking system extending over all the States of the Union; but it would require much investigation on the spot to enable any one to form a notion whether the correspondence between these banks enables them to economize currency as much as the English system of London agencies. In France and most continental countries the cheque and clearing system can hardly be said to exist except in some of the large towns. Paris has an incipient clearing house, and the Bank of France, moreover, makes transfers between clients to the extent of two or three millions daily. All banks will to a certain extent economize currency, and those of Amsterdam and Hamburg have for some centuries carried on a system of transfers, the true prototype of our system.

Considerable changes, it is true, are taking place in the mode of conducting business in some parts of the Continent. Professor Cliffe Leslie, who is well known to be intimately acquainted with the economical systems of the continental countries, attributes the rise of prices in Germany in a great degree to the quicker circulation of the money, and the freer use of instruments of credit. In the *Fortnightly Review* for

November, 1870 (pp. 568-9), he says:—"The improvements in locomotion and in commercial activity which have so largely augmented the money-making power of the Germans, have also quickened prodigiously the circulation of money; and the development of credit, likewise following industrial progress, has added to the volume of the circulating medium a mass of substitutes for money which move with greater velocity. A much smaller amount of money than formerly now suffices to do a given amount of business, or to raise prices to a given range; and to the increased amount of actual money now current in Germany we must add a brisk circulation of instruments of credit. Were the circulating medium composed of coin alone, whatever the amount of the precious metals issuing from the mines, or circulating in other countries, and whatever the price of German commodities in markets abroad, no rise in the prices of German commodities at home could take place without additional coin to sustain it."

So different, then, are the commercial habits of different peoples, that there evidently exists no proportion whatever between the amount of currency in a country and the aggregate of the exchanges which can be effected by it. Even if we had reliable statistics of the amounts of currencies, such data should be regarded as indicating, not the comparative abundance or scarcity of money, but the degree of civilization, of providence, or of complexity of banking organization, in the country.

Conclusion.

From all the above considerations it follows that the only method of regulating the *amount* of the currency is to leave it at perfect freedom to regulate itself. Money must find its own level like water, and flow in and out of a country, according to fluctuations of commerce which no government can foresee or prevent. The manner in which paper notes may be used to represent and replace part of the metallic currency should be strictly regulated, because otherwise belief in the existence of metallic money is created when there is no such money to warrant the belief. But the amount of money itself can be no more regulated than the amounts of corn, iron, cotton, or other common commodities produced and consumed by a people. It must be allowed, indeed, to be no easy matter to discriminate precisely and soundly between those points at which the legislator must interfere in the management of the currency and lay down a fixed rule, and those points at which perfect freedom must be maintained.

A comparison of our present laws regarding currency and trade, with those which existed in this country from the tenth to the fourteenth century, will show a curious double progress. Many things which our ancestors attempted to regulate by law are now left free by general consent, and other things which they left free, or nearly so, are now strictly regulated. The rates of wages, the price of the quartern loaf, the exercise of various trades, were then the subject of legislation, though we now know that they cannot be properly brought within the scope of legislative control. On the other hand, an endless diversity of weights and measures were formerly used in different parts of the country, and little or no attempt was made to reduce them to any system or precise definition. Almost every important town, too, had its mint in the earlier centuries, and barons and great ecclesiastics often exercised the right of issuing their own money. There are still a very few persons who advocate free coinage; but, by almost general consent, the work of coining metallic money is now, in every civilized country, committed to the care of the state. We provide for a uniform system of coins with the same care that we establish a national system of weights and measures. But while we thus take the greatest care of the metallic currency in one respect, we have utterly abandoned all the futile attempts which were in former centuries made to bring bullion into the kingdom in order to set the mint to work.

We must deal with the paper currency in an analogous manner, and regulate it both more and less than hitherto. Private issues should disappear like private mints, and each kingdom should have one uniform paper circulation, issued from a single central state department, more resembling a mint than a bank. The manner of issuing this paper currency should be strictly regulated in one sense; the paper circulation should be made to increase and diminish with the amount of gold deposited in exchange for it. At the same time, no thought need be taken about the amount so issued. The purpose of the strict regulation is not to govern the amount, but to leave that amount to vary according to the natural laws of supply and demand. In my opinion, it is the issue of paper representative notes, accepted in place of coin, which constitutes an arbitrary interference with the natural laws governing the variations of a purely metallic currency, so that strict legislative control in one way leads to more real freedom in another. I am quite willing to allow, however, that questions of great nicety and subtlety arise in this subject, and that only in the gradual progress of economic science can they be finally set at rest.

INDEX.

A

ABRASION of coins, 83, 157, 164
Aes, 41, 45, 52; *rude*, 53; *grave*, 91
African Barter Company, 2
African money, 93
Agent banks, 259
Agio, 72, 200
Alternative standard, 137
Aluminium, 132
American money (see United States)
Amsterdam, banks of, 200, 221, 254
Aristotle on money, 88
As, 22, 91
Assignats, 202, 228, 232, 246
Australian sovereigns, 154
Austrian money, 126, 136, 140
Austro-Hungarian money, 148, 160

B

BABBAGE, CHARLES, 267
Bagehot, Walter, 92, 322
Bankers' bank, 256, 292
——— cheques, 242
——— competition of, 311
Bankers' Magazine, 322
Bank money, 200
Bank-notes, 239; weight of, 203
Bank of England, 111, 114, 222; monopoly of coinage, 117; supplies silver coin, 118; bullion office, 212; bank-notes, 215, 313; in 1839, 317; bankers' deposits, 322
Bank of France, 231, 338
Bank Charter Act, 116, 222, 225, 312
Bank shares, speculation in, 210
Bank-system, single, 252; complex, 255; branch, 257; agency, 259
Barter, 1, 6, 8, 77, 189; restoration of, 288
Belgium, money of, 49, 103, 130
Bernardakis, M., 196, 198
Billon, 125
Bills of exchange, 191, 214, 299; history of, 300; trade in, 302
Bills of lading, 207
Binary system, 181
Book credit, 251
Boulton and Watt, 121, 123
——— letter of, 65
Branch banks, number of, 258
Brazil, money of, 147
Bronze coin, 128; French, 74; English, 110, 129, 164; stagnation of, 131; penny, 124
Buenos Ayres, paper money of, 234
Bullion report, 230
——— trade of Bank of England in, 117

Burmah, money of, 44, 89
Byzantine money, 29, 195

C

CACAO nuts as money, 26, 33
Canadian money, 73
Capital, derivation of name, 23
Carthaginian money, 197
Cash, Chinese money, 58, 65, 90; ambiguity of word, 249, 323; proportion of in payments, 285
Cattle as currency, 22
Cent, 187
Centime pieces, 124, 128, 185
Certified cheques, 243
Chambre des Compensations, 279
Chattel, derivation of name, 23
Cheque and clearing system, 192, 242, 283, 337
Cheque Bank, 243, 290
Cheques, 240; circulated in Queensland, 241; crossed, 243
Chevalier, M. Michel, 30, 57, 69, 86, 92, 137, 202, 245
Chili, 147
Chinese money, 58, 97, 142, 148, 197
Clazomenian money, 204
Clearing House, 257; London, 202, 337; of the world, 303
Clipped coins, 199
Coal raised in Great Britain, 310
Cognizability, 40
Coin, 17, 25, 27, 57
Coinage, amount at English Mint, 163
────── Act, 76, 105, 107, 116; of United States, 146
Coining, invention of, 55; a royal prerogative, 65; of bank-notes, 318
Colonial currencies, 134, 147
Colouring of coins, 126
Compensatio ad pensum, 90
Compensatory action of double standard, 139

Composite coin, 127
────── legal tender, 101
Confederate States notes, 233
Conveyance, cost of, 35
Copper, 35, 45; price of, 110, 123; objections to, 125
Corn as money, 25, 35
────── rents, 326
Counterfeit, coin, 59; sous, 126
Counting boards, 161
Country bankers, supply of silver coin to, 119
────── clearing, 261
Courcelle-Seneuil, 86, 137, 139, 198
Cours forcé, 76
Cowry shells, 24, 33, 71
Credit, 238; and debit exchanges, 278
Currency by weight, 88
────── weight of, 130

D

DECIMAL system, 172, 175, 182
Demurrage, 116
Denarii notched, 80
Denmark, money of, 140, 147
De Parieu, M., 174
Deposit banks, 199
Diamonds, value of, 36
Divisibility, 38
Dock warrants, 207
Dollar, 93, 95; valuation of, 72; sizes of, 156; American, 172, 174, 178, 187
Double standard, 136
────── eagle, 156, 159
Drachma, 54
Ducat pieces, 151, 156
Dumas, Ernest, 63
Duodecimal system, 181
Duplication, method of, 162

E

EAGLE, 156, 159
Economist, 326, 332

INDEX. 345

Efficiency of currency, 336
Egypt, money of, 147
English money, 98
Etruscan money, 53
Exchange, 8; medium of, 4; ratios of, 5; theory of, 10
Exchange and Mart, The, 4

F

FARR, Dr., 157
Farthing, 97, 110
Fee, derivation of, 22
Feer-Herzog, M., 95, 137, 158
Fineness, of silver money, 103; remedy in, 109; of gold and silver, 151; of gold, 158; of French silver money, 154
Finland, money of, 149
Five-franc piece in gold, 178
Five-pound piece, 159
Florin, 97; English, 160, 176; Austrian, 174
Formosa, money of, 58
Fourpenny pieces pawned, 213
Franc, 171, 174, 185
Free-banking school, 314
Free-issue system, 230
French money, 71, 76, 99, 124, 127, 128; copper money, 103; amount of small money, 130; currency, 144; mint, 169; commission of inquiry, 174
Functions of money, 13, 16

G

GAMING, 39
Garbling, 81
Garnier, M. Joseph, 30, 86, 92
German empire, monetary system, 104, 126, 129; nickel coinage, 50; demand for gold by, 140; fineness of proposed crown-piece, 152; wear of coin, 159; reform of monetary system, 180, 279; bank law, 226, 318

Gladstone, W. E., 16, 21, 43, 318
Glasgow, pig-iron stores, 210; settlement in iron market, 283
Gold, beauty of, 34; characteristics of, 47; bullion, 116; probable discoveries, 143; standard, 174; weight, 202; value, 315
—— coin, deficiency of weight, 111
Goldsmiths' notes, 201
Government bonds, 246
Graham, Professor Thomas, 133, 153, 177
Greece, money of, 147
Greenback currency, 179, 232
Gresham's Law, 64, 80, 99, 112
Guernsey market notes, 204
Guinea, value of, 98, 103
Guinea-pieces, 28

H

HABIT, force of, 32, 78, 214
Halfpenny, 110
Half-sovereign, 107
Halifax currency, 74
Hamburg, Bank of, 200, 221, 254
Harris, essay on money, 30
Hatchett, experiments of, 153
Hebrew money, 45
Hendriks, Frederick, 137, 172
Herschel, Sir John, 133
Hertz, James, 290
Holland, money of, 135
Homogeneity, 37
Hudson Bay Company's trade, 20
Hungary (see Austro-Hungarian)

I

IMPRESSIBILITY, 40
In-clearing, 266, 272, 278
Indestructibility, 36
India, money of, 95, 142, 148
Insurance broker's business, 251
Interest on bills, 245

Interest, loss of, 284
International money, 167
Iridium, 36
Irish money, 52
—— banks, note issues of, 313
Iron money, 35, 43, 96
Issues of provincial banks, 313
Italy, money of, 103, 129, 130, 142, 216
Itzibu, Japanese coin, 84

J

JAMAICA, nickel coinage of, 50
Japan, money of, 58, 84; iron money, 43; new metallic currency, 147

K

KESITAH, Hebrew coin, 89
Kobang, 84
Kossuth's bonds, 233
Kreutzer pieces, 126

L

LACEDÆMONIAN money, 35, 195
Land reserve, 259
Langton, William, 286
Law, John, 228, 313
Lead, 43, 44
Least current weight of coins, 107, 111, 157
Leather money, 20, 127, 195, 197
Legal tender, 76, 107; single, 96; multiple, 98, 327; composite, 102; limited in silver coinage, 110, 145
Leslie, Professor Cliffe, 316
Life of sovereign, 157
Light gold coin, 111, 113
Liverpool, Lord, 102, 108, 136
Liverpool Clearing House, 269
—————— cotton market, 281, 282
—————— use of cheques in, 280

Livre, 89
Locke on credit, 238
Loi du 7 Germinal, an XI., 100, 110, 144
Lombard Street Clearing House, 263
London, banking system of, 192; goldsmiths, 221; bank agencies, 260; Clearing House, 262, 265; drawing upon, 304; centralization of financial business in, 305; foreign bankers in, 307
Lowe, Joseph, 328
Lowe, Robert, 105
Lubbock, Sir John, 265, 285

M

MACLEOD, H. D., 230
Macute, 71
Maize, as money, 25, 27
Manchester Clearing House, 269, 277, 279
—————— use of notes in, 286
—————— cotton trade, 288
Mancus, 71
Mandats, 228, 234
Manganese, 132
Marchandise banale, 4
Marco Polo, 197
Maria Theresa dollar, 79, 156
Mark, 71; new German coin, 180
Massachusetts, money of, 44, 99
Maundy money, 109, 125
Measure of value, 5, 13
Medium of exchange, 4
Melting gold, cost of, 38, 48
Metals, declining values of, 42; alloys of, 51; equivalent weights of, 123
Metallic value, 75
Mexican dollar, 79, 169, 170
Mil, 176, 186
Miller, F. B., 154
Milling of coin, 60
Milreis, 184

INDEX.

Mint, the English, 120; regulations for coining gold, 116; cost of, 165
Mirabeau's proposals, 100
Monetary, Conference of 1867, 177; Convention, 144-5, 173; technology, 134
Money, of account, 70; Anglo-Saxon, 70; definition of English, 77; representative, 191; definition of money, 248
——— market, 322
Monnaie d'appoint, 122
Montesquieu, 71
Morison, K., 280
Moxon, T. B., 321

N

NATIONAL BANK currency, 224
——— debt, 246
New South Wales, token money in, 195
New York Clearing House, 278
Newcastle Clearing House, 269
Newton, Sir Isaac, 98
Nickel, 49, 132
Nix, E. W., 269
Nominal value, 75
Norway, money of, 72, 78, 126, 140, 147

O

OBOLUS, 54
Oil as currency, 25
Ora, 71
Osmium, 36
Out-clearing, 266, 270, 278
Oxen as currency, 21, 33, 35

P

PALGRAVE, R. H. INGLIS, 325, 286, 314
Paper money, 236

Parallel standards, 95
Paris Clearing House, 279
Patina of bronze, 129
Peag currency, 33
Pecunia, 22
Penny, 110, 123, 124; weight of, 45; composite, 127; penny and ten-franc scheme, 176
Percy, Dr., 132
Persian money, 56, 59, 198,
Pheidon, inventor of money, 56
Picking and culling, 81, 112
Pig-iron warrants, 208, 210
Platinum, 48
Porcelain coins, 42
Portability, 34
Porter, G. R., 330
Portugal, money of, 147, 171, 184
Postage stamps, 233
Post-office money orders, 294; savings bank, 297
Pound and mil scheme, 176
——— sterling, 89, 171, 174, 184
Precious stones, 37, 40
Price of silver, 141, 143, 163
Prices, variation of, 315, 325, 332
Profit on coinage, 111
Promises, specific and general, 209; freedom of, 211
Promissory notes, 206
Prussian historical money, 63

R

RAILWAY Clearing House, 280
Ratio of exchange, 5, 10
Reciprocity of trade, 299
Recoinage of French bronze money, 128
Rei, 184, 186
Remedy, for sovereign, 106; for shilling, 109
Reserve, minimum, 223; proportional, 223; documentary, 227; real property, 228; bankers', 322

Returned cheques, 266, 276
Ricardo, David, 314
Ring money, 54
Roberts, W. C., 132, 133, 137
Rogers, Rev. J. E. T., 73
Roman money, 45, 85, 122
Rouble, 71
Roumania, money of, 147
Rupee, 148
Russia, early currency of, 20; platinum money, 48; metallic money, 71, 149; paper money, 202, 232, 235; government bank, 222

S

SALT as money, 28
Savings banks, 296
Scales, use in making payments, 88; in counting coin, 161
Scotland, currency of, 142; banking system, 257, 319; bank-note issues, 313
Scrope, Poulett, 3_9
Seignorage, 74, 163, 181
Sequin, 151
Seyd, Ernest, 110, 116, 121, 137, 157, 173
Shilling, 71, 108, 176
Siamese money, 55
Silver, 46; penny of, 86, 70, 97; English coin, 75, 96; supply of coin, 118; ratio of value to gold, 108; price of, 137; wear of, 158; weight of, 202.
Singapore, money of, 94
Skat, derivation of, 23
Skilling, 126
Skins as currency, 20, 33, 196
Slaves as currency, 23
Smith, Adam, 200
Sou, 186
Sous de cloche, 128
South American money, 93

Sovereign, 105; light, 113; weighed at Bank of England, 116; weight of, 153; Australian, 154; least current weight, 157; international currency, 170
Spanish dollar, 94; money, 147
Spencer, Herbert, 34, 64, 82
Stability of value, 38
Stafford, William, 30
Standard of value, 14; fineness of silver, 75; fineness of gold, 105
Steel coins, 138
Stephenson, Robert, 280
Stock certificates, 247
Stock Exchange Clearing House, 281
Storch, Henri, 33, 196
Stycas, 52
Sumner, Professor W. G., 236, 318
Sweating of coin, 114
Sweden, money of, 129, 140, 147; copper money, 45, 58, 97; rixdaler, 95
Switzerland, money of, 103, 145; small money, 134; wear of gold coin, 157
Sycee silver, 148
Syracusan money, 203

T

TABULAR standard, 328
Tael, 90
Tallies of exchequer, 196; tally checks, 296
Tartar money, 198
Ten-franc piece, 176, 187
Theory of political economy, 10
Threepenny pieces, 125, 155
Thrimsa, 71
Tin money, 44, 127, 203
Tobacco as currency, 27, 33, 202
Token money, 74, 83, 194, 203
Tooke, Thomas, 314

Tower of London, 201
Trade, expansion of, 310
Tradesmen's tokens, 65, 103, 195
Truck, *troc*, 3, 7
Turgot, 53
Turkey, money of, 147

U

UNITED STATES, money of, 49, 72, 94, 101, 129, 178, 183, 187; ratio of gold to silver, 146; thickness of coins, 155; interest-bearing currency, 246; National Bank currency, 224
Utility, 9, 32

V

VALUE, 9, 11; measure, 5; standard, 14; store, 15; stability, 38; unit, 67; sense of, 68; intrinsic, 75; metallic, 75

Vaughan, Rice, 30
Virginian money, 202

W

WAGES paid by cheque, 295
Wallace, A. R., 2
Walras, Léon, 10, 30
Wampumpeag currency, 24, 33
Warrants, gold, 189; pig-iron, 208
Webster on paper currency, 236
West Indies, money of, 93
Wilson, Rivers, 177
Winkler, Dr. Clemens, 132
Wolowski, Louis, 1, 100, 137, 139, 140, 235, 318
Wooden money, 29
Wood's halfpence, 75
Wrottesley, Lord, 175

Z

ZEND AVESTA, fees mentioned in, 23

BIBLIOLIFE

Old Books Deserve a New Life
www.bibliolife.com

Did you know that you can get most of our titles in our trademark **EasyScript**™ print format? **EasyScript**™ provides readers with a larger than average typeface, for a reading experience that's easier on the eyes.

Did you know that we have an ever-growing collection of books in many languages?

Order online:
www.bibliolife.com/store

Or to exclusively browse our **EasyScript**™ collection:
www.bibliogrande.com

At BiblioLife, we aim to make knowledge more accessible by making thousands of titles available to you – quickly and affordably.

Contact us:
BiblioLife
PO Box 21206
Charleston, SC 29413

Made in the USA
San Bernardino, CA
13 March 2017